Baker Handbook
of Single Adult Ministry

Other books by Douglas L. Fagerstrom

Single to God
The Lonely Pew
Single Adult Ministry

Baker Handbook
of Single Adult Ministry

Edited by Douglas L. Fagerstrom

Foreword by Bill Flanagan and Jim Smoke

Baker Books

A Division of Baker Book House Co
Grand Rapids, Michigan 49516

© 1997 by Douglas Fagerstrom

Published by Baker Books
a division of Baker Book House Company
P.O. Box 6287, Grand Rapids, MI 49516-6287

Printed in the United States of America

Library of Congress Cataloging-in-Publication Data

Baker handbook of single adult ministry /
   Douglas L. Fagerstrom, ed., foreword by Bill Flanagan and Jim Smoke.
   p. cm.
   Includes bibliographical references (p.).
   ISBN 0-8010-9027-X
   1. Church work with single people. I. Fagerstrom, Douglas L.
   BV639.S5B35 1996
   259'.08652—dc20   96-44807

For information about academic books, resources for Christian leaders, and all new releases available from Baker Book House, visit our web site:
www.bakerbooks.com/

Contents

Contents

Contents

Contents

Foreword

This book is not the last word on how to minister to single adults. Nor is it the first. However, it is the most comprehensive resource for single adult ministry. It reveals the experiences in the trenches of dedicated leaders in churches large and small across America who have given many hours a week loving and caring for single adults.

It is also the perpetual dream of some of us who have been around long enough to have asked the question: "What's a single adult, and what's a single adult ministry?" This book attempts to address some of the many "who, why, how, and what" questions being asked regarding single adult ministries.

Its authors are and have been on the front line of this emerging ministry that began in the early '70s. They are pioneers. They are still learning, also. They care deeply about the ministry and those who share it with them.

This is not an answer book. It is merely a guidebook. Use it with wisdom and prayer! It should motivate you and expand your vision. It will provide the first step in many areas of single adult ministry.

We dedicate it to the millions of single adults in our society without whom this ministry would not exist.

Jim Smoke

In 1971 I inherited a small, struggling single adult ministry as a part of my work. At that time only a few people had a prophetic vision of the need for reaching out to single men and women. Just a handful were beginning to understand the emerging phenomenon of the vast, growing army of single adults in America. As the 1970s began, you could have counted the single adult ministries in local churches across the country on the fingers of both hands.

Through the next few years, leaders began to develop and share ideas. By the mid-'70s, a few conferences and publications were available. But not until the early 1980s did a national network come into being. You hold in your hands a book that is one of those valuable materials. A focused ministry with single people has now come of age in the church, and the tools to accomplish it are now available. Those of us who have specialized in this area for a long time are privileged to share with newer leaders some of the principles, methods, and ideas that we have learned.

I am deeply appreciative and thankful to the men and women in single adult ministry whose expertise, effort, and creativity are reflected on these pages. Continued power and blessings to these colleagues and partners in ministry who are taking single adult ministry to a new and higher level of sophistication and excellence. Power and prayers, also, to those who read and apply the content of these pages into Christ-centered ministries with single people across America and beyond.

Bill Flanagan

Preface

In our mind's eye we can see the Lord Jesus walking past the gate of the sheepfold in pursuit of the one lost sheep. That one is alone and afraid. That one is in danger and pain. That one is lost. The shepherd's role is to find the sheep, nurture the sheep, bind up its wounds, and bring it back inside the gate to protect it and help it to grow.

The shepherd does not leave the sheep alone or leave the sheep in want. The shepherd does not condemn the sheep as wayward but "restores his soul" and places him back with the rest of the sheep.

Single adults are without question the fastest growing subculture of our world. Second to that is the senior adult phenomenon, and many seniors are also single.

The church of Jesus Christ has not kept up with the singles boom. The percentage of singles in the church is not close to the percentage in society. The church must catch up if we are to reach this large and wonderful mission field that God has placed before us.

We must learn about and love single adults.

We must discover and understand their needs.

We must remove the myths and overcome our fears.

We must reach out with hearts of compassion and acts of mercy.

We must share the gospel of Jesus Christ with a generation that is in pursuit of love, peace, and intimacy.

It is from the church (God's people) that single adults can discover from God's Word who they are and what their gifts are, receive love and encouragement, and find help in their time of need. It is here that ministry begins and lives are changed.

A Ministry to Adults

Singles are adults. One half of America's adults are single. Yet, we tend to treat the single adult as a single adolescent. Interchangeably this book uses the terms "adult single" and "single adult." The key word in understanding the needs and ministry of the "single adult" is the word "adult." Singles see themselves as adult first and single second. Even single adult parents see being a parent and living as an adult ahead of their singleness. Ministries will do well to do the same. Singles want to be accepted as they are, adult men and women with adult problems and adult situations. They learn as adults learn. They cry and laugh as adults. They lead as adults. They are adults.

A Beginning

This book is a starter manual for single adult ministry. For the ministry just beginning, it is a comprehensive resource for discovering who single adults are, what needs they have, and how to start a ministry with them. For the established ministry, it provides the foundation and outline for beginning new programs and gaining a fuller understanding of what must be done in ministry.

A Comprehensive Guide

It would be impossible to provide the last or inclusive word on the multiplicity of singles ministry needs in one volume. Many books have been written on each subject that is here covered in one or two brief chapters. However, our purpose is to provide an overview of each of the needs, major concerns, and areas of singles ministry that are most significant. This book will be a guide to establish direction, clarity, purpose, and design in single adult ministry.

Deep Conviction

Each of the authors in this book has deep love and compassion for single adults. They have served well in the trenches. They have agonized, wept, shared, and grown with singles from coast to coast. They speak to us from their hearts, experience, and biblical conviction of God's call to ministry with adult singles. You will learn from them. Listen closely to the voice of God's shepherds who know well the Good Shepherd.

Dedication

This book is dedicated to Jesus Christ, the Good Shepherd, who binds up the wounds of every single adult and brings the lost into his forever family. I give deepest gratitude and love to my wife, Donna, and daughter, Darci, who have loved singles with me for the last seventeen years of ministry. And I extend humble appreciation and God's richest blessing to the authors of this book, my dear friends in life and ministry, who I know dedicate this book to single adult leaders and all single adults everywhere.

My prayer is that the single adult ministry will continue to grow and reach single adults around the world with the good news of Jesus Christ. Thank you for sharing that prayer with me and many others. Welcome to the team of single adult ministry leaders.

Doug Fagerstrom

Part

The Need for a Ministry
with Single Adults

1

Today's Single Adult Phenomenon: The Realities, Myths, and Identity

Carolyn Koons

Growing up in America always meant that your dreams would come true, and you would be right in step, walking the aisle to wedlock, eventually owning your own home, raising 2.5 children, owning an R.V., a speedboat, or a small vacation cabin, and living happily ever after. The dream was a Noah's ark (two by two), "traditionally marrying" culture. However, in the last several decades, marital patterns have changed, creating a new singles subculture. Along with such major societal changes came new attitudes, stereotypes, myths, and often misunderstandings.

The Value System: Singles in a Couples World

Everywhere we look we see a couples world, and there is pressure to keep it that way. At the same time, our society is changing, and at times there is a contradiction of values. On one hand, we highly regard individualism, being unique in thoughts and actions, and being competitive. On the other hand, we promote community, conformity, and group consensus. For some, marriage is instrumental in fulfilling the socialization process, drawing us closer to the norm or community.

17

As marriage is viewed as a positive, "right" choice, singleness becomes a negative, "wrong" choice, or a failure to achieve a state that is normal. Many singles feel pressure from society, parents, and themselves to fit in with society. This begins the eternal search to find "the magic one-and-only." "Waiting on God for the perfect person" and the attitude that "marriage is God's perfect will" is often proclaimed from the pulpits today, laying on tremendous guilt while impacting the self-esteem of thousands of single Christian men and women.

Historical Attitudes on Singleness Since 1900

Throughout history singles have comprised only 2–3 percent of the adult population until their drastic increase over the last thirty years. Since the early 1900s, society's awareness of singles has increased, and its attitudes have changed. From 1900 through the 1920s, single women, no matter what their age, were labeled "old maids," a term rarely heard today. During the '30s and '40s, the Depression years, single women were called "spinsters." Society tried to attack the "problem" of female singleness (seldom were single men focused on) by writing major articles addressing the issue: "Does It Hurt to Be an Old Maid?" "Alarming Increase of Old Maids and Bachelors in New England," "Family Parasites: The Economic Value of the Unmarried Sister," "The Sorrowful Maiden and the Jovial Bachelor," and "There Is No Place in Heaven for Old Maids."

The 1950s and '60s saw a turn as divorce increased in America. Articles took more of a questioning or coaching approach: "How to Be Marriageable: Results of a Marriage Readiness Course," "A Spinster's Lot Can Be a Happy One," "When Being Single Stops Being Fun," "How to Be Human Though Single," "Study Disputes Images of the Happy Bachelor." Lists such as "129 Ways to Get a Husband," "Six Ways of Being an Old Maid," and "Six Ways to Meet a Man" were published.

The "new morality" of the 1970s unfortunately labeled singles as "swinging singles," which helped widen the growing barrier between married and single adult groups. Articles began to reflect a more aggressive singles lifestyle: "What Women Should Know about Single Men," "A to Z List on Where to Find a Man," "Humanizing the Meat Market," "Celebrate Singleness: Marriage May Be Second Best," "Movin' On—Alone," and "49 Million Singles Can't All Be Right."

The 1980s carried an even different image of singles. Some articles referred to them as the "growing" singles, hard workers, physically active and healthy, affluent, and introspective. The categories will still continue to change. However, it appears that singleness is here to stay. Never again will America be a 97 percent married and 3 percent single adult population.

Myths and Stereotypes

Society forms myths and stereotypes about each of its subcultures. Society's attitude toward singles clusters around several specific notions about the nature of single people and their lives. These notions tend to promote a negative or unfair image of the single life. However, no one should categorize or label singles, for any reason. They are unique and different, as are all men and women. They need the freedom to shape their own self-images without being hampered by myths.

The following are some of the more common stereotypes of singles.

All Singles Are Lonely

Because marriage has been considered the norm and culture has often romanticized marriage as a blissful, all-consuming relationship, singleness was thought of as just a passing phase to be resolved by the ultimate state of marriage. Singles are considered second best, unfulfilled, maladjusted, irresponsible, and immature at best, so it seems obvious that all singles must be lonely.

Studies comparing married and single adults showed that loneliness did not seem to be caused by the lack of having someone with whom to do things. (People may equate loneliness with being alone because they are uncomfortable being solitary and discovering their unique selves.) The determining factor was whether or not a person had someone with whom to share his or her problems—a kind of kindred spirit. The significant find was that singles, especially never-marrieds, were the least likely to associate being alone with loneliness.

On the other hand, those recently divorced associated being alone with loneliness and also felt they had lost someone with whom to share their problems. Married people associated poor quality of and lack of communication in their marriage with loneliness. Pairing did not necessarily eliminate loneliness.

All Singles Want to Get Married

Historically it has been assumed that women are more dependent than men and need the security that a mate could provide. It used to be an economical, sociological, and psychological necessity that women marry. Some people have preached that singles are only "half" persons, intended to spend their lives finding the other half in order to become one, or more precisely, whole. God never created "half" people. Our responsibility is our relationship with God, to mature in his grace and wisdom.

As times change, men and women are finding more options, more freedom, and more career opportunities.

Overall, Single Men Are Irresponsible

Society has a tendency to label anyone who does not conform to its expectations or standards as irresponsible. A few studies have attempted to indicate that the thirty-nine-year-old single male group is one of the most irresponsible segments of society (highest crime rate, arrest rate, drug rate, entrance into mental institutions). But the 1980s provided a whole new perspective on male singleness. Since then, young, educated single men have been running major companies. Singleness offers men a time of freedom for education and career. Men, often "taken care of" by Mom, aren't necessarily looking for just another person to take care of them. With home conveniences available, or as they learn cooking and living skills, men are more apt to take their time to wait for just the right woman to spend their lives with.

Singles Are Sexually Frustrated

A national questionnaire dealing with problem areas and frustrations of singles was given to both married and single adults. The results indicated that marrieds perceived that the number one problem singles face was sexual frustrations and expressions. Given the same questionnaire, singles ranked sexual frustration fifth place among their problems. The "swinging singles" image and singles bars have promoted a stereotype that singles are sexually active. There is the reality that some singles are sexually active. Many are living together. This is an area that must be addressed in the church. Studies indicate that Christian singles are more sexually active than had been assumed, though not as sexually active as the national average of singles. Still, the swinging single appears to be in the minority.

Sexuality and intimacy are two areas that must be addressed with singles. It also needs to be noted that marriage does not preclude sexual frustration.

The Singles Industry

Single people comprise the largest concentrated pool of sales prospects in the country today. It is, therefore, not surprising that a singles industry has emerged to multiple billions of dollars each year. And it is an industry that is growing. Singles apartments, bars, dating services, magazines, and vacations are just a few of the singles products available. Singles are the biggest purchasers of sports cars, condominiums, and fashions; are the greatest frequenters of restaurants (often going eight to ten times a week); and are the target of most major movies, television advertisements, and health clubs. Singles go where singles are, singles are spending more money, and singles are setting the trends.

The Church's Response

In order for the church to minister to singles and be a viable church in the twenty-first century it must redefine its mission and ministry. We need to rethink our biblical and theological roots and develop a new perspective on singleness. The church also needs to expand its term "family," moving from a traditional family definition to one that includes singles, widows, single-parent families, extended families, expanded families, step families, and blended families. We must become the family we are—the family of God!

And, in order to minister to today's singles, the church must also think in new patterns of ministry. Specialized ministries, time slots and church buildings, glamour programs, multi-staffs, and family ministry programs must be reevaluated in the decades to come.

Most of all, myths and stereotypes must be erased throughout each of the segments of the church in order to become community, a place where one can find help, strength, healing, and wholeness.

Single Adult Identity: Uncharted Territory

Few men and women actually set out to be single, yet close to one half of all adult Americans find themselves in this uncharted lifestyle. Singleness was thrust on many of them by a death or divorce, and they may feel ostracized or branded. Other singles don't want to be single and try frantically to alter their status. Many are teased about being single: "I can't believe you're not married yet!" And to others singleness is a provocative, sought-after, and flaunted lifestyle.

The American culture is highly educated and well-informed and understands human growth and development. Psychologists, sociologists, family therapists, and educators have been able to study human growth from conception to death. Each discipline describes growth by identifiable stages, phases, and benchmarks, producing thousands of books on the topic.

Developmental theories are based on a marriage model. Traditionally in America, it has been expected that 97 percent of the population would grow up following all of the "normal" developmental stages through high school into the next steps of dating, courtship, marriage, and children. With the rise of the singles phenomenon, the more than 50 percent divorce rate, and other sociological effects, these developmental patterns no longer apply. Developmental stages of single adults are not the same as developmental stages of married adults. This developmental gap contributes to the misunderstandings surrounding singleness and the growing social gap between single and married adults in America.

Major sociological and psychological literature states that serious research about singles is noticeably missing from the field of family sociology, though there are a few studies dealing with divorce. While not completely ignored by most writers on the family, singles are defined in terms of their relationship to marriage. Social psychologists are accustomed to referring to singles as "those who fail to marry," or as "those who do not make positive choices."

If singleness is discussed at all by these writers, it is generally in terms of stereotypes and assumptions. They see singles as hostile toward marriage or toward persons of the opposite sex; not having cut the umbilical cord from their parents; possibly being homosexual, unattractive, or having physical and psychological reasons for not finding a mate; afraid of involvement or commitment; lacking social skills for dating; having unrealistic criteria for finding a spouse; unwilling to assume responsibility; and the list goes on.

A divorced person is defined as someone who failed at marriage, could not adjust, or is unable to relate. No wonder approximately 80 percent of divorced people remarry within the first two years following their first divorce.

A New Awakening

America is changing. The singles phenomenon is a large part of this change. The statistic of over 70 million single adults is staggering, as it has many implications for the American culture. Trends predict that more than 50 percent of adults today will spend some significant time during their adult lives as divorced or widowed singles. One fourth of all U.S. families are single-parent families. And there are over 11 million blended families in the U.S. today.

Our concept of family is being redefined, reevaluated, and expanded to include singles, single parents, extended families, expanded families, and blended families. These individuals are looking for programs and ministries to assist them with the course and journey of their lives.

The Who of Singledom

It is important to understand that singles do not fall in one large group called "single adults." Today's single adult belongs to one of four very different groups, each with its own subgroups, varying needs, pressure points, and social and emotional concerns. Singles today are never-married; widowed; divorced; and separated. It is important to identify and understand the unique needs of each of these groups in order to minister effectively to them.

Why So Many Singles?

The increase in the number of single adults is a complex phenomenon, some of which is related to the reasons why men and women marry. Some of the reasons for marriage include the bond of love or sex, mutual aid in the struggle for existence, and the desire to have children. In today's urban and industrial age, modern conveniences, a career emphasis, the changing role of the family, the increased divorce rate, changing lifestyles, the women's rights movement, and fewer available men have made marriage less imperative as a means of providing love, aid, or children.

Though single lifestyles still carry a lot of uncertainty and conflicting messages, singles today are learning more about themselves and the world around them. As they live the single experience, they are able to identify three primary reasons for maintaining singleness: commitment to career, independence, and not meeting the right person.

Some Challenges of Singleness

While singleness has definite advantages, it carries with it some definite disadvantages as well. These include loneliness; an identity in the context of a married society; a tendency toward or preoccupation with self; a pattern of going it alone; and outside pressure or criticism and misunderstanding from family and friends.

Singles list five struggles that seem to take precedence in their lifestyles. The biggest frustration is in "being left out" or not being "included" by couples because of their singleness. Singles want to be part of the church, families, events, and leadership. They do not want to be thrust into singles-only groups. As Britton Wood states, "Singles want to be the church too." They want to be included equally as whole, growing people.

The second struggle for singles is finances, especially if the single is a parent and head of a household. Seventy-five percent of single-parent women find themselves on welfare in order to survive. There is no potential for two incomes. Singles also can get caught in the "me-now" syndrome, buying and doing things for themselves—now. Good financial counsel is needed.

Finding rewarding friendships is a third problem for singles. A rewarding friendship is one in which the friends can share, be honest, laugh, and cry—not a friendship in which one person is constantly pressuring the other to be paired off in an opposite-sex relationship, nor in which questions about a same-sex relationship arise. Maybe one of the biggest challenges facing the church today is to understand the concept of community and friendship for both marrieds and singles, young and old.

Single parenting responsibilities ranked fourth for both the custodial and noncustodial parents. Balancing work, parenting, and financial pressures while maintaining some form of social life and friendship is a major challenge.

Finally, singles have to deal with their sexual pressures. They indicated that the first four struggles consumed so much of their time and energy that sexual pressure ranked considerably below them. They admit to some sexual frustration but say that "being restricted sexually" had tended to make them "more creative and active in other ways."

Seasons of Singleness

The lack of an identity, caused by the lack of developmental information and combined with questions about their goals and needs, encourages many singles to desire marriage. Some simply fear that singleness might be for a lifetime and believe that "the grass is always greener on the other side of the fence." Singleness needs to be viewed as a season of time. A season is unpredictable, without a specific length, and with various opportunities. And indeed this season, for some, may be for all of life.

A season of singleness provides freedom to grow, for some a time for healing and renewal. Perhaps this is a time to celebrate or reflect. This can be a time of seeking understanding, perhaps to deal with some painful scars and memories of the past. For some this season may feel like winter, but perhaps that is needed for growth.

Seasons have beginnings, middles, and ends. Singles may find themselves going through various stages of singleness. Some might be in the stage of single parenting. Many are pursuing the stages of education or career. These stages may overlap each other, but each has its own distinct characteristics. There may be the inclination to move through a particular stage too quickly, trying to change it, not understanding it, not taking the opportunity for growth and change. The greatest challenge for singles and those who walk beside them is to understand the stage in which the singles find themselves and seize the challenge to become God's whole person.

Establishing a Biblical Basis
for the Single Adult Ministry

Bill Flanagan

A careful examination of Scripture reveals a deep concern for the fatherless (children who have been orphaned or who are with just one parent) and also for widows and the unmarried—individuals who, in their singleness, are struggling or perhaps desire to be married. The apostle Paul teaches that in whatever state we are to be content (see Phil. 4:11). As he writes to the Corinthian Christians in his first letter we gain a glimpse of his convictions about singleness. Chapter 7 is an important one for careful study by singles leaders.

Biblical Principles for Ministry

There are no more specific biblical principles for a single adult ministry than there are for many other significant ministries in the church. Therefore, it is important to look at an overview of the directives the Scriptures give to us for ministry in general. All Christians have a mandate from Scripture for ministry. A scriptural mandate is mandatory because the Bible is not only our focus, but also our final authority for all that we believe and do.

One of the most powerful and succinct passages teaching biblical ministry principles is the concluding verses of Peter's Pentecost sermon (Acts 2:14–39). The Christian community is challenged by the following verses to grow in four different dimensions. Each of these areas of focus has particular application for single adult ministry.

Grow in Numbers (Acts 2:41)

We read in Acts 2:41 and 47 that the Lord added daily to the community new lives that were touched and changed by the gospel. The fact that people were being "added" clearly teaches that the disciples already had something going. Therefore, single adults don't need to build a church of their own but, rather, need to become integrated into the church as it exists, making it even more complete and balanced.

This verse teaches that 3,000 people were drawn to Jesus Christ and added to the body in one day. That means evangelism was a significant part of the ministry. This raises the subject of our vision as well as our preparation to handle growth and integrate new people meaningfully into a congregation. Our ministries must be geared to grow, but the best way to grow in numbers is to keep focused on individuals. We are called to be shepherds, not ranchers. A shepherd knows his flock by name, while a rancher only knows how many head there are in his herd.

Grow Up (Acts 2:42)

We are called by God to grow in our personal and corporate spiritual life. The early church did this in four basic ways as taught in the text:

1. in the teaching of the apostles
2. in fellowshipping together
3. in the breaking of bread
4. in praying for one another

A single adult ministry, as any ministry in the church, needs to be a part of the total Christian life. Therefore, it is appropriate that our groups reflect the social, relational, sexual, recreational, intellectual, and spiritual dimensions of who we are as children of God. Single adult ministries that are biblically focused should not be narrowly tuned to spiritual development but open to the totality of the human experience.

Grow Out (Acts 2:43–45)

The early church had a mission. It did not exist for itself alone but reached out into the world with the message of Christ and with works of compassion and love.

Single adults are a mission field, but it can be equally true that single adults have a mission. They exhibit a special awareness and sensitivity that the church vitally needs to hear to accomplish its evangelistic task with tact, wisdom, and compassion. A single adult ministry, therefore, should never exist to meet only its own needs. It must exist to serve the larger community, seeing it as a mission field with deep spiritual and human needs.

There is always a beautiful tension and balance between our Lord's command to "come" as well as "go." Come and get your needs met. Come and meet new friends. Come to events that offer stimulating opportunities for personal growth. But at the same time "Go." Go into the world to work and play, to be disciples of Christ. If all we are saying is "Come," sooner or later we will stagnate and die.

Grow Together (Acts 2:46–47)

The early church was a family, a community of togetherness, support, and encouragement. Few saw themselves as "Lone Ranger Christians." Faith to them was always personal but never private. They were a people in process, growing together.

An important goal or measuring stick one can apply to any ministry is the exclamation of outsiders echoing an expression heard in the early church, "See how they love each other."

Growing together in the biblical sense means that single people be integrated into the whole life of the congregation, not as a satellite appendage or "little leper colony." A church or ministry that is pleasing to God and that is focused biblically is one that grows in each of these four ways. The whole church includes those who are young and old, black and white, handicapped and healthy, male and female, educated and ignorant, rich and poor, married and single, focusing its energies together to bring praise and glory to Jesus Christ.

Practical Guidelines for Using Scripture in Single Adult Ministry

A singles ministry that keeps itself biblically focused will probably have several ways of utilizing the Word of God in its regular program.

Single Adult Class

Any singles ministry that involves a considerable number of people will center in a class, usually on Sunday morning, taught by a pastor or trained layperson. This class will focus on the Scriptures and will interpret biblical materials in the context of the issues of daily living that apply particularly to single adults. Usually these classes are ongoing in nature and are not focused on single adult issues as a steady diet. Most singles get bored with this and want to move on to other more important biblical studies.

Small Group Studies

Singles ministries that are growing in their Christian discipleship will employ small group experiences. The covenantal groups exist not just to study the Bible, but also for fellowship, personal sharing, and prayer. Many singles groups have small group ministries that utilize *open* groups where people can come and rotate in and out on a regular basis. These groups are particularly helpful for new people. Also, covenant groups that are *closed* after they are formed may be a crucial part of a ministry to develop trust, intimacy, healing, and spiritual growth.

Over the years, single adults have been turned off by churches that look down their noses and metaphorically hit singles over the head with their large ninety-pound black Bibles. It is a biblical axiom that we accept people where they are, not where we think they ought to be. All of us need to be wary of using Scripture to judge, to justify, or to prove our point of view. While the Bible "is useful for teaching, rebuking, correcting and training in righteousness, so that the man of God may be thoroughly equipped for every good work" (2 Tim. 3:16), it is equally true that Scripture is to be taught and used with care and compassion. The church exists to build up and not tear down, to welcome and not exclude.

We need to continually endeavor to build a strong biblical base and rationale for dealing with some of the difficult issues of our time, such as divorce, relationships, sex, and remarriage. Singles do not want pat answers in response to these issues but want to discover God's will for their lives within the healthy tension that often exists between grace and the Law.

Part 2

Needs and Issues
of Single Adult Ministry

Dating

Harold Ivan Smith

Dating has been labeled the scourge of modern single adult society; few singles think well of the process. After all, many don't want to be dating in the first place—they'd rather be married.

The Big Question

I have an acquaintance who opens every conversation with one question: "How's your dating life?" The previous conversation could have been on trivial aspects of the levitical Law or on car prices; his curiosity is undaunted. Many single adults get annoyed by similar questions from married believers.

There's a classic toothpaste commercial that asks, "How's your love life?" The person with a mouth full of sparkling teeth sounds off a list of superlatives: "Great! Super! Incredible!" Then the announcer sternly demands, "How's *your* love life?" Reluctantly another person confesses, "Awful." (There are a lot of nods in the audience.) Fortunately there's hope for the guy: Consistent use of brand X toothpaste will make him very dateable. The commercial closes with the hero wandering into the sunset with a beautiful woman at his side (probably late for a Bible study). The moral of the story: Use *this* product and you won't be sitting home watching this commercial.

Once upon a time, dating was relaxed, fun, adventuresome, even inexpensive. There were set rules that assisted the process toward the inevitable—marriage. Supposedly, someday when one least expected it (that's why grooming aids are so essential), Prince or Princess Charming would come sweeping into one's life to the strains of "Ah, sweet mystery of life, at last I've found you." Furthermore, dating had a goal: "And they lived happily ever after."

For many single adults, the most troublesome aspect of adult dating is the memory residue from adolescence. Have you ever drunk a glass of milk, then noticed the filmy residue on the glass? Because most adolescent dating left a lot to be desired, the residual effects cloud the adult experience.

Some single adults complain that dating is like dividing up for softball in the third grade. "Somebody pick me, *please*," the softball and dating candidates plead. Softball wasn't much fun when the two captains argued, "You take him!" "No! You take him!" Dating can bring similar rejection.

The Big Picture

Some singles leaders have constructed intense "biblical systems" of dating. Unfortunately, dating was beyond the comprehension of Moses, Abraham, and most of the biblical authors. Proof texts won't be helpful to everyone.

However, I would suggest the following guidelines for leaders.

Face the reality of dating. Adult dating can be a pleasure or the pits. Singles cannot pretend that they are not adults or are not single. Nor can they avoid the basic need for relational living. Single adults are not designed to be lone rangers. Even the masked man had his faithful sidekick, Tonto.

Enlarge your understanding of dating. Help your single adults see dating as an opportunity rather than a problem. That requires a positive spirit and some creative suggestions for healthy dating habits and ideas.

Help singles express and work through negative feelings. Some single adults have a dating life that leaves nondaters envious. Many insist on sharing tidbits over coffee and doughnuts on Sunday morning. As a result, "So how come I don't date?" will be the question in the singles' minds all during your session. The reality is that a single can tithe, teach Sunday school, have an incredible figure and personality, live at the best address in town, have the correct doctrinal conclusions on everything, and still be dateless!

They will respond, "It's not fair!" Your response may be little more than, "Life isn't fair." Some singles will cry, some will be depressed, others will perhaps covet their neighbor's dating. Appreciate their pain of datelessness and so help them work through negative feelings.

Help singles give up the grand illusions. Some singles may still be searching for the perfect match! However, by this time in their life, expectations of Prince or Princess Charming may have changed. Some are tempted now to settle for the discount; some are motivated by desperation. Help them find a happy medium. Ironically, the single may be more emotionally and spiritually mature at this stage of life and therefore be more likely to be Prince or Princess Charming to someone.

The Big Realities

What are the realities that single adults face in dating?

The old rules don't apply. Maybe singles want dating referees in striped shirts to keep the process moving and fair. You can help the newly single person make sense of the bewildering changes in dating practices. Many divorced and widowed people have been stunned by the sexual expectations in dating today. Help the single adult confront that reality.

Some professional teams have difficulty early in a season with the new rules. Rules change. Today women do ask men out. Certainly that frightens many traditional males. So they hibernate.

For yuppie-oriented singles, dating must be squeezed into a busy work schedule. Some prefer to date people who are in the same or similar line of work. Moreover, there is more spontaneous dating, which doesn't necessarily mean the asker is taking the askee for granted.

A lot of people aren't dating. It is safe to take bragging about dating and divide by four. People often exaggerate in describing their dating life. It is equally easy for some single adults to be oversensitive about dating, to be too hard on themselves. Have them ask themselves, "Am I really the only person in my neighborhood who isn't dating?"

Some dates aren't worth the hassle. Too many single adults live by the notion, "A bad date is better than no date!" Wrong. That notion may explain the significant increase in what is termed "date rape"—when a date turns into a wrestling match and ultimately into rape.

Just how creative is the dater? In singleland there are psychopaths, neurotics, abusive personalities, people who "hate" the opposite sex. The more desperate one is to date, the more likely one is to encounter one of these. Too many single adults have put themselves into situations and then prayed for deliverance.

There are singles who are so focused on themselves that they do not have time to get in touch with another person. How many monologues can a single survive?

Finally, some singles think that x expenditure of funds on a date automatically entitles them to a corresponding portion of intimacy. Too many do not understand the word no, or *NO!*

Finances are important. There is a common but dying tradition that males should pay for the date. That may have been true in adolescent dating, but in today's world, a single who insists on maintaining that standard will watch a lot of TV reruns, dateless.

Many single men are not, contrary to popular opinion, rolling in dough. Rent, taxes, insurance, car expenses, utilities take a disproportionate share of any person's income (especially if you add child support and alimony). Women who reach for the check—who seriously offer to pay—and men who are not threatened by such, date more.

When/then thinking is unproductive. Some singles think, *When I lose twenty-five pounds, then I'll date,* or, *When I get a new job . . .* or, *When I change singles groups, then . . .* This thinking makes dateless evenings a little easier to handle because one can say to oneself, *It's really my fault that I am sitting here, dateless.*

"Possessive" dating is the discount of dating relationships. A lot of dating is a flea market for bartering fringe benefits. Some singles become so attached to the fringes that they cannot terminate unwholesome relationships. Possessive dating means, "I don't have to worry about Friday night—we'll do something," regardless of the emotional commitment of the daters.

A lot of men want to date women who can cook or sew or clean house. Some women use men for home maintenance, automobile repair, or security consultations. Some people manipulate others as a basic survival tactic. But with the fringes come the strings that become ropes. Christian singles who date must realize that those they date are equally loved by Jesus. Therefore, any manipulation or exploitation is unthinkable.

Help your single adults develop skills to carefully evaluate the "emotional portfolio" of individuals they date.

Some men are Mama's boys. In a world where macho is important, some men are desperately confused by the new rules and expectations of women. Some are looking for a mother rather than a wife. Some men become prisoners to shyness to such a degree that a date is an incredible psychological hurdle. Some men do not know how to treat a woman. They envy the finesse of their friends, even self-indict, asking, "Who would want to go out with me?" Some desperately fear rejection.

Remember, for bona fide Mama's boys, Mama has home-court advantage and a decisive head start.

The Big Confusion

If a single is tightly clinging to a fantasy of Prince or Princess Charming and has heavily invested in that fantasy, what does he or she do to "tide oneself over" until the tardy Charming arrives on the scene? Just as a snack may reduce one's cravings for food until mealtime, so there are individuals who seek "relational snacks" or minirelationships.

So, the individual invests enough to keep the door ajar but not enough to be exclusive. The unspoken philosophy is, "I won't commit myself to you long enough to see if there is potential for a lasting relationship. Besides, someone better may come along and it would be difficult to dump you gracefully. So, let's just be friends, OK?" Many single adults want riskless, hassleless dating. Some become comfortable with the uncomfortable. But the essential element in relationship building and maintenance is risk.

One difficulty with relational snacks is misunderstood intentions. The "snack" hopes "If I keep giving and giving, eventually he or she is going to fall in love with me." A lot of single adults have "special" friends. Some proclaim to the married world that that is one of the luxuries of singleness. However, one or the other of the "pals" could have unspoken romantic intentions. This can lead to hurt.

Another kind of dating is "agenda" dating—i.e., dating only serious candidates for marriage. Agenda dating is unproductive. Dating should enhance friendships, and friendships are a good way to evolve into marriage.

Then there is the dating done by "transitional" Christians. Transitional Christians confuse everyone. There are a lot of undisciplined Christian single adults who have accepted Jesus as Savior but not as Lord of their dating. So, they walk in both worlds, but not firmly in either one. Christian singles who date have a commitment to wholeness in Christ Jesus that they must not compromise.

Christian singles who date must be alert to "snowballing" relationships. They should not hesitate to ask for a time-out. Christian singles who date must watch their language. They should not say, "I love you" without understanding the significance of the words and the potential for misunderstanding. Different people mean different things by those words. Christian singles who date need to realize that other single adults compare their witness on Saturday night (and any bragging or commentary on dating) with what they profess on Sunday mornings. Christian singles who date cannot ignore realities, but through faith in Christ, they can deal with those realities redemptively.

Goal and Career Planning

Jon Clemmer

The biblical model for planning and goal-setting is set by God himself. It is evident that God establishes clear personal tasks and goals for himself, and he always accomplishes them (Eph. 1:11).

God has also laid a solid foundation of goals and plans in the way that he administers his will and designs through his children (2 Cor. 4:7; Eph. 3:20). God then holds us personally accountable for our time usage and talent development (Matt. 25:14–30).

God has ordained that the Christian life is not neutral in the service of Christ. He has an action plan that we must endeavor to discover and follow (Jer. 29:11–14). We must resist the enemy in the pursuit of Christ-honoring goals and objectives (1 Peter 5:8).

Goal-Planning

Types of Goals

1. *Long-term goals.* These are goals that involve one's whole life and every aspect of it. They tend to reflect our values in terms of what is important or not important to us as far as the big picture is concerned. These should include all the major areas of one's life such as personal, developmental (including spiritual), social, fam-

ily relational, vocational, recreational, financial, and communal. Singles need to think in terms of long-term goals. So many singles tend to put life on hold until they marry.

2. *Intermediate goals.* These are goals that involve every aspect of one's life over a specific period of time. Three years is a good length of time within which to accomplish intermediate goals; this seems long enough to notice significant progress but short enough that an individual can manage personal life choices during that time.

3. *Short-term goals.* These are goals that can involve every aspect of one's life or one certain aspect of life at the present moment. The question has been asked, "Suppose you were to find out today that you only had six months left to live. How would you change your life?" Asking this question can force a person to weed out the insignificant goals and priorities in his current lifestyle and refocus on the truly important things. Or, there may be one need, dream, or commitment that requires special attention. It alone may become the short-term goal.

Seeing Dreams Become Realities

The secret to getting large tasks done is to break them down into smaller, manageable increments. There are classically three levels or strata of planning necessary to accomplish larger goals or tasks.

1. *The objective.* The objective is the vision, event, large task, or idea that one wishes to see become a reality. An objective can almost never be accomplished by completing one task alone. (For example, My objective is to hold a weekend retreat for 200 single adults at a resort two hours from the church.)

2. *The goal.* The goal is one of a limited number (three to ten) of tasks that, when all accomplished, will guarantee the accomplishment of the objective. A goal can rarely be accomplished by one task alone. (For example, My goal is to line up a retreat location for 200 single adults, 2 hours from the church.)

3. *The action step or strategy.* One of a limited number (one to ten) of tasks that, when accomplished, signal the completion of the step. These are small enough increments that each can usually be accomplished by one task alone. (For example, My action step is to call five different conference and retreat centers and inquire as to cost and availability.)

Using Your Time

Planning is key to success. Many singles have large amounts of discretionary time and, as a result, often waste large chunks of it and then feel guilty. Singles especially need to consider the following principles of time usage.

1. *Plan your time.* Just as you plan your money (set up a budget) or your vacation (line up transportation and accommodations) so you need to plan your time on a quarterly, weekly, and daily basis. I recommend three hours for the quarterly planning session, one hour for the weekly session, and one half hour for the daily session. But, regardless of the time spent on planning, the point is to plan. Each should be made in light of long-term, intermediate, and short-term goals you have already established as well as your priorities within each category. Such planning will give you confidence in making and keeping personal time commitments.

2. *Plan your tasks.* Many singles tend only to schedule their appointments or commitments where other people are concerned. However, they will accomplish their personal tasks far better if they also schedule in time to do certain tasks in which only they are involved (e.g., personal devotions, paying bills, etc.).

3. *Set priorities.* In the classic pamphlet on time management called *Tyranny of the Urgent*, Charles E. Hummel states, "The urgent things of life often crowd out the important." How true this is for all people—especially singles. One way to keep the important tasks on top of the list is to arrange your To-Do list. Each To-Do list, whether kept on a daily, weekly, monthly, quarterly, or annual basis, can be arranged item by item, so that the most important items get done first. To do this, you can use the A-B-C system. In this system an *A* placed next to a numbered item on a To-Do list means it is absolutely essential, and that it will pay high dividends in terms of goal accomplishment when completed. A *B* placed next to a numbered item means that it is important and worthwhile but not vital. This is an item that, if left undone, would *not* create serious problems. A *C* placed next to a numbered item means that it is of limited value. *C* items are often there merely for future reference and can often become *B* items

and then *A* items as time changes priorities. Beside the A-B-C method of arranging priorities, a check mark is very crucial to denote an urgent item that calls for immediate action and that cannot be left undone. The check mark allows one to go back and reemphasize some priorities as time passes and they become more crucial. Again, the point is not *this* system of numbers, letters, or checks, but *some* system of writing things down and maintaining order and balance.

4. *Evaluate your priorities.* It is good to set time aside weekly, monthly, and annually to see if you really are accomplishing your goals with the priorities set. This can be a time of real encouragement or chastisement as you see whether or not you have disciplined yourself to follow a plan.

We all need assistance in planning and setting goals. The singles leader can be a great model to the singles. The result is fulfillment and satisfaction of growth and maturity. This is a marvelous ministry from which many singles will benefit.

Career Counseling

For many singles there is great concern about career goals and the destination of their lives in a vocation. Career counseling is near the top of the list of issues that a singles minister deals with regularly.

Many singles are very young (eighteen to twenty-five) and are just embarking on new career adventures, yet there is a high level of concern and doubt about "this job being the right one." Some singles enter the job market with an already high level of dissatisfaction in life. Therefore, the job is added to the same list of life's frustrations and question marks.

Singles are on the move. Many are not planted geographically or relationally. Their options for friends and scenery are wide open. Their career is not always a number-one priority. Added to that is a lack of financial commitments. As a result, career transition and mobility are more likely.

Other singles need to work just to survive. Some are recently divorced and have to reenter the job market. Education and skills might be few. Counsel is needed.

Pastoral Counseling

When counseling single adults on career choice, evaluation, and change, try to focus on the following issues:

- Discerning God's will according to biblical principles
- Including personal enjoyment as a criterion
- Handling inappropriate pressure from parents and friends
- Evaluating past experiences in the job market
- Soliciting the opinions of close friends and relatives
- Getting sophisticated *personality* testing done through a reputable Christian counselor
- Getting sophisticated *vocational* testing done through a reputable counselor
- Considering any limitations in ability or education
- Determining whether further training is needed
- Getting the hard facts regarding the current job market
- Keeping your faith in Christ strong (see James 1:6–8)
- Knowing the principles behind a call to full-time ministry

Resources on Career Counseling

There is a wealth of material on the market dealing with every aspect of career planning. Many professional singles will read these books or attend specialized seminars and conferences on the subject. Therefore, you don't need to be an expert in the literature. But it does help to be able to point singles to some books that will help them get started. The two books I recommend are:

What Color Is Your Parachute? Richard Nelson Bolles, Ten Speed Press, Berkeley, Calif., 1984.

The Three Boxes of Life, Richard Nelson Bolles, Ten Speed Press, Berkeley, Calif., 1981.

The final and most valuable resources are the leader's prayers for, encouragement of, and perseverance with the single in transition. Your support and possibly a support group of God's caring and loving people are most significant.

Finances and Housing Needs

Andy Morgan

Divorce is considered one of the most traumatic and stressful experiences a person can encounter. Therefore, there is no doubt that when people go through a divorce, they will face major emotional, psychological, spiritual, and physical changes. Add to that the trauma of relocating, paying bills, possibly changing careers, upkeep of home and automobile, and perhaps raising children alone or "long-distance."

This chapter deals specifically with some of the financial and housing issues that the divorced person faces. The basis of this chapter is the result of surveys and conversations with over four hundred single adults. The purpose is not to be exhaustive or scientifically accurate; instead the chapter is intended to inform, to help make us aware of certain areas of need that a single adult may face, and to give some concrete suggestions that can be used by ministers, churches, counselors, and single adults themselves. Some suggestions will be able to be put into place with little effort—just a few phone calls; whereas other suggestions may involve a major effort by the church or a particular ministry.

Of the many problems that the single adult may face, finances and housing may cause the greatest amount of stress. Housing came up over and over again in surveys as the main financial need during divorce, because a house or rental payment is usually the largest payment anyone makes in a month. Coming up with a security deposit was also mentioned; that amount is usually needed over and above the usual monthly payment.

What Singles Have to Say

Though the financial side of finding a new residence is extremely important, the housing issue is also emotional: "We've shared this home all our married life. How can I possibly move out?" "How can I take the kids out of school in the middle of a school year?" "All my friends live in this town. How can I move where there are only strangers?" "A three-room apartment after a seven-room house? What will I do with all my things? These and memories are all I have left." Many—too many—major decisions have to be made, usually in a short amount of time, adding more stress to an already stressful situation.

Housing is the "biggie," but there are also several other financial needs that have to be dealt with, any one of which can cause a financial structure to come tumbling down. A home without heat, lights, or water is not considered much of a home in America. Utilities need to be paid every month. Thankfully, some of the utility companies are willing to help people work out a payment plan, so that service is not discontinued.

Putting good food on the table three times a day is another area where changes may have to be made. Shopping becomes a chore— sometimes a nightmare—because you now have $35 to spend on a week's groceries and you used to have $135. Name brands may have to go; and that '29 Depression story about "adding another potato and some water to the soup" now becomes true again.

Automobiles and insurance are also part of the "American way." You must get a job if you didn't have one before, you must be able to drive to that job, and your car must be insured. Do you borrow from relatives? Just when you think you have your monthly budget worked out, one of these six-month bills comes around and throws it all out of whack. If you're lucky, the kids' medical bills are still covered, but your routine checkups with the doctor and dentist may have to be postponed.

Clothing is another area of concern. Again, your values and ideas about being in style may have to change. You may have to start making do with last year's styles, rummage-sale bargains, and hand-me-downs from relatives and friends. Pride takes another step backward.

So far, all we've discussed are basics for survival. What about vacations? Spending money for the little extras? Savings in the bank for a rainy day? (Overnight, *all* your days may become rainy days!)

Though there is no guarantee, most often the noncustodial mate is able to take the kids someplace special for vacation. And you are happy for them . . . almost. "Santa Claus Dad" and "Disney World Mom" become real. Often the custodial parent is just getting into the full-time job market and hasn't had time to acquire a paid vacation. So the competition for the kids' hearts, the jealousy, the "this is not fair" syndrome sets in at the same time as all the financial worries.

If you are fortunate enough to be able to get all the basics under control, often there isn't much, if anything, left over. Fun times become creative, because movies and dinners out and bowling and concerts are too expensive. Walks, bike rides, puzzles, minitreats at McDonald's, and trips to the park all take on a new meaning.

If your sense of security was wrapped up in mutual funds or savings accounts, you literally may be forced to move it out of the bank and into the hands of God. The story of Job becomes precious. If you're strong and can hang on long enough, you can say, "If he could do it, so can I."

When asked what organizations helped the most when facing the financial, housing, and emotional trauma of a divorce, it was surprising how few people found the help they needed through the church. This is a shame because the Bible says, "Religion that God our Father accepts as pure and faultless is this: to look after orphans and widows in their distress and to keep oneself from being polluted by the world" (James 1:27). The widows and orphans (fatherless) of the twentieth century include our divorced people and their innocent children.

What the Body of Christ Can Do

The church can, and more importantly *should,* take a very active role in helping to restore a person's life to a sense of wholeness and stability in the midst of one of the major traumas of life. To do this the body of Christ needs to first open their hearts and minds to areas of ministry that are unique and challenging. Second, the church must do something.

There are many ways that the church or a particular ministry can help. The main tool would be a committee that would handle the networking involved. In times of great stress, it can be very difficult to know where to turn. There are so many questions and seemingly so few answers. The church, through this committee (possibly only one person in a small church), could be the "pool" where those who are dying of thirst could come for a drink. This pool should be full of refreshing water and surrounded by many cups.

One cup could be a "housing" cup. There could be a network within the church of people who have short-term housing available. "How many rooms?" "Are children and/or pets allowed?" "How would expenses be handled?" are all questions that could be asked of people who were willing to open their homes. An index file would be kept and referred to as needed. Perhaps people vacation in Florida every winter and would appreciate having someone in their home for six months to take care of things. Others might have a room or two that they would like to rent out for as long as necessary. This "housing cup" could also contain a directory of the different types of homes and apartments that are available in the area and a contact person in the real estate field who would alert the church to places as they become available.

A second cup could be a "food and utility" cup. Again, knowing where to get help is sometimes as important as being able to do it yourself. "How does one apply for food stamps?" "I hear about government programs that help the needy. Where are they? How do I get in touch with them?" "Food pantries, cheese and milk programs . . . how do I connect with them?" "I've received notice that the gas is being shut off. What now?" If the church had the answers to these questions, the distressed person could avoid the countless headaches and the days and weeks of "letting your fingers do the walking" that it might normally take. When even getting out of bed becomes a chore, facing numerous organizations, all asking numerous questions, can be overwhelming. And frightening. And humiliating. And just plain difficult.

Another cup could be labeled "maintenance." Homes and cars and furnaces and water heaters have a way of breaking down—always at a bad time. The church could possibly work out a deal with a local mechanic who would work on cars through their referral at a discounted rate. Another file or "yellow pages for the church" could be kept on individuals who would be willing to help when a divorced person in their church had a breakdown of a mechanical, electrical, automotive, or plumbing nature. The church could also host a seminar on basic car maintenance or be able to recommend such a class through their community adult education program or junior college.

The fourth cup could be the "benevolence" cup. Every church should have an emergency fund, monies set aside for just that purpose: groceries, medical bills, rent, utilities, whatever is deemed an emergency. Most churches have a few people (even one person would help) who are willing to give extra financial support. Missions should begin in your own backyard, and I believe that the local church would be willing to help if they knew the money was going toward real needs. Or the church could build into its budget an "emergency account." A percentage of the offerings could be set aside weekly for certain emergencies. So in addition to supporting its buildings, staff, and programs, the church would be in a very real sense looking after orphans and widows in their distress.

A "resource" cup is number five. Additional support could be offered through valuable resource contacts: a banker willing to offer financial counseling; a lawyer who could offer legal advice; a list of phone numbers and prices of local day-care centers; names and numbers of those available for babysitting; crisis center and hot-line numbers; a list of classes offered by the community colleges that are geared to helping singles get back on their feet; women's resource centers, and so on. Most metro areas have church-related agencies that can help. Find out what they are. Keep a file of them. Find a dedicated person in your church who has a heart for the hurting and can keep this file current.

Finally, the church should have a "healing" cup. Having financial needs met will relieve much of the stress of a divorce, but certainly not all of it. The emotional pain cuts deeply. Healing of the heart takes longer than healing of the broken-down water heater. Where should a person turn then? First, last, and always to his church family. As in the other areas, the church can have much to offer.

One of the most difficult aspects of facing crisis and change is embarrassment. When a person who has been accustomed to buying the best cuts of meat and the softest toilet tissue now has to apply for food stamps, a tremendous amount of emotional upheaval erupts. Some would rather starve themselves than have to face this type of embarrassment. Part of the responsibility of the church is to accompany singles through the process of financial assistance so they know it's OK to experience special needs; that it's OK to receive help. Then, and only then, will the church be able to support singles emotionally as well as physically to work through the process of starting over.

Churches can offer a support group of individuals who will walk through the issues and problems with a hurting person. They could provide counseling within the church or have a network of counselors and services who can deal with identity and crisis issues. They also need to help the divorced person form a new base of security. Something God asks of all of us (but is often ignored unless we are forced into it through a crisis such as a divorce) is that we move from our materialistic mentality to a spiritual and relational mentality. How is this accomplished? Through spiritual counseling and teaching people that they need to focus on their relationship with Christ, who is their only true security. Human beings being what they are, it is easier to trust what they can see and feel and touch—their homes, their jobs, their retirement accounts. When these artificial supports are knocked away, it's time to take a good hard look at faith. How strong and deep is it? Is it real? Can God be trusted? A church should be able to guide a person to the answers to these questions.

None of these suggestions for how a church helps its hurting through housing and financial and emotional needs are difficult. They just need a little organization and a person or two who are very dedicated to answering God's call to serve in love; people who are not called to judge or condemn or belittle, but to love.

6

Guiding Spiritual Growth

Jim E. Towns

Many adult singles today claim to be religious. Yet, there is a distinct difference between being affiliated with the religion and having a personal relationship with Jesus Christ! Spiritual life and vitality is sought by many who claim to be Christians. They are seeking to know their Creator personally. However, many are confused. Others are thirsting for spiritual refreshment and guidance.

Nonscriptural Concepts

Even though they feel a need to know God, some people have immature concepts about who God really is. Currently there are several inadequate, nonscriptural concepts about God and spiritual growth.

Spiritual yuppiedom. If you have all the appropriate material possessions and position, then God will be happy to have you on his team.

Spiritual Santa Claus. God is keeping a list and checking it twice to find out who has been naughty and nice. If you live right, then only good things will happen to you.

Spiritual chance. God is a "slot machine in the sky." You put money in the offering, pull the prayer handle, and he will pay off sooner or later.

Spiritual computer. God is a giant computer in the clouds. You punch your problem tape, run it though the computer, and God will kick out solutions at church.

Spiritual policeman. God is a policeman who keeps you in line. God is watching and hoping you will mess up so he can crack you over the head with a club.

Formal Sunday event. Perhaps one of the most common misconceptions that people have about God is that he is a formal Sunday event. In other words, spiritual growth and vitality begin and end in worship, ritual, form, organ music, and sermons.

A Scriptural Concept

It is imperative that we communicate to our singles a scriptural concept of God. It is not possible to have an appropriate, healthy relationship with God without having a scriptural understanding of who he is! A distorted idea of him will cause a distorted response to him. A right response to God will come from a right understanding of him.

Scripture reveals God as Father-Son-Spirit. Throughout time, God has been revealing himself. Scripture gives a progressive revelation of his nature. The first expression of God is as God-Father, who is the creator, ruler, and sustainer of the universe—and me! In the Bible, God progressively revealed himself as *Elohim*—the supreme, all-powerful God; *El Shaddai*—the almighty God; *Jehovah-Jireh*—the Provider; *Jehovah*—the Redeemer and Lord; *Jehovah-Rophe*—the Healer; *Jehovah-Nissi*—the Banner of Victory; *Jehovah-Shalom*—our Peace; *Jehovah-Rohi*—our Shepherd; and *Jehovah-Shammah*—our God who dwells with us. God-Father loves us so much that he not only gave us life, but also provides for us.

The second expression of God is as God-Son: Jesus Christ, Savior, and Lord of those who trust him. The greatest revelation of God is given to us through Jesus Christ. He came to tell us about our Father in heaven. But more than that, Jesus Christ came to provide the way for us to be united with our Father.

The third expression of God is as God-Spirit: the illuminator of the Scriptures and enabler of his people to perform his works. Just as holy men of God were inspired to write the Scriptures, we must trust the same Spirit of God to illuminate us in order to understand spiritual truths. The Holy Spirit convicts us of our need for Jesus the Savior, and Jesus unites us with the Father.

Who's Right?

In the Christian faith there is a battle between legalism and libertinism. The carnal Christian boasts of his liberty. The spiritual Christian boasts of his slavery to Jesus. Many singles will confuse legalism for fundamentalism and libertinism for liberalism.

In legalism, people get caught up more with the means than the end. To these people, the Bible is only a rule book. They live by the letter of the law while often ignoring the spirit of the law. There are those who make an oversimplification of scriptural truths. They live by surface responses rather than getting the deeper meaning of what God is really saying. Then there are some who give easy answers for tough questions. They have a list of fifty Scriptures and recite answers without thinking and praying. They spiritually cop out, not really knowing a word from God on a specific situation. These people need to consider the spirit of the law as well as the letter of the law.

In libertinism, people view the Bible as only a guidebook for freedom. This group seems to be drowning in freedom. They say, "Once saved always saved, so I can do anything I desire." They have the carefree attitude of "I don't care what others think." This misses the point because the point is not what others think of us but what they think of God because of us!

Guiding Spiritual Growth

Whether spiritual guidance is one-on-one or in a group, the wise minister or counselor will first realize that single adults are not overgrown youth. They are adults and must be treated as such. Yet, the leader has an important role and responsibility to provide spiritual guidance resulting in spiritual growth.

Some singles try consciously or unconsciously to manipulate spiritual growth. Sometimes through deliberate design, singles set out to try to *make* God do what they desire. The following components of proper spiritual growth can be misused to try to manipulate God:

The Scriptures. Some people go to the Bible and demand that God fulfill the passage MY WAY in MY TIME! This is being presumptuous even from the "name it and claim it" perspective.

Prayer. Many people think that if they pray hard enough or long enough, God will have to give what is demanded. Or they use a Bible verse and say, "God, you said it; you have to do it."

Praise. Some people try to manipulate God through praising. They think that if they truly praised the Lord, he would have to change situations and meet demands.

Bargaining. Many people try to make a bargain with God. They say, "God, if you will do . . . , then I will do. . . ."

There are many marvelous methods of Bible study, prayer, and praise. Excellent study guides and programs are readily available. However, spiritual growth begins with a desire to know the Blesser rather than trying to get a blessing. The answer for producing spiritual growth is not in formulas, conducting meetings, and so on. Many people seek to live off such formulas. These singles may be "miracle hoppers" and "meeting jumpers" who are searching but spiritually shallow. Spiritual depth is realized when God's truths and plan for living are appropriated.

In counseling, teaching, and preaching, we need to maintain that spiritual growth occurs when we let God be God in our lives. The wise minister and counselor will go beyond the Band-Aid approach. He or she will cover the basics of Christ's saving gospel, being sure the single adult has trusted Jesus as Savior and Lord. Then helpful tools (Bible study, memorization, meditation, and prayer) can be given as helps to grow in a living, vital, personal faith in Jesus Christ.

7

The Single Adult Lifestyle

Harold Ivan Smith

Ultimately, lifestyle is a choice. Several factors compete for consideration in that choice. First, there are numbers. At the time this nation was founded, approximately 6 percent of the population was unmarried; a single adult was highly conspicuous in that society and, therefore, highly suspect. Today, more than 40 percent of the population is unmarried. There is safety in numbers, so more singles may choose to remain single. Single adults are the trendsetters, particularly those who are yuppies or baby-boomers.

Second, materialism can influence the choice of lifestyle. As a group, singles account for billions of dollars in disposable income. Single adults spend their dollars on eating out; liquor sales; automobile sales; and vacation sales. One in six home buyers in the U.S. is single. In fact, single women have emerged as the fastest-growing group of new home buyers.

Third, mobility is a factor in lifestyle. Singles may find themselves living, by their choice or an employer's choice, halfway across the continent from their families. How are they to shape their lives?

Three Basic Lifestyles

I believe there are three basic lifestyles common for singles, some of which overlap.

Mate-seekers. These single adults are committed to the notion that life begins when they get married. The agenda of singleness is to find a mate, and some would add, "the sooner, the better." Singles events and groups are places to meet someone. The mate-seekers often define themselves by their dating or deep desire to date.

Self-seekers. These single adults are committed to getting ahead or concentrating on their career. This is typical among the host of single adults labeled "yuppies," or young urban professionals. They work longer hours, pursue more leads, make more sales presentations, and do more billings than a married person who has a family to go home to.

Some who are not professionals are still self-seekers, in that their lives revolve around themselves.

Kingdom-seekers. These single adults are committed to relational and spiritual development and maturity. Even if they perceive singleness as negative (and few kingdom-seekers do), they realize it beats other options. Kingdom-seekers generally see their singleness as a season. Many kingdom-seekers become vitally committed to single adult ministry and other ministries in their churches. They take Paul's admonition seriously: "An unmarried man is concerned about the Lord's affairs—how he can please the Lord. But a married man is concerned about the affairs of this world—how he can please his wife—and his interests are divided" (1 Cor. 7:32–34).

This single adult would say that, if marriage happens, it will be a pleasant surprise. If it doesn't happen, it will not be a bitter disappointment.

Profiles of Christian Singles

A Christian single is frequently identifiable by what he or she believes; by how he or she behaves; by where he or she belongs; and by how he or she budgets (spends) money and resources.

There are distinctive lifestyles common among single adults. Some are transitional, others are more set, particularly in older single adults. Here are general personality sketches that help determine lifestyle.

Joe/Josephine the right. This single adult always has to have the last word. Anyone who disagrees with this person is on a collision course. He or she has a strong need to be right—regardless of the subject.

Milton/Mildred the nice. This person never complains, never finds fault, and never says no to any request. The Miltons/Mildreds keep many single adult groups surviving. They have a strong need to be liked and will avoid choices that threaten their popularity.

Arthur/Alice the sensitive. This single adult has feelings that can spill over (or erupt) with the slightest jar. He or she may have a permanent chip on their shoulders. This person has unfinished business and unresolved conflicts.

Ben/Beth the successful. This single adult equates one's self-worth (at the moment) with his latest success or coup in business or relationships. The more successful she is, the better she feels. He or she is willing to do almost anything to get ahead or to climb the ladder. Sometimes, the need to be successful is stronger than the need to be ethical or have a correct view of the source of self-esteem.

Dan/Dinah the attention addicts. These single adults need a lot of attention to ward off loneliness, anxiety, and boredom with their single status. Some Dans and Dinahs are hypochondriacs. They would rather get negative attention than be ignored. They deal with details and expect you to listen to long recitals of problems and insults. They can be a disruptive influence in a group because they alienate emotionally healthy single adults.

Steve/Sally the strong. This single adult has to perceive him or herself as a "strong" individual who really doesn't need the group. She views other single adults as either strong or weak. He pushes himself to the max, whether at work or in a "friendly" game of tennis. The need to be strong may be misperceived by others as aloofness or arrogance.

Paul/Pris the spiritual. This single adult is a Christian's Christian. She tosses around Greek nuances and C. S. Lewis quotes. He keeps a running tally on everyone's spirituality. This person may "carry a burden" and is "glad to do it!" He or she has a strong need to be publicly recognized as a spiritual person.

Chris/Cynthia the intellectual. This single adult prides him or herself on knowing where everyone stands on every issue. He has never once said, "I don't know." She has an opinion on everything and can be very verbal. This single adult does not want to be caught unaware or uncertain on any topic.[1]

All of these single adults have enormous potential. They become a challenge to the single adult leader. How can we reach them? Unfortunately, some leaders ask, "How can I CHANGE them?"

The leader should urge them to work for balance and vulnerability in their lives. For some singles, their success or intellect or strength is a shield behind which they hide. They will only let down that barrier and allow themselves to be known and loved in response to the persistent kindness of a leader.

Formulating a Christian Lifestyle

To develop a distinctively Christian lifestyle, one has to face several challenges.

To reject the materialistic hedonism of contemporary single culture. The goal is to say, "I am more than what I own, drive, wear, possess." The single adult must constantly evaluate the "trinkets" so prized by a single adult subculture.

To define oneself by other than a vocation or job. The first question many singles ask is, "What do you do?" Some professions gain immediate status, while others do not.

To treat all people with dignity. It is easy to be a "with-it" single in a single adult fellowship or group, to consider oneself slightly superior to others in the group. Racism, age discrimination, elitism, and sexism die slowly among single adults.

To be a good steward of one's talents and resources. Single adults need to be aware that God has expectations of how they can share their resources in kingdom-building. Paul wrote, "Therefore, as we have opportunity, let us do good to all people, especially to those who belong to the family of believers" (Gal. 6:10).

To extract good from every situation. Some single adults seemingly have accumulated more than their fair share of life's lumps and bruises. Some have social, financial, psychological, or emotional handicaps of some degree. Some let others continue to use them as doormats. Some have never learned to defend themselves.

But every situation can be perceived as either a problem or an opportunity. The single decides.

To develop a network of cheerleaders. The single adult needs other single adults and married adults for a strong balance in his or her life. Single adult ministry offers a laboratory of sorts to examine and fine-tune one's lifestyle. Single adult groups have been tremendous motivators for change and growth. But growth always occurs more expediently and orderly in the climate of affirmation.

Questioning a Lifestyle

A single adult group must lovingly call into question its lifestyles, whether individually or corporately. Alfred Montapert has formulated some questions that are a good resource for such an examination or evaluation.

- Am I doing the things that make me happy?
- Are my thoughts of noble character?
- How can I simplify my life?
- What are my talents?
- Does my work satisfy my soul?
- Am I giving value to my existence?
- How could I improve my life?[2]

To that list I would add this question: Is Jesus Lord of my singleness? Am I seeking *first* the kingdom of God?

Paul's words summarize the need for guidance in building, maintaining, and evaluating a lifestyle: "Make it your ambition to lead a quiet life, to mind your own business and to work with your hands, just as we told you, so that *your daily life* [or lifestyle] may win the respect of outsiders" (1 Thess. 4:11–12, italics added).

Part **3**

Ministry with Single Adults

Singles Helping Singles

Rich Kraljev

Where are singles in America? You'll find them in restaurants, singles bars, clubs, and health spas by the thousands. Sundays you'll find them in the pews of virtually every church in America.

What does God say about single adults and their lifestyles? Jesus referred to the single state as a unique and special kind of gift (Matt. 19:11–12). For those without children the single life can be a time of *simplicity* because of not being responsible for a family; of *energy* that flows with greater flexibility from available time; of *opportunity*—never before has there been a time such as now with so many singles in it.

Unfortunately today this vast resource pool is going untapped in some respects by both single adults and the church. Many adult singles tend to minimize their own potential, and because of a lack of understanding, many churches are turning singles away because they don't fit conveniently into traditional molds and comfortable stereotypes. Because we are stewards of the gifts God has given us, single adults and Christian leaders need to be challenged to discover and put to good use such a deep well of talent and ability! What do singles have to offer?

- in many cases, compassion and sensitivity to human need born from brokenness and subsequent healing

- a profound appreciation for the renewing grace of God forged from their own redemption and restoration
- an ability to look at life with realism and a sense of humor
- a variety of spiritual gifts and abilities for ministry
- flexibility and creative energy
- a desire for evangelism and discipleship of the unchurched singles of the community
- a loyalty and dedication to Christ's church and its local leadership that manifests itself in commitment, follow-through, and faithfulness

Here are some practical suggestions of ways that singles could use their resources.

Ministry One to Another

- Because many have experienced the breakup of marriages, singles who have healed and are trained can become adept at beginning and developing a divorce recovery ministry. Widows and widowers can help much the same way.
- With proper direction and preparation, trained single lay counselors can help meet the real needs of their single brothers and sisters.
- Many single adults are gifted teachers and speakers and can lead Bible study classes geared to other singles. Small group ministries led by single adults in homes, the church, office buildings, and restaurants create a sense of continuity and community for single adults.

Support and Healing One to Another

- Singles who have become successful at single parenting are ideal leaders for single parenting support groups.
- Support groups for those afflicted by eating disorders, sexual abuse, and compulsive behaviors are well within singles' abilities to provide help and facilitate discussion.

- Singles can pool their resources and be a real help to each other in cooking, auto repair, moving, house maintenance, and so much more.

Outreach One to Another

- Trained and organized into teams, single adults can be effective in personal peer evangelism.
- Singles can meet a great need in our society today with compassionate ministries to shut-ins and the hospitalized.
- Singles can fill a big gap by acting as friends and role models in Big Brother and Big Sister programs.

Having Fun One with Another

Singles have deep relational needs. Single adults can plan and stage activities of a social nature that create great excitement. Camps, conferences, hikes, rafting trips, tours, and excursions near and far are all possibilities when singles are given leadership.

Building the Body of Christ Together

- Single adults are productive and fruitful. They can be biblical tithers and an asset to church finances.
- Singles are stalwart prayer partners to the church and each other.
- Many singles are skilled professionals in the business world and have much to offer administratively to committees and planning organizations.
- Singles can set the pace for ministry in many areas of the church.

The possibilities for single adults in ministry to each other are endless. The only limiting factor is lack of vision and willingness to use this great untapped resource. It's time to cease looking at singles as a liability and open our eyes to the great asset they can be to each other and the church.

Marrieds Helping Singles

Doug Calhoun

In Christian ministry a gap often exists between adult singles and married couples. Age alone does not seem to be the cause of this separation. Marriage establishes a demarcation line between a couple and their friends who are single. Divergent interests and commitments begin to place them into two separate worlds. Children add complexity to the lives of couples, intensifying the already present desire to have more time by themselves. How can there be a meaningful ministry between these two groups?

The concern of this chapter is the important effect married couples can have in the lives of the single members of the church. Both marrieds and singles are *adult* members of the body of Christ first, with a specific relational status second. This is a fairer perspective than consigning singles to some stage of ongoing adolescence until they get married. Marrieds may not consciously perceive singles as less-mature, but they may subconsciously have accepted the worlds idea that married people are more responsible.

Recently a group of three singles and a young married couple met for dessert. Two of the singles were older than the couple. Yet on more than one occasion the married couple asked the singles, "What do single people think of . . . ?" as though they expected some nonadult response. The couple finally remarked,

"We really are all the same age!" That discovery of mutual adult-hood was somehow a surprise! Mutuality in Christ is a goal for all believers.

Why Help?

Scripturally, married people, like all Christians, live under the injunction "to love one another." After a couple gets married, the tendency is to pull out of other relationships and to focus only on the marriage. The notion that love is a quantity that we must hoard prompts people to carefully invest their love in their marriages. Somehow, though, the married couple must think where they can serve beyond their own family unit. That service will enrich them.

Ecclesiastically, the complete segregation of people into age groups or preference areas falls short of the true marvel of the redeemed community of faith. Paul's grand picture of Christ's body in the Book of Ephesians constantly portrays the oneness and interdependence of the members of Christ (Eph. 2:11–22; 3:6, 14–15; 4:3–6). One of the strongest evidences of the power of the reconciling gospel can be demonstrated when "natural" group barriers are broken down or ignored because of Christ. While recognizing the distinctions between marrieds and singles, the ability of each group to relate to and serve the other reflects the presence of God at work.

Many singles will eventually marry. The interaction between the two groups allows important learning opportunities for singles to observe Christian marriage at work. How crucial this is today where a growing percentage of singles come from broken families and homes without a biblical basis. Modeling does not demand perfection; rather, it requires people who are willing to live their lives before others in a shared fashion.

What Needs Help

Transience hallmarks our generation, particularly the single person. Employers feel little regret shipping off one of their unattached workers to another city. The relocation costs are much smaller than for a married person, and the supposed ease in uprooting makes for a quick transition. The business industry relies heavily on the young adult population to be mobile, flying between major metropolises. Though strategically true, this attitude fails to realize the cost to these people. Such uprootedness usually results in being some distance from family and friends. The lack of roots in the community creates loneliness. Many such individuals have to live without any support system in their immediate area. A couple or family has its own enclave to rely on, but the single person must fend for himself.

Another facet of single individuals' existence is their living arrangements. Most either live alone or with other singles whom they rarely see because of schedule conflicts. This isolation suits the normal desire of this age for independence; but an equally strong, though conflicting, need for belonging remains unfulfilled. Perhaps the forced separation from home brings welcome relief, or perhaps not. Either way, many singles desire to have someplace where they can be a part of a family. Relating only to other singles can result in being unconnected with a broader scope of life. Knowing and being known still remain as key concerns of an adult single.

It should be noted briefly that marrieds have needs of their own that single people may help meet. For instance, a couple cannot fill each other's total need for relationships. They can become ingrown and unserving in their outlook. The freshness brought by a single person and the initiation to serve can bring a new vitality and appreciation to the marriage.

Ways Married Couples Can Help

From the start it is important to stress that a "program" is not what is needed, rather, a way of life, a building of friendships. The first step is simple—opening one's home to single adults. The single person may need a place of refuge or rest from his own world. The focus may be conversation or games or politics or hobbies or study. Whatever avenue is used, there is opportunity for the building of relationships that will benefit all the people involved; the fundamental idea is to develop acceptance of each other and to cultivate trust.

What may begin as a casual acquaintance between a couple and a single adult has the potential of becoming a meaningful friendship, with both the husband and wife. Being able to offer safe relationships with each spouse individually or together presents a unique opportunity for the single person to develop relationships uncomplicated by romance. If the couple is older, the pattern may resemble that of parent to child; if they are closer in age, it can simply be a strong peer relationship. These friendships can be very formative in interpersonal skills and self-evaluation. By creating a sense of belonging, the couple provides the single with a place to know and be known safely.

Adult singles without children should be brought into whole family life. If the couple has children, encourage the single person to develop relationships with them. Kids have a way of lavishing love and affection on anyone who takes the time to be with them. Parents already know the joy this love brings. Sharing this gift with singles who may be lonely can be like administering a life-saving drug; it can bring meaning and hope back into their lives.

All this indeed calls for a growing level of trust and communication between each person and a willingness to allow God to work. Sharing disappointments or resolving conflicts with each other are as important as any gift one could give to the other. The relationship cultivated between the single adult and the couple becomes a school for learning love in all its fullness. The reality of a lived-out marriage can correct the idealistic conception of marriage or redeem the shambles left from a broken marriage or a broken family in childhood.

The mutuality of this friendship appears in the ways people learn to give to and receive from each other. The ages of people concerned affect the avenues this mutual service manifests itself. Besides what is inherent in the previous suggestions, a couple can especially help by connecting a single person with the broader church congregation or the community. Explaining traditions or upcoming events, sitting with them at meetings, inviting them to participate in planning or putting on programs—all these are ideas to involve someone who is new and having difficulty plugging into the scene.

One other specific service is providing counsel for the single person. This should probably come about slowly in the relationship and at the request of the adult single. In any relationship, friends have to earn the right to be heard and to develop trust before they can speak the truth in love. A married couple can provide helpful insight for a single person. If couples are open to this, the opportunities will present themselves.

Ways Churches and Pastors Can Help

The attitudes of the church leadership occupy a pivotal role in the life of its congregation. To build the kind of interaction discussed in this chapter will take attitudinal as well as program changes. Regarding attitudes, the manner in which comments are given about singles' events or congregational affairs can carry the connotation that singles are not really part of the whole church. The implication can be that singles are great to have around when the church needs a labor force but not when it's considering leaders or board members.

For example, a church can sponsor a Dinner-for-Eight program on a monthly or bimonthly basis. Arrange to have two couples and four singles from the church meet for dinner. The interchange creates meaningful relationships that might not have happened otherwise. In the Sunday school program, offer electives that are available to all adults plus some specifically targeted for singles or for marrieds. The same idea holds for small group Bible studies; try to provide a balance for the needs of both. Giving singles responsibility in the church affirms them and builds the church. Are singles on the governing boards? Singles certainly have more to contribute than simply being baby-sitters in the nursery or waiters at a banquet.

In discipleship, relationships between singles and marrieds are key. Many singles want someone they can look up to in the faith. Many couples can learn much from adult singles. An older Christian can provide what the individual's parents were unable or unwilling to give him. Encourage the older women to train the younger ones in the Lord (Titus 2:3–5). Also in terms of general church activities, this may mean giving consideration to specific publicity for the singles to be included (e.g., "Church Family Night"—how can that be reworded to convey welcome to singles?).

Are the singles meaningfully included in the planning and concerns of church retreats or summer "family" camps?

The wise pastor and congregation will sense the potential for the future of their church when looking at singles and will cultivate the interchange between marrieds and singles.

Cautions to Be Considered

Building healthy relationships takes effort and commitment. A couple can probably handle only a few (two or three) such relationships at any given time. The loyalty and perseverance they offer to a few people carries more value than many superficial acquaintances. To avoid overextension, each person needs to feel free to honestly communicate with the others. Asking too much too soon of the single or married person will dampen the enthusiasm for the friendship. It may be in order at the beginning stages to more explicitly spell out what is being offered or expected, without sounding too stiff (e.g., if the couple or single has children who require attention early in the morning, explain why this puts a time limit on the evening's activity).

The married couple (especially if they have children) will be tempted to see the single person only on the couple's own terms or timetable. While to some extent this may need to be the case, the underlying attitude fails to connote equality or mutuality. Similarly, people should resist a one-sided or one-directional approach to the relationship; namely, we, the married couple will now help this "poor" single person. Instead, both parties should try to engender a spirit of discovery and loving service to each other.

The couple must guard against these relationships substituting for their own marital relationship. It may be easier to talk with that single man or woman than one's own spouse, but that is no excuse for failing to give energy and time to work on one's marital bonds. In the end, this kind of tension and its proper resolution will demonstrate the work involved with marriage, and that is a needed lesson for everyone.

One can easily see that the downside of this tension could be the start of an affair. Yes, it is possible. Hopefully, fear of what may happen will not hinder folk from building good friendships with the opposite sex that honor God. Spouses must discuss how they feel about the husband getting close to a single woman, or the wife to a single man. It may be helpful for the couple to agree together on a method of bringing this issue up for discussion before the pressure of the event itself.

While there are many advantages to mutual caring, both parties should realize that friendship is not simply free baby-sitting, a laundry service, a hotel, or free restaurant. Such things may be given to each other, but beware of any emotional blackmail to obtain them.

Conclusion

The ability and commitment to developing long-term and loyal friendships benefits all those involved and the church as a whole. Somehow Christ always gives us more capacity to love and to give, even when we think we have reached our limits. To offer such care between singles and marrieds brings health, challenge, and growth in our obedience to our Lord, and a valuable perspective on life and marriage.

10

Help for Single-Parent Children

Jim and Barbara Dycus

There are millions of children in the United States. They bless our lives daily as we come in contact with their enthusiasm, energy, and joy. Yet almost one third of these children are living in one-parent homes.

How Are They Different?

What do we need to know about these kids? Are they any different from other kids? Is a traditional Sunday school ministry enough for them? Or do they need some specialized ministry that zeroes in on their special needs?

The evidence says that they do! Even the Bible shows the benefit of special ministry to single-parent children.

It appears that both Ishmael, the son of the patriarch Abraham, and Timothy, the spiritual son of the apostle Paul, were single-parent children. Ishmael grew up to be the leader of a great and mighty nation (see Gen. 21–25). Timothy grew up to be the leader or the pastor of the first-century church in Ephesus where Paul calls him, "You, man of God" (1 Tim. 6:11).

Both men were raised by their mothers. They both had a godly heritage and training. They both had one parent, yet God was absolutely faithful to demonstrate his grace and love to meet their every need as well as to provide them with a future and a hope.

Timothy had some specialized ministry from a man who became his role model and who loved him profusely. This is evident in the way Paul addressed his letters to Timothy. Paul began every letter the same way: "Grace and peace be unto you." Eleven times he uses that salutation. But only in his letters to Timothy does he add: "Grace, mercy, and peace" be unto you. Paul gave Timothy a ministry of mercy that met the special single-parent child needs he had.

Paul teaches us to "see to it that no one misses the grace of God and that no bitter root grows up to cause trouble and defile many" (Heb. 12:15). In order to follow that advice with single-parent families, we need to understand their special needs.

Emotional Needs

The child who loses a parent has an emotional response to that loss. These emotions are normal but are largely negative. They include grief, sense of loss, guilt, rejection, anger, depression, loss of self-esteem, confusion, and fear of change. In order to recover from these negative emotions, the child needs help *identifying* the emotion, *understanding* the emotion, and *learning to make a positive response* in place of the negative one.

Family Living Needs

A child's security is tied up in the stability of the home. When an event disrupts the stability of the home, the child's security blanket is ripped away.

The stability can be restored, even in a one-parent home! But adaptations to a new form of family life need to be made. These include living with one parent, becoming more independent, accepting more personal responsibility in the management of the home, adapting to financial changes, and learning to effectively communicate with family members. Ministry must provide tools and practical help in each of these areas.

Relationship Needs

Divorce or death creates some problems for a child in his or her ability to establish good relationships. Because the loss has caused a feeling of rejection, the child begins to defend himself against another loss. The walls go up and it becomes more difficult to trust, love, or accept a new relationship.

Single-parent children need help in learning to build positive relationships. And in order to help, we have to first gain their respect and trust! That's why for these children a Sunday school relationship won't be enough. We need to be prepared to offer unconditional acceptance in a megadose, until children take down the walls and let us in.

How Can the Church Help?

It's obvious that we *need* to help. How do we do it? The biblical example of Hagar and Ishmael gives us some goals for our design. (See Genesis 21:17–20.)

Recognize the Need

"God heard the boy crying" (Gen. 21:17). We begin to help by recognizing the need to help.

To do this we need to decide how we feel about divorce and children of divorce and really understand what the Bible teaches about the family, divorce, and children's needs. Don't forget to dig into forgiveness and God's grace. We need to catch a vision of the need in our local community, and especially our local church.

Unconditionally Accept

"Lift the boy up and take him by the hand" (Gen. 21:18). We have to do some lifting and some hugging to let children in crisis recognize that we accept them, just as they are—just where they hurt! Decide where your place is with them and how much you have to give. Do this before you begin to minister to them. They can't take another rejection while they hurt.

Develop Positive Responses

"I [God] will make him into a great nation" (Gen. 21:18). We can help the child of divorce begin to make a positive response to

his hurt, to have acceptance in place of grief, stability instead of loss, freedom from guilt, love instead of rejection and anger, worth instead of worthlessness, reality instead of denial, security instead of fear, forgiveness instead of blame, understanding instead of confusion, and new relationships to dispel the loneliness.

Understand Specific Needs

Hagar "gave the boy a drink" (Gen. 21:19). Ishmael had a specific need that she was able to meet. We have to deal in specifics with the children of divorce or loss. Discover their needs. Find them out from the children. This requires long-term relationship-building with child and parent.

Encourage Spiritual Growth

"God was with the boy as he grew up" (Gen. 21:20). We need to "be there" too! Paul was with Timothy. How did Paul help Timothy? He led him to Christ, instructed him, advised him, charged him, praised him, loved him, encouraged him, laid hands on him (moving Timothy into ministry). Paul obviously made the difference in Timothy's life. Today, single-parent children can experience the same difference.

Establishing an Ongoing Ministry

Ongoing is the operative word here. We're not talking about some flash in the pan that singles out the child and makes him feel different but something to which he can belong.

Develop One-on-One Relationships

Before the child who hurts will open up and let us in, we have to build a relationship with that child. It helps us both. We need to get to know this child, his special needs, where he hurts the most, where he'll let us in. The child finds acceptance to dispel his feelings of rejection, love to chase away the worthlessness, and role modeling to lead him into godliness.

Let the single-parent child tag along with you, help wash your car, bake cookies, or play with your kids. Let the child (children) talk to *you*, instead of you just talking to her (them). Remove the unnatural, restrictive classroom setting and have some silly fun! You needn't do it all alone; get several from your congregation involved in one-to-one relationships with children of divorce.

Specialize Your Ministry

Build a ministry that meets the special needs of single-parent kids. Three natural areas of ministry follow:

1. *Crisis intervention.* This begins with recognizing and dealing with the immediate negative responses to the loss.

2. *Recovery assistance.* The child must be taught positive biblical responses for the negative.

3. *Life management assistance.* Now that the crisis is over and the child has begun recovery, he or she needs to know how to manage life beyond the hurt. He or she must now be taught self-government, how to make good choices, how to understand God's plan for each family member and then be led into a program with a plan for spiritual growth (i.e., Sunday school, family devotions).

Meshing Children's and Singles Ministries

Ministry to single-parent children can be a vital part of singles ministry. Single parents need to be in singles ministry, but many cannot leave their children to attend. Have them bring the kids! Offer ministry to the kids each time your singles meet.

Have workshops and learning centers for the kids during divorce recovery sessions or fellowship activities for them when you have social activities for the adults. Plan a kids' retreat while their parents attend the single adult retreat. Encourage your single adults to be one-on-one role models. Let the single adults who are blessed financially help the single parents and children who aren't.

Follow the advice Jesus gave in Matthew 18:5–6: "And whoever welcomes a little child like this in my name welcomes me. But if anyone causes one of these little ones who believe in me to sin, it would be better for him to have a large millstone hung around his neck and to be drowned in the depth of the sea."

The Role of the Senior Pastor

Bud Pearson

Every singles ministry in a local church, to be successful, must have the wholehearted support of the senior pastor. The entire congregation will develop feelings and respond to single adults in the same way that the senior pastor does.

The Senior Pastor Sets the Tone

He leads to provide an atmosphere of acceptance. An openhearted welcome to all single adults whatever their status is the goal.

Often single adults are hurting deeply. They need a listening ear and an understanding response where genuine concern is evident. A loving and caring pastor models this attitude. The senior pastor is the shepherd who leads his congregation in caring for all the sheep.

He leads in welcoming single adults as part of the family of God. Every single adult is either a believer or a potential believer. To receive each person as someone loved by God is to fulfill the role God has for us. The family of God needs to be viewed as open to all. For this to be a reality, there can be no second-class citizens because of one's status in life. The Lord Jesus opened up his world to all people, and a congregation can be led to do the same by the senior pastor.

He leads in including single adults in the ministry of the church. Including single adults in the life of the church means opening the doors of all ministries in the body of Christ. Every believer needs to fulfill his or her calling, and the church that truly accepts single adults also accepts the responsibility of placing them in meaningful roles in the life of the congregation.

The Senior Pastor Conveys the Need

He conveys the importance of a single ministry to the ruling body of the church. He points out the facts of the huge population of single adults and their need for meaningful relationships with others. He makes the ruling body aware of the potential for evangelism and the opportunity of the church to fulfill its role to all people. The Great Commission includes single adults.

He conveys how to minister to singles. Single adults are often wounded. Nowhere in society are people equipped to heal hurts like the church is prepared to do. The senior pastor, by being with them, speaking to them, having them in his home, etc., leads the congregation in this ministry of healing. He leads the church to be the church—reaching out, loving, and sharing Christ with people who are open and ready to listen and receive.

The Senior Pastor Determines Support Level

He supports singles by his messages. He speaks to and of singles in his messages, letting the congregation know of his love and concern for all the people.

He supports singles in announcements. He promotes them and their programs from the pulpit. This gives credence to their programs and serves to highlight the reality that they are a part of the church.

He supports singles by publicity. He makes sure that there is space in bulletins, news sheets, and church publications for singles programs and events. This not only serves to inform, but also gives the congregation an awareness that single adult functions are as important as all other ministries of the church.

The Senior Pastor Guarantees Leadership

The senior pastor takes the steps necessary to launch single adult ministry and assure its continuation. There are options in leadership.

A full-time singles minister is best. When possible, this assures a more adequate counseling, learning, teaching, and training program for the ministry. Many churches are now catching the vision for singles ministry and are preparing for it. This fact assures a bright future for reaching the single adult population and provides many churches with the opportunity to consider their role in it.

A married couple can serve. This may be a first-time married or remarried couple. They must be sensitive to the needs of single adults. With a desire to serve and be used in singles ministry, a couple can fulfill this role very well, as has been demonstrated in many churches.

Other possibilities exist. Whoever it is, a high regard must be maintained for the person or persons who lead a singles ministry. They must know and feel that they are a part of the church's ministry team, and they must be included as such. The senior pastor must lead in giving equal status to the singles leaders so that they and the single adults will know that they are a part of the church in the fullest sense.

The Senior Pastor Must See the Potential

Singles serve, and they serve well. Many single adults have available time. They also want to feel useful. Serving others can be an integral part of the healing process for one who is divorced or widowed. Churches with effective single adult ministries are those in which single persons have been given opportunities to serve, not only in the functions of the single adults, but in the larger body.

It has been amply demonstrated that, when given the opportunities, single adults are a blessing to the church. At one time, our local church reported that 35 percent of its choir members, 40 percent of its teaching staff, 30 percent of its ushers and greeters, and 60 percent of its paraprofessional counselors were single adults.

Perhaps the most significant thing of all is that single adults bring a spirit of acceptance, love, and caring to a church. Some have hurt deeply and, through that hurt, have in the truest way become wounded healers. The senior pastor will do well to recognize this and desire to be close to the singles in their personal lives and in their service to the Lord. The senior pastor, in a society that includes more than one single person for every married couple, will do well to lead his congregation into a ministry with single adults. He holds the key to the success or failure of the ministry to singles in the church that he pastors.

12

A Profile of the Single-Adult Minister

Timm Jackson

His men had just returned from their first assignment. They seemed to talk all at once as they shared excitedly with him their reports. His plans were to be alone with them for a day . . . a trip to a deserted piece of land . . . a time of rest and lunch . . . a little instruction to help them grow. It was going to be a great day. But the crowds found him and his "schedule" was tossed aside, for a major miracle was about to occur (Mark 6:30–44).

This little scenario in Christ's life on the day of the feeding of the 5,000 reminds us again of his greatest attribute—his obedience to God. Many of us would choose rather to have a manual of how-to's, an easy problem-solver we could flip through in search of the perfect approach to "ministry for the moment." However, Christ seems to show us throughout the Gospels that a choice toward obedience needs to precede any direction we could ever take. Let's go back to our opening story.

Here Christ chooses to minister to the masses through teaching and later on, feeding. An inspirational afternoon such as this would never have occurred if Christ had chosen the way of the "dayplanner" schedule. Instead, he obeyed God's direction and ministered to thousands, as well as to the original focal group, his disciples.

We can learn much from Christ's life. Single-adult ministers have been given the seemingly insurmountable task of reaching a specialized group of people with the claims of Christ so they may in turn affect their world. But the challenge is no greater than what Christ saw on that hot day on the shores of Galilee.

Jesus' Way

It is easy to look at a world of hurting, stressed-out, lost, or lonely singles and feel helplessly inadequate. One may even think it is ridiculous to consider approaching such a segment of society without years of accumulated credentials, abilities, and tolerances. Yet, Jesus made a difference. We must learn from him. The following were modeled by Jesus Christ.

Spiritual preparedness. Be godly (2 Peter 1:5–7). Jesus cherished his personal privacy for those times of spiritual renewal. Direction that comes from moments of personal communion with God gives perfect protection and incredible inspiration.

A compassionate spirit. Jesus was "moved with compassion" (Mark 6:34, KJV). When we develop a tenderness toward our singles, all else fades away—tiredness, apathy, and ineptness. We begin to see a mission, gain a larger perspective, and feel a challenge to positively minister once we have learned how to care for people.

Versatility. Throughout his life, Jesus showed tremendous versatility. He lost sleep, overlooked mealtimes, and changed agendas to accommodate people. Programming is useless if it looms as a giant over the needs of people. Give yourself the joy of being able to break away from the daily drudgery and get actively involved in the lives of people.

Vision. Jesus saw the crowd as sheep without a shepherd. As we gain a proper perspective of our mission, we too will see our "crowd" as singles who need to be led to the Savior with life-changing growth. We may also begin to see the needs of each individual as uniquely his or her own. Singles come from a variety of church backgrounds and life experiences. It is most rewarding to learn how to relate to each one. Also, a ministry to singles becomes a real challenge in dealing with new attenders. Because of their often sensitive situations, they call for a special touch of concern by the minister. If you can develop a "sight" that "feels" the needs of others, you will probably see your ministry become greater than just your church constituency as it encompasses a total community. People will love filling your vision!

Teaching. How discouraged Jesus must have been when his disciples stated *their* solution to the crowd's need for food. Even the fresh return from their preaching trip couldn't change their hearts enough, for they said, "Send the people away." Yet, Jesus chose to patiently teach them, allowing them the opportunity to watch his solution become reality. His response, "You give them something to eat," showed he still wished for the Twelve to inherit his ministry. Don't be afraid to share ownership of the ministry with your single adults. The camaraderie will be greatly worth the effort of patiently discipling others into the inner workings and commitment of ministry. And allow yourself the relief of being accountable to someone for your own spiritual growth. A teacher is a student. You must personally grow as a disciple of Jesus Christ.

Organization for a purpose. When Jesus was faced with the feeding of the 5,000, he was prepared for it. He divided the mass of people into specifically numbered groups. You too need to plan for your "miracle." Don't just think being "led by the Spirit" will do it all for you. You will be more useful to the people if you have freed yourself from details so you can think about their personal needs. Set an atmosphere for ministry that will lend itself to positive decisions being made for Christ. Organize your life and program of ministry. That shows your love and concern for both.

Speaking out in support. When Jesus said to the disciples, "You give them something to eat," he was also representing the needs of the humble people to his own men. Don't be afraid to do the same for your singles. Enhance their reputation to your pastor and accept any opportunity to share their stories with the congregation.

Let the church board know of your belief that the singles in your church are among the most important people there. It will help any churchgoer who is on the outside of the singles' world to better understand the validity of an adult singles ministry. It will also comfort your people to know you care enough to verbalize your support to others.

Servanthood. Jesus became the first short-order cook of all time when he fed the 5,000. As Christ, our mission here on this earth should be that we have "not come to be served, but to serve" (Matt. 20:28). Let your people know what a blessing they are to you and how you feel privileged that God allowed you this opportunity to minister and be ministered to. If people start to put you on a pedestal, knock it down! You're not involved in ministry to be a king, but to be a servant. Jesus' choice of a servant's role gives us a great example to follow.

The Other Way—Corrected

You may still feel inadequate for service as an adult singles minister. Perhaps you have many sentences coming to mind beginning, "But . . ." The following responses are fallacies regarding the requirements of a capable adult singles minister.

A singles minister should be unmarried. False. Though a single can say, "I've been through that too," a married couple also can remember their days as singles. A married minister and spouse bring a balance of ministry perspective and life experiences to both never-marrieds and formerly-marrieds. If marriage is a single person's goal, the married minister can help from both sides of the altar, as a former single and now married. The singles can see that the minister chose, with God's direction, to be a part of the single's ministry. Being married does not negate genuine servanthood.

A singles minister should have a seminary degree. False. This may be helpful, but it is not required. Many have not had seminary training. Many seminaries are limited in courses that offer training in singles ministry. Some have come into singles ministry from other careers, feeling a special burden for adult singles. One may have experienced divorce. God can use us with all of our accumulated life experiences. Yet, biblical knowledge is an imperative to be a minister to any people group. If one feels unqualified educationally, seminary is a good consideration, but you may also want to consider other excellent training resources and programs.

Lack of experience will impair my work with other staff. False. What will limit you is your lack of love. If you can convince your peers that you feel your ministry is one of the most important ministries of the church, they will learn to respect you. It may take time, but staff relationships can build a foundation of support that will prove invaluable to your mental health. Don't be afraid to share with them your conflicts, dreams, and disappointments. It will make you believable to them and they will become friends that last forever.

I get too burdened by the counseling. You don't have to suffer from overload. One of the great designs of specialized programs and workshops, such as divorce or grief recovery, is that you can affect many people at once through a group experience. As your people train themselves to become better listeners, the load will decisively change. You may also have professional counselors in your area to whom you can make referrals. The minister should set counseling limits. It cannot be accomplished by one person.

Singles ministers need to have a high energy level. False. No one ever has enough energy. What you need to do is plan ahead. Learn to become versatile. Recruit and train quality, dedicated people to share the programming load with you and you will be amazed at what can be accomplished without your personal attention. Learn to be a good steward of your time and energy. If God wanted you stronger, he would have made you into a superman! Develop wisdom in knowing what you are best at, delegate responsibilities where you are less qualified, and go on from there.

A person should be highly creative. False. There are ways to have creative programming without being creative yourself. Look for other people's ideas. Investigate other churches that have had successful programs. Ask your singles for ideas. Don't be afraid to learn from others. And remember, a loving program is much more important than creativity.

A Christlike Profile

Singles ministry is a modern-day parallel to Christ's feeding of the 5,000. Many singles are among the neediest people in society today. Choose to project a personal profile that is in the likeness of our Lord and Savior. It will carry you toward the reality of fulfilling your portion of the Great Commission.

An Overview of the Single Adult Organization

Timm Jackson

Simply said, singles ministry is a ministry of one to one. It is one person drawing from another out of the storehouse and surplus God has given. Organization and structure become most effective when the "one to one" takes precedence. Take a person who is needy, fill that need with a tiny seed of hope from another, and you have begun a fascinating journey—you travel toward reaching God's great goal of making disciples. Whether your group numbers ten, one hundred ten, or one thousand ten, your best first step will be inviting other singles to help you fulfill the Great Commission—one to one. Jesus, in his last days on earth, gave us these special words, "You, then, are to go and make disciples of all the nations and baptize them in the name of the Father and of the Son and of the Holy Spirit. Teach them to observe all that I have commanded you and, remember, I am with you always, even to the end of the world" (Matt. 28:19–20 PHILLIPS).

Develop a Purpose Statement

Deciding to help individuals effectively reach out to others means requiring changes to occur. Begin by writing your own philosophy of ministry. Here is an example:

Our singles ministry is in existence to provide a place and a message where modern-day single adults, with or without children, may be attracted to the claims of Christ, both personal and corporate, in a nonjudgmental, nonthreatening, loving, problem-sharing and -solving atmosphere that helps them deal authentically with their needs. The goal is that they will choose to make Jesus Christ not only their Savior, but also their Lord.

A statement of purpose such as this will help clarify and crystallize your focus of and approach to ministry. It will also give you a solid base and vehicle for fulfilling the Great Commission and evaluating what is being accomplished. This gives you a *ministry with a mission.* The purpose must be biblical. It must rest and stand on an authoritative foundation.

Develop Personal Involvement

As each person does his part, we discover a simple yet marvelous and rewarding principle: Give of yourself to others and your own needs will begin to be met. People need to be needed. If a person senses she is important, she has found a definite "comfort zone" in which she will be able to grow. As time goes on, that feeling of support will broaden to the point that the single person will want to relate to more people than those just like herself. Perhaps a woman is thirty-six and divorced with two teenage children. Initially, she will feel most comfortable with those in like circumstances. If, however, she receives a feeling of personal significance and thus begins to reach out to others from her "comfort," she may soon broaden her "zone" to include other single parents. Perhaps she will begin to relate to an older female who enjoys helping others. Eventually, this single parent will probably find herself happily involved in church activities, such as singing in the choir, or teaching a Sunday school class, or serving on a board or committee. She has found many options in which she can be a part of fulfilling the Great Commission.

Develop Ownership

Involving singles in a ministry and organization with a mission also helps each person claim ownership of the ministry. Call something your own and it suddenly becomes very important. It is a special gem to the possessor. It needs protection. It is handled carefully and looked after with love. The more a person claims ownership, the more supportive he will be of your calling and his role of action as a leader and as your coworker.

Singles claiming ownership cause an organization to become efficient. One paid clergy cannot have all the expertise that is needed to lead a well-rounded program. Realizing you are weak in some areas is OK. Let your people use their years of accumulated life experiences for the ministry's benefit. Besides, we all need to learn more. As more people become involved, you will discover a more positive environment is created in which to learn.

Develop a Ministry for Adults

A ministry with a mission to singles must be a ministry for adults. Singles have gained much experience with which to reach out to others. They are also in the process of gaining even more valuable experience. The sooner that experience is put to good use, the more effective your ministry will be. Singles are not teenagers, nor are they a second-class adult subgroup.

Develop a Creative Atmosphere

Let your organization be a ministry that creates. There will be ingenious people around to help you grow your own ministry, giving you less need for a ready-made format. Use someone else's ideas for a guide to get you started. Once you have developed a plan for programming, a schedule, and a budget, don't be afraid to reevaluate each with your group of leaders. Experiment with ideas. Allow yourself and your leaders the freedom to fail. But always keep your philosophy of ministry in mind and aim toward your goal of fulfilling the Great Commission.

Discover the Needs

Your experiments will have a great chance to succeed if you first consider the needs of your singles. Send out a questionnaire, inquiring about their status. Are they mostly never-married, divorced, or widowed? What is the median age? Are they financially burdened or well-off? Programming should be the response to these needs as well as other interest points.

Geographic needs may also be taken into account. Does your church reach out far beyond its own city? If so, you may want to occasionally go to the constituency or take into consideration their transportation needs.

Develop a Multifaceted Ministry

The world of single adults holds many different types of people. Because of this, you will also want a ministry with many facets. A large, impact-type program with Christian-oriented entertainment is a great draw to introduce the public and local community to your church and your ministry. Seminars will greatly enhance your ministry. These are short-term learning experiences that can either be weekend happenings or weekly series. Singles need to be learning. Parenting, finances, and self-esteem are good topic ideas, as well as divorce recovery and grief workshops, which will probably become a staple of your programming. These times of learning will not only draw people from the community, but also will give you a tremendous opportunity to present the gospel in a positive and relaxed setting.

An ongoing learning experience is also helpful to your organization, such as a Sunday teaching experience with a pastor or layperson who can effectively apply God's love in a practical response to life's relationships and problems.

You may also want to consider specialty groups. These are often requested by the constituency because of the comfort zones that they create. For those who feel something in common, you may want to consider groups such as never-marrieds, single parents, or those who are widowed. Age-oriented activities are also conducive to creating a comfort zone among most singles. Specialty relationships such as prayer partners or big buddies or caregivers may be considered.

Small group studies, such as talk-it-overs, where people are not tied in with a series but come when they can, are great for many singles groups. The topic can be secular with a Christian orientation that lends comfort to people, no matter what their religious backgrounds may be. A topic such as "laughter" may open people up to what true happiness really is or how God longs to be a part of our everyday lives and bring joy to us. Bible studies or Christian book studies are also great for small group interaction and can be taken to any geographic location. All of these cause a great camaraderie since each study is subject-oriented and attracts people with common interests. Small-group experiences greatly enhance your base of spiritual ministry.

Sports are valid contributions to a ministry in that they are non-threatening to the average non-churched single but offer great opportunities to see the Christian faith in action as people become acquainted with a church campus. A relaxed atmosphere where we can be ourselves opens us up to great ministry opportunities.

Retreats and getaways serve a wonderful purpose of taking people away from many of their everyday problems. Here they may seriously consider the claims of Christ and, consequently, make major spiritual commitments. Singles often have limited income for vacations, so such trips are helpful for their emotional well-being.

Develop Leadership

Last, your organization must be a ministry that develops leadership. You have the opportunity to develop the strongest, most capable leaders a church has ever experienced. Singles may experience the extremes of life. They may have had financial difficulty. If problems with children existed they might have stood alone in resolving such problems. If loss and rejection have been a part of their lives, they probably felt it more than those who are married because of the lack of a "buffer" to comfort them in those moments. Consequently, singles will learn of God's grace and power in a way that marrieds often do not. Give them a chance to become part of the ongoing singles ministry as a part of the church. Let them be a part of its budgeting, its inner workings, its government, and they will show a tremendous commitment. The liaison and input they offer will greatly benefit the whole church as time goes on.

Develop a system of accountability with job outlines, reports, evaluation, and goal-setting. Plans, goals, minutes, and other important information about the organization and ministry should always be in written form for all participants.

Should your leadership staff be large or small in numbers? Make your decision based on what is most comfortable for you, the leader. If you should choose to use a small staff, make sure the other singles still feel a sense of ownership of the ministry. Make every person important, just as they are in God's eyes. Develop good systems of communication and training for your leaders. Remember, recruitment is an ongoing process.

Should you use male or female leadership? Use both because both are so well-equipped to serve and commit to you. However, if you are trying to build up the number of males in your group, feel free to put males up front, on stage, and at the door greeting people. It will immediately demonstrate that guys in the group are important and it will draw more men to the ministry.

Organization and structure are necessary because they are tools with which to achieve a great goal for God's purpose. Focus on the individual—and he or she will in turn focus on another. Organization and structure will help you keep your eyes realistically on your goals as you effectively fulfill your Great Commission.

Recruiting and Training Leaders

John Splinter

Each ministry situation is different. Each has its own "personality." Therefore, it is important to give some thought to the makeup of both the pool of leaders from which one will be drawing and also to the group to which ministry will be offered. Before recruitment begins, a complete evaluation of needs, of present ministry, of people resources available, and of mission statement is most helpful. This is where you begin, realistically and ideally.

After having done a complete analysis of your group and your overall approach to ministry, it is critically important to begin targeting your ministry. Begin slowly. The best approach is to start with one ministry at a time: one well-researched, well-thought-out ministry. You may wish to have only one ministry for singles, or you may wish to have several approaches to ministry. Ask yourself right from the beginning just what you desire to accomplish.

Not all singles will respond to any one program. What you target will determine who comes, what age they'll be, what their personal backgrounds will be (divorced, never married, etc.), and what level of self-management they possess.

Two common mistakes made by new singles ministries include one ministry that does not target anything, so it starts up with a solid core group of people and drops off to less than one half of what it originally started with; and a ministry that targets too many things, tries to grow too quickly, and does not develop the leadership necessary to sustain and grow the ministry, so it dies prematurely from lack of support and leadership.

It is very important to tie leadership recruitment to specific life experiences. For example, the most empathetic divorce recovery leaders will be the formerly divorced. Sports programs will be best run by people who are keenly interested in the specific sport. Look for people who have direct experience and interest in the area of need you are trying to fill, or else people whom the Lord has blessed with special sensitivities and gifts (see Eph. 4:11–12).

Selection

Be selective in your request for volunteers. At certain levels of leadership, it is better to hand pick those whom you feel will do the best job rather than simply to ask for volunteers (see Matt. 9:9; Mark 1:17). If you simply ask for volunteers rather than developing a careful training and selection process, you could end up with people with limited skills and experiences, or with spiritual gifts that do not match the job outline.

Don't be afraid to ask the people who are busy already. They're probably the ones best suited for the job. They're highly involved with life. Yet give them the opportunity to change roles, stretch their ministry, or say no.

Exciting people usually create exciting ministry. The inverse is equally true. Create a climate of enthusiasm. Stimulate and motivate your people. Encourage the people with vision and positive energy to lead.

Expectations

It is essential that churches or singles groups become the best possible places for training and resources. Here are some thoughts in that direction.

First, give leaders a job outline or job description. It may be very simple or brief. However, leaders need to know what is expected of them, what they are responsible for, and to whom are they accountable.

Next, give leaders a vision or objective, for example: "This is the need. These are the gifts I see in you, gifts that can meet this need. This is how the Lord could use you within this ministry. This is what it will take to get the job done. This is where I'd like to see your ministry within the next six months; the next year." It is always important to communicate the vision or the objectives of the ministry or program. (See John 1:42. Christ had a vision for Peter long before Peter could see it.)

Never under-ask. Don't be afraid to tell your leaders that their involvement is going to cost them something. It will at least cost their time, prayers, and thought.

Ask for a definite commitment, a specific time period. For example, you may tell a leader that a specific task will take five hours per week, and the duration of the task will be one year.

Give specific task objectives, and use a time frame for completion, for example: "Next week at this time we'll be needing. . . . By next month at this time we'll be at point . . . and you'll need to have accomplished. . . . By four months from now . . . "

Training

Equip your leaders with the best possible tools. Churches should have the best resources available—films, books, tapes, periodicals, videos, and so forth. Buy or rent resources as needed, because it is very important to equip leaders for their tasks.

Don't be afraid to ask volunteers to give their own money to purchase resources. If they're committed to a task, they'll probably be willing to participate financially to help see the task accomplished. However, work on developing an adequate budget within the ministry to provide for leadership development, training, and resources.

Involve community resources such as professional counselors, program training personnel, community colleges, and the like. There are a host of resources within most communities. Identify and tap them, as they will add much to your ministry to single adults.

Encourage your leaders to visit other churches that have successful singles ministries. Help your leaders attend seminars or training workshops that pertain to singles ministry, singles needs, and singles identity. Develop your own leadership courses, seminars, workshops, or retreats. This is an area of spiritual discipleship.

Send your leaders out with a vision for the task, prayer support, encouragement, training, and resources to accomplish the task. See to it that you have given the best possible training, done by the best people in any particular field, so your volunteers feel well prepared for their tasks.

Evaluation

As you turn your leaders loose to accomplish their objectives, build in regular "checkpoints." For example, hold monthly executive leadership meetings with committee chairpersons only. However, regular contact with most of your key leaders whether they are chairpersons or not is a necessary ingredient in maintaining strong leadership teams.

Focus much of your time on building, supporting, and evaluating leadership on a regular basis rather than spending your time running the various programs on your own. The more programs or ministries you hope to develop, the more important equipping others becomes.

Team Building

Build leadership teams as well as individuals. Get leaders involved in training others to assist them in their objectives and eventually to take over for them. This gives you the opportunity to recycle the leaders into other ministries.

Ask your leaders to continually be recruiting new leaders to assist them, and encourage your leaders to be on the lookout for new resources that may be of help in building the ministry or program.

Organize your leaders into management or operational committees, with one person acting as chairperson and each person on the committee being given a specific task, or reason, for being on the committee.

Ask the leadership teams to stay with the program until they accomplish their objectives, grow the program or ministry past its present size, and replace themselves with leadership of equal or superior potential.

An Atmosphere of Freedom

Help your leaders understand that it is very important for people to use the gifts that God has given them in ministry (Matt. 25:14–30). Create within your ministry the "ministry-identity" of service, rather than the identity of coming to the church just to be "nurtured."

Give freedom to your leadership teams once they're created. Let them own the ministry (see John 17). Don't feel a need to immediately rescue them if they flounder. Let them struggle and grow to set their ship back aright. Keep encouraging them toward the ministry objective. Keep equipping them. But let them own it.

Rotate your leaders, moving people from subcommittee up to vice-chair, to chair, and then out to new challenges. This process will take time. Be patient.

Allow leadership teams to chart new directions as they see the vision for ministry. Create an atmosphere that encourages input from the bottom up. Active democracy encourages active participation.

Additional Leadership Principles

Need dictates ministry. If a program or ministry is dead, leave it for a new program. If there's a need, it will succeed, and God will raise up leaders to meet the need.

Hungry people make poor shoppers (and leaders). People who are too close to acute trauma should be avoided for leadership positions until they stabilize. Chronically traumatized people need to recover from their own traumas before being given leadership responsibility.

Use married people too. Married people can be as effective in leadership to singles as singles can be, but select couples as carefully as single leaders.

Expect turnover. Singles ministries are often transdenominational and highly transient. Expect an annual turnover as high as 50 percent.

Integrate. Singles leaders should be integrated into the church and onto church boards. Work toward developing integration into the church body. Many times singles are seen as outside the church, and they feel it.

Grow leaders. Grow your ministry leadership team by accepting individuals as they are when they come to you and taking them to the next step in their own spiritual growth, whatever that step may be.

Avoid burning out your best leaders. One or two responsibilities are plenty for most.

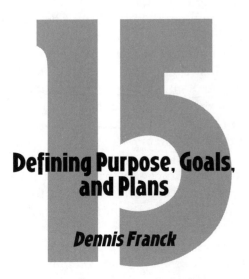

Defining Purpose, Goals, and Plans

Dennis Franck

Imagine a ship setting out to sea without a course, or a plane taking off without any specific destination. It would be potentially disastrous. So it would be for a ministry without distinct purpose, clear goals, and definite plans. Any ministry needs to have these elements, and ministry to adult singles is no different.

Purpose

Purpose can be defined as an aim, an intention, a reason for existence. The purpose for ministry to adult singles can be simply stated: *to develop healthy Christian singles.* Three ways for achieving this are suggested.

Provide an Accepting Ministry

An atmosphere of unconditional love and acceptance needs to be provided and sensed at all times. People need to feel acceptance without condemnation. The example of Jesus in John 4 with the woman at the well shows Jesus accepting, forgiving, loving, and ministering to a woman who was divorced five times and now living with a man. He did not judge or condemn her.

This attitude is desperately important because of the varied backgrounds of the people you will be ministering to. Some may come in the midst of a divorce or separation from their spouses. Some may have lost their spouses through death. Others may have never married. Some currently may be living with persons of the opposite sex. There may be individuals who are involved in homosexual relationships. Drug addicts and alcoholics may attend the group. Single parents who have lost their mates through divorce or death or who have never married may come. People who are socially handicapped, mentally handicapped, and physically handicapped may appear. In addition to this, individuals from every church background and theological persuasion may come. Many of these people's situations present issues that are major controversies. However, all of these people *desire* and *deserve* our unconditional love and acceptance. Without that, it is doubtful they will return.

Provide a Whole Ministry

To foster the purpose of wholeness, ministry to adult singles needs to develop four elements: the spiritual, the social, the emotional, and the educational. Each element is a key part of the total ministry and will play a vital role in contributing to the development of people's lives.

A spiritual atmosphere and thrust should be foundational. When this is present, the group will be known for its biblical basis and Christian emphasis. The Christian emphasis can be portrayed in every aspect of the ministry (music, prayer, classes, retreats, etc.).

Since adult singles desire fulfilling relationships, various types of social activities and opportunities for fellowship can be offered. Their needs of support, friendship, learning, relating, dating, and mating will begin to be fulfilled from within the social network provided by the ministry.

The need for individual emotional growth can be met through counseling with the minister or leader or through counseling with other adult singles. Many times singles are each other's own best counselors because of the knowledge they've gained from similar experiences.

Educational growth is needed concerning managing money, raising children as a single parent, preparing for a permanent relationship, determining identity, understanding sexuality, and other areas. These issues are often discussed in one-to-one relationships but could also be in class settings.

Provide a Growing Ministry

A third means of contributing to individual wholeness is to provide opportunities for personal growth through discipleship and involvement in the ministry. As leadership people and support people are developed, those involved feel a personal sense of contribution and importance. They derive joy from assisting in a ministry that provides help and healing to people.

Involving many individuals also eliminates burnout of a few and brings a feeling of ownership: "This ministry does not belong to the leader; it is ours! We are responsible for its success or its failure."

A natural consequence of personal growth is group growth. As people assume responsibility for the ministry, the group will begin to grow spiritually, numerically, financially, etc. The reality of people helping people will influence and foster corporate growth. As individuals grow, the ministry will grow.

Goals

Goals can be defined as set objectives that achieve a purpose. Goals need to be determined that, when met, contribute to the enhancement and achievement of the ministry's purposes.

Whom Are We Targeting?

Either at the onset of the ministry or sometime in its early stages, a decision will need to be made concerning whom is going to be targeted. Will you be providing a ministry mainly for those in *your church?* Will you endeavor to reach the *unchurched?* Will you accept adult singles from *other churches?* Some people will probably come from hearing about your efforts. It should be made clear that you are not trying to get people out of their churches and into yours but that you are only providing for a need that may not be met somewhere else.

What Needs Are to Be Met?

Another issue that needs to be considered concerns the type(s) of adult singles you are trying to reach. The term "adult single" includes individuals eighteen years and up. If the decision is made to plan for the ages eighteen to thirty, it will mean ministering mainly to the never-married person. If the goal is to attract mainly the adult between thirty and fifty-five, it will mean ministering primarily to the divorced person.

Within each of these age groups, however, all three types of adult singles are present. There are people in their forties, fifties, and sixties who have never married. There are those in their twenties and thirties who are divorced and widowed. Even more complicated is the fact that, within all age groups, there are people who are currently separated from their spouses. There are also single parents who are single either by divorce, death of a spouse, or who have never married but happen to have children by adoption, circumstance, or design. (These mainly fall into the twenty to fifty age bracket.)

Many of the needs and struggles of the adult single are similar, regardless of the reason for singleness. Five basic needs are:

1. Spiritual—to know God through a personal, vital, growing relationship with Jesus Christ.
2. Relational—to learn to relate to people of all ages in casual or intimate relationships with the same and opposite sex.
3. Emotional—to maintain emotional stability in a complex world.
4. Directional—to find direction in the many areas of life.
5. Financial—to learn to effectively manage money.

These basic needs should be clearly identified and established as goals set for the ministry.

Plans

It has been said that "those who fail to plan, plan to fail." I believe this is true. Definite plans achieve specific goals that fulfill clear purposes. A *total ministry should be planned* as soon as possible, *but developed in stages.* Establishing and directing a ministry to adult singles is a very complex and challenging undertaking because of the many issues that adult singles face. An effective, need-fulfilling ministry does not happen overnight. It takes time to develop. Be patient and allow time for it. Several things must be considered in the planning process.

Leadership. People to assume various leadership roles will need to be found, appointed, trained, and motivated. Are potential leaders currently present or must there be a waiting period? Consider what kind of person is needed for the position. This may be determined largely by the type of activity (Bible study, social, retreat, publicity, etc.).

Time frame. Consider the timing when you are planning for the ministry. Is there currently verbal and moral support or must those be developed? Is the need for this particular segment of the ministry present already, or is the intention to begin it first and expect those who will benefit from it to come? When is it possible to begin?

Finances. Is there currently enough money for this ministry, or will it have to be raised? How will it be raised, and by when? Has the church or sponsoring organization budgeted for it? If not, what would it take to get them to? Or, will the ministry be self-supporting?

Facilities. A ministry to adult singles can be developed one of two ways—inside the church building or campus, or outside the church building or campus. Since there is not an overabundance of these ministries in most areas of the country, location is a very important factor. There are several advantages and disadvantages either way you choose.

In the Church—Advantages

- Meeting room(s) at no cost
- Availability of storage space

- Visibility to the church body (the sponsoring church begins to understand the purposes of the ministry)
- Spiritual image and thrust easy to maintain

In the Church—Disadvantages

- Attracts lesser percent of the unchurched—many are reluctant to step into a church because of stereotypes
- Misunderstanding of purpose from leaders of other churches— they may think you are proselytizing or that people may leave their churches and go to yours, even if the ministry does not meet on a regular church day
- Possible scheduling conflicts

Out of the Church—Advantages

- Attracts a higher percent of unchurched people
- Attracts a higher percent of other-church people whose churches have no ministry to adult singles
- Community witness—the public may eventually get the impression of a city-wide ministry and a true caring for people
- Parking space (depending on scheduling)

Out of the Church—Disadvantages

- Finding a suitable room(s); considerations include location, image of the establishment, seating, availability of refreshments (purchase or bring in), location of restrooms, and other items depending on preference and need
- Storage availability—props and materials may need to be taken out of the building after each meeting
- Lack of church leadership support—may not allow a ministry out of the church; the sponsoring church may not benefit numerically and financially
- Possible scheduling conflicts
- Image of the ministry—both churched and unchurched people may have false images of the group (these may include "A Dating Club," "A Losers Group," "A Swingers Group," "A Spiritual Clique," "A Lonelies Group," and others)

Curriculum/materials. Ten to fifteen years ago, resource and teaching material for developing a ministry to adult singles was difficult to find. It may still not be as easy to find as other types of materials (for youth, children). However, more writers are responding to the ever-growing need for resources.

When seeking resource material, be sure to obtain material that is *geared to adults.* Some people mistakenly assume that the word *single* refers mainly to the young adult, ages eighteen to twenty-four (the college-age person). These people can indeed be single. However, a very high percentage of adult singles are between the ages of twenty-five and seventy-five and are single because of divorce, death of a spouse, or never marrying. These people's needs and interests are distinctly those of adults and most of the time differ from those of college-age adults. Using material that is mainly geared to the college-age person would reach only a small percentage of America's single adults.

It would be wise to ask leaders of other single adult ministries what materials they use. It is always helpful to obtain a good recommendation before purchasing or using a particular book or tape. For practical ideas on networking through NSL consult the appendix on page 353.

Evaluation

In the final analysis, two questions must be answered. Evaluation is imperative to discover whether or not goals have been met and the purpose fulfilled. The two questions are Is there *effective ministry to* people? and Is there *effective ministry for* people?

For the answer to the first question, look closely at what is happening in the individual lives of people. Are lives being changed and people being made whole? Is there an attitude of enthusiasm among the people? Are there continually first-time visitors attending? Are individuals being treated warmly, respectfully, and with genuine hospitality? Are the current programs really meeting the definite needs of the people? These should be evaluated to determine the effectiveness of *ministry to* people.

For the answer to the second question, look closely at what is happening in the group. Are there many kinds of involvement opportunities, both for leadership people and support people? Are people really ministering to each other by giving encouragement, prayer, and counseling? Is there a genuine feeling that this ministry belongs to the people and not the pastor or leader? These should be evaluated to determine the effectiveness of *ministry for* people.

Building Community in a Single Adult Ministry

Jim Smoke

The average singles group in America turns over its population from 40 to 60 percent every six months. Knowing that statistic makes it rather difficult to think and plan for long-term community building. The people who seem to stay longest in any singles group are usually the leaders. Because they are in leadership together, they tend to form a very tight community of support and caring for one another. The struggle to form community beyond the leadership team is a difficult one that most leaders struggle with. The answer to the age-old question of what draws people together is as varied as weather patterns. One thing does remain constant: People need the support that belonging to a community gives. The following are a few key principles that have been learned and demonstrated among many singles ministries in recent years.

Community does not happen by legislation. You cannot *make* people become important to one another in a loving and caring fashion. Building community is a process that takes an endless amount of time. There is little or no sense of community in the forming of a new group of singles. People cannot belong to one another until they really know one another. Using group dynamics and group gymnastics does not make a community.

The leaders must model what they want the followers to become. Jesus' final commands to the disciples contained the admonition to "love each other." In the best of times, that is seldom easy. In tough times, it can be virtually impossible. The tenor of any ministry is set by the leadership. If there is dissension in leadership, you can be sure there will be tension in the ranks. Since leadership is usually "up front," their community patterns with one another are highly visible. I have had people tell me they wanted to be in leadership only because they were envious of the spirit of community the leaders had with one another.

Building community is a teaching process. Community should come from a biblical base with the model of Jesus and his relationship with the disciples (Luke 22:7–14; John 13:1–17; Acts 4:32–35; Philem. 14; Heb. 10:24–25; 1 Peter 5:2). You always teach your people what you want them to do and be. Then you model your teaching. It is easy to become fragmented in a singles ministry because there is little or no emphasis on community. Sports teams spend as much time building community as perfecting their athletic skills. That is why when one team member gets in a scuffle with an opposing player, the bench usually empties as the rest of the team comes to the rescue.

Building community is based in building healthy relationships. Many people lack relational skills or have been hurt so deeply that they fear any form of relationship. You cannot build community with everyone by walking on eggshells. Life is about relationships. Building them involves risks. There are no guarantees. Our teaching process must include teaching people how to build healthy relationships.

Good communities last because they become solid friendships. I still meet yearly for a dinner with about forty of my former singles ministry leaders from the early '70s. And we will continue to do that each year because we were and still remain a community. Common needs, interests, dreams, and struggles brought us together. Those same things hold us together, and the ties have strengthened over the years.

People only support what they help create. A sense of belonging comes from a sense of ownership. People need a good reason to attend, join, participate. Yes, I know there will always be a crowd content to just be sideline spectators. They are everywhere in life and they usually run from responsibility. Leave them alone with their reasons and concentrate on those who want to be involved. Community comes from involvement, not from passive observance. Whenever you can, give your people a reason to be at your events and programs. Make sure the reason goes beyond just filling the seats.

Fellow strugglers build a solid community. There is a dynamic of shared experience or shared trial that draws people closer to each other. It needs little explanation; it just happens. It is true in Alcoholics Anonymous and it is true in divorce recovery work. Brought together by their shared suffering, when strugglers then experience healing, they help others who need it, and the bonds of community through caring become even stronger.

Building community does not mean having one big happy family. In a singles ministry, it means having one common objective and having many happy families. There is more mystery concerning what draws people into different communities than there is explanation. The important thing is that people find a place to belong. We all search for that place or places where we know we belong, feel comfortable, fit in. We are never hesitant to go where we feel secure and accepted. A sense of belonging seldom happens overnight. We need to test the waters to see where we belong best.

Joining a community can be difficult for some. One of the dynamics of any singles group is that many of the people attending it have lost their former communities and have little or no sense of belonging anywhere as they pass through your door. They need to hear someone say, "There's a place for you here. You will be loved and accepted and you will find a home." Many single adults are in transition, experiencing a difficult time. They often wander from group to group, looking for a safe place to pitch their tents and camp for a while. Any group of singles could be described as containing those who have lost community, those in search of a new community, those who have found a new community, and those fearful they will be nomads from community for the rest of their lives.

Building a community is a slow and often torturous process, but the finished product is worth the process!

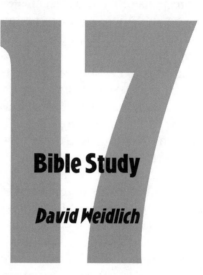

Bible Study

David Weidlich

Single adults need security, fulfillment, healthy relationships, and help with raising children. These are important needs, and adults want more than just opinions when it comes to providing solutions.

An old cliché says, "Consider the source." A person may be quite capable of teaching truth using science, psychology, and philosophy as sources. But how can people know whether what that person is teaching is true? A lot is based on the trustworthiness of the source.

The Bible, Our Textbook

The Bible claims complete trustworthiness for itself. It was written by God who is, after all, the author of all truth. When correctly interpreted and applied, the truth of Scripture is a powerful and profitable tool (2 Tim. 2:15; 3:16).

You cannot have that confidence if you are teaching the latest discoveries reported in a journal written by men or women. What you're teaching may prove to be helpful. Or, time and further discoveries may prove that you were unhelpful. However, if you are accurately conveying the truths of the Bible, you can't go wrong!

Christians are given the responsibility of teaching others about God and his expectations of people. Jesus left his disciples with the words, "Go and make disciples of all nations" (Matt. 28:19). Jesus' followers were called *mathetai*, "disciples." The word means "learners" or "pupils." So the process of disciple-making is the process of producing learners or pupils of Christ. If people are expected to be learners, there must be teachers.

A ministry to single adults must include biblical teaching. A church does well to be concerned about singles, but if they aren't offering biblical solutions to life's problems, they're not training disciples. Therefore, the Bible is our number one textbook in training and nurturing single adult disciples.

Learning is considered tedious to many because the goal of many teachers—in and out of the church—is merely to transfer ideas from the teacher to the student. Certainly, that's part of it, but the Christian's goal in ministry is to make disciples mature in Christ (Col. 1:25, 28–29).

With that in mind, we can see that Christian teachers must teach certain facts from God's Word and life's situations, but they must also encourage and motivate their students to apply and practice those ideas in real life. Not only is that the right thing to do; it's what people need the most.

Jesus, the Master Teacher

In discussing how best to teach the Bible, we should not forget that Jesus was himself a Bible teacher. And what an effective one!

The most influential teachers are those who not only communicate facts well, but who also communicate love and concern. Jesus certainly did. Who wouldn't listen to a teacher who said, "I am the good shepherd . . . and I lay down my life for my sheep"? (John 10:14–15). Students learn much more effectively when the teacher communicates genuine concern and warmth.

Jesus not only taught a righteous lifestyle, he lived it! His integrity taught what mere words could not. He modeled what he taught. His attitude and last words on the cross, "Father forgive them," added immeasurable impact to his teaching love for one's enemies. Teachers must be models of the actions and attitudes they teach.

Jesus' teaching style involved constant interaction with his pupils. They were free to interrupt or ask questions. Often he asked them questions to guide them toward truth. He taught from the Scriptures (Luke 4:17–27). He employed parables, discussions, and natural, everyday situations and events (Matt. 13:34–35) in his lessons. He motivated the disciples to think and discover for themselves. This produced confusion at times, like when he left them so they could ponder the meaning of a parable or "hard saying." But in the long run, he was more effective than if he had only dispensed factual data to his disciples. They *discovered* God's good Word for themselves.

Principles for Effective Teaching

The example of Jesus and the insights of modern educators can be used to draw out several principles about effective teaching.

Pray. Continually seek God's guidance as you prepare and teach. Ask the Holy Spirit to guide you and your group into the truth (Eph. 1:17–18).

Let go of the reins. Too often teachers continue bottle-feeding their students long after their students are able to feed themselves. Give up your desire to have control. People are more motivated to learn when they share in ownership of the learning experience.

Be a facilitator. Teachers need to see themselves less as dispensers of knowledge and more as facilitators who point fellow-learners to the truth (Christ). The teacher is still an important part of the learning process. But the role is different. He or she is a guide, consultant, and resource person. Remember, singles are adults. Adults learn best through personal discovery during the journey.

Accept the role of motivator. Show *why* people need to learn something by asking questions that arouse felt needs. Or use a case study that parallels their experience followed by the question, "What would you do in this situation?" Use questions to open their minds to new possibilities, not to lead learners into parroting expected answers.

Encourage participation. Let students dialogue in an atmosphere of freedom and acceptance. Give them ownership of the learning experience by allowing them to formulate their own thoughts and goals. You might ask, "What is it that you want from this study?" Also, encourage them to evaluate the learning experience from time to time.

Use a variety of techniques and materials. Include small group discussion, role plays, readings, lectures, interviews, drama, music and art activities, research activities, tests, and writing assignments. Create learning activities, not learning passivities.

Always emphasize application. It cannot be assumed that adult students will naturally and correctly apply biblical principles to life situations. We must help them. For example, ask, "How does Paul's discussion of humility apply to your relationship with your ex-spouse?" Or, "Name one thing you will do this week that shows humility." Use assignments to encourage the integration of new attitudes and skills in life situations. Remember, assignments are best carried out when learners participate in designing them. A group may want to assign themselves to memorize a verse or carry out a service project.

Evaluate and encourage. Learn from your teaching experiences and improve your teaching skills. Also help learners feel a sense of progress toward goals by reviewing and affirming their achievements. Divide learning into distinguishable segments and, at the end of one, celebrate!

Forms of Bible Study

God's creativity in making people is limitless. We're all different, and all groups of people are different. But several general forms that teaching may take seem to apply to all people in all cultures and situations.

Large group study. In this form, communication is necessarily more one-way, though not exclusively. Recognize the diversity of your group and gear your studies to be broader in application. The larger the group, the less commitment you can expect. For this reason, make each session a self-contained unit to include even those who haven't attended before. While doing a series, keep it short; three or four sessions is a reasonable length.

Topical lessons work well in a large group context because you are better able to meet the felt needs of those participating. However, Bible book studies should not be ignored. Many people won't come unless they can see right away that there's something in it for them. So address a subject that a wide variety of singles would be interested in—relationships, sex, career success, single parenting, or money management. Start with these felt needs and then present a biblical perspective on these issues. For simplicity and impact stick with one appropriate passage of Scripture as your main text and apply it faithfully to the issue at hand.

Small groups. This form provides for more flexibility. Groups can be more homogeneous; that is, made up of people who have many things in common. This way, you can meet specific needs. For example, you may have a group for career women, one for never-marrieds, one for single parents, one for new Christians, one for people who are not (yet) Christians, and one for any combination of people. People are generally attracted to people who are like themselves and they will make a stronger commitment to the group.

The success of a small group is largely dependent on its leader(s). The best leader is one who will take the role of a pastor, or shepherd, to care for needs of the individuals in the group. He or she must maintain a balance of control and freedom. Group members must own the group, but the leader must hold individuals accountable to the group and to their goals.

Small groups provide for more flexibility in studying. In a group of dedicated people you have a good context for an in-depth inductive Bible study. Or with a group of single parents you can study what the Scriptures say about parenting. So the application can be more specific according to the common needs of the group.

Cramming. Another effective form of Bible study is called "cramming." Of course, cramming isn't highly recommended in academic circles, but if it weren't for this method, many college students wouldn't learn anything.

The same principles can be transferred to informal education by holding conferences, seminars, and retreats. People are more likely to commit to a one-time experience for a long period of time than to an equal amount of time stretched out over several weeks or months. These "cramming" sessions are good opportunities for intense study with application to specific needs. For example, you might hold a seminar on money management where scriptural attitudes and principles are studied, or a weekend retreat where 1 Corinthians is taught as it relates especially to singles in sexual morality, relationships, marriage, spiritual gifts, and more.

The task of Bible study is not an easy one. Sadly, many teachers are content to go for the quick rewards of serving up popular but ultimately unsatisfying spiritual food. Jesus has called us to make disciples, and this can only be done by teaching people about God and his expectations of us and then motivating them to respond through faith and obedience.

Go and make disciples. Jesus says, "And surely I am with you always" (Matt. 28:20).

18
Developing Small Groups

Jeff McNicol

The development of small groups is not a new phenomenon. However, the realization that small groups are a crucial aspect of vital, growing ministries is. Churches and other organizations are focusing on groups with fewer participants and have experienced great benefits as a result. This approach is particularly effective in singles ministry.

What Is a Small Group?

Numerically. It is quite difficult to suggest a specific size that is optimal for every single adult small group because no two are alike. Yet there is a range in which small groups function most effectively. This range is approximately from four to twelve participants. More than twelve will tend to stifle interaction, causing the group to become dominated by just a few.

Functionally. If one were to reduce all the functional benefits of small groups to a single word, it would be *interaction*. Nearly all of the other positive elements are an outgrowth of the interaction possible in small groups. Not only does it encourage personal interaction between members of the group, fostering relationship building, it also aids in increasing personal ownership of the group. Once a person considers it "his" or "her" group, his or her commitment and desire to make it successful increase significantly.

The Need for Small Groups

Interrelationally. The relational interaction of the small group for singles is important because for some members this may be the only source of support. Each of us has certain needs in our lives, and it helps to know that others are aware of them. A group of caring individuals can listen to those needs and provide comfort. Beyond being a place to share needs, a small group has potential for deep camaraderie among all its members. I have experienced a great warmth and love from the singles I work with and have also seen group members support one another emotionally, physically, financially, and spiritually. A support structure such as this takes time and an investment of ourselves in the lives of others, but the results can be life-changing and well worth the effort.

Functionally. Small groups are very conducive to member participation. A larger group essentially becomes a teacher/listener environment, failing to encourage discussion. With the smaller group, however, it is feasible that all those present can take part. There is also the opportunity of prayer on behalf of all the others in the group. One additional exciting aspect of the smaller group is that personal follow-up can be done with relative ease. After praying for someone, let that person know you are thinking of him or her. Chances are that your concern alone will provide comfort.

The Leadership of Small Groups

Developing leadership. Leadership is not something a person is born with; rather, leaders are trained and taught. Learning to be a leader is not much different from learning any other skill; with practice and perseverance, leadership skills can be developed. For this very reason, potential future leaders must be given opportunities to "try their wings" and serve in leadership. Sharing the leadership is an absolute necessity in singles ministry. Due to the high turnover, unless we are nourishing leadership replacements, we will be left without small group leaders.

Choosing a leader. How do we go about recognizing a potential small group leader? We must begin with prayer. If God wants us to have a singles ministry, he will provide the necessary personnel. We, however, must be in a position to recognize God's provision. Praying for the Lord's guidance is the first step. There are also certain characteristics that suggest leadership qualities. One such quality is vision. One who does not have a good idea of where the small group is headed and what its purpose is will probably not lead well. However, vision can be caught by the potential leader. Additional leadership qualities include a love for God, spiritual maturity, affinity for others, a pleasant personality (not necessarily outgoing), diligence, and a willingness to be a team player.

The leader's role as facilitator. Within the small group setting, it is preferential to think of the central figure as the facilitator. It has been stressed that interaction is the major function of small groups. If a leader operates as a dictator, that interaction will not take place and the small group may as well be a large group. If the leader is a facilitator, however, he will only enhance the group, teaching others to lead in the process.

Modeling leadership. The leader must model leadership to others. There are a few specific principles to be kept in mind. First of all, it is crucial to invest time and effort into potential future leaders. Essentially it is a discipleship process whereby one leader trains another, who trains another, and so forth (2 Tim. 2:2). Second, when modeling leadership, it is important to demonstrate a teachable attitude. No one has all the answers, and to pretend we do will only diminish our credibility in the eyes of others. Remain open to the ideas of others.

How to Implement and Sustain Small Groups

Getting started. The best place to start is with prayer, seeking God's direction for the small group(s) you are planning to initiate. When the time comes to determine who the group members will be, group people according to common interests or backgrounds.

Some extra effort in this area will certainly be time well spent in the long run. Within the given parameters, determine what would be the most effective number of participants for your specific situation, and stick to it. Once the group reaches the maximum number, start and build a second group. If numerical growth is a goal, two groups of six have a greater growth potential than one group of twelve simply because a group already at its maximum number will not tend to be "growth minded." The final key in starting is to recognize the needs of the people within the group and make the group's purposes very clear. Hidden agendas will only serve to frustrate a group focusing on a separate purpose. The leader and group must share and ultimately agree on a purpose and plan for the group. This in turn will develop ownership, and the group will move forward with a common focus.

During the actual group meetings, there are two overriding approaches in presenting material, namely the use of constants or variables. Constants are necessary to give the group continuity from week to week. It gives group members focal points to recognize and keeps the meetings from becoming disjointed. On the other hand, the meetings also need variables. Without variables, the group will become dull. There needs to be a balance, and it is the leader's responsibility to maintain that balance.

Moving forward. The small group should never be satisfied with the status quo. There must always be a sense of direction plus a feeling of achieving goals and moving ahead. Group vision and ownership will help to accomplish this. As with any ministry or organization, goals give direction to small groups. A small group will tend to flounder if members do not have a clear understanding of the goals. Another hint in this area is to ask for and expect involvement. A small group needs commitment from its members. If someone wishes to be in a group, you have the right to expect some level of involvement in due time.

Terminating. In a chapter on developing small groups, you might be surprised to find a discussion on terminating the small group. However, it is an important, often overlooked, necessity in many groups. No gathering of people is guaranteed to be successful forever. Even the best small group can reach the point where its goal has been reached and effectiveness has run out. This is nothing to be ashamed of, but for the sake of all involved, do not be afraid to admit it and dissolve the group.

Potential Dangers for Small Groups

Individual domination. The strength of the small group is found in the interaction it can generate. When one individual dominates the discussion, it will be a setback to the group. The dominator may not be the "official" group leader.

Lack of focus. Without clear goals and purpose, the group will lack direction. Continually emphasize the group's goals as it meets together.

Superficial relationships. There is a measure of vulnerability for members of a small group. It is, however, that risk of showing others who you are inside that transports the group from superficial relations to a more meaningful involvement in one another's lives.

Forced transparency. Because of the risk involved in sharing oneself, we must be careful not to force it. Nobody shares his or her innermost feelings with someone he or she has just met. A level of trust and acceptance must be attained before intimacy will emerge.

Growing beyond a small group. Once a group gets too large, it can no longer be effective as a small group. Too many members will kill the group. Determine your boundaries, and when you reach the maximum, form a new group.

Cliques. All cliques are not bad. The formulation of a small group in and of itself is a clique. However, if different cliques form within the small group, it could be devastating. Inner cliques could create an atmosphere where open interaction cannot take place.

Dead groups. Many small groups reach the place where they cease being effective. To force the group to continue will only frustrate those involved. Let dying groups die, and allow their members to move on.

Small groups are a significant means through which ministry to singles can take place. The support, fellowship, and interaction provided by such groups will serve to meet many needs in the lives of single adults.

A Balanced Ministry

Chris Eaton

Balance is as important to a ministry as it is to a high-wire walker. Even just a slight shift to one side or the other may create a disastrous imbalance. Therefore, the leaders of a singles ministry should think *balance* every step of the way. Unfortunately, too many ministries do not start thinking about balance until a fall has occurred, and at that point, the damage may be irreparable.

Balance Defined

One reason balance sometimes escapes the planners of a ministry is that it seems an element too vague to incorporate into the planning. Therefore, it is wise to begin with a rather simple working definition:

Balance in a ministry is the meeting of both the social and spiritual needs of the participants in such a way that the two are viewed as inseparable.

The ideal ministry treats social and spiritual needs as interdependent. This philosophy is especially important in a single adult ministry, where social need is so much more apparent. The mistake often made in the planning of ministries is to view these needs as separate.

For example, a spiritual time is planned once a week and a social time is planned once a month. There is a "fun" time and a "serious" time. Yet in the Scriptures the two go hand in hand. Certainly relationships play a vital part in a person's relationship with God (for example, examine all the "one another" references in the Scriptures).

A well-balanced ministry is reached when spiritual growth and relational development (community building) are both happening in some way at *every* function of the group. Sometimes there will be more social than spiritual emphasis, and vice versa, but the emphases need to be balanced out in the end. Just as it would be ridiculous for the high-wire walker to continually lean in one direction, so also it is foolish for a leader to allow a ministry to continually lean in one direction.

The Importance of Balance

The importance of balance to a ministry can be illustrated by the results of both balance and imbalance.

Balance

Individual growth. Participants will be growing in their spirituality. They will not just be learning material, rather they will be developing a "cutting edge" relationship with Jesus Christ. Learning is always more effective in the context of a community. In a community people are challenged not only to learn but also to put that learning into practice.

Group growth. When there's balance in a group, there will be more of an interest in visitors, an interest not only in their spiritual state, but also in their relational situation. Obviously when there's an interest in the visitors, a larger percentage of them will return to the group. To be quite honest, the reason some single adult ministries stagnate is simply that there is nothing worth coming back to. When balance is evident there will be something for almost everyone.

Imbalance

The group is "too" spiritual. The primary focus is inward. The emphasis is only on the spiritual dimension. *Motto: Study!* The characteristics of this group are:

1. Social element sought elsewhere. The need is still there and has to be met. A program may be great on Sunday morning, but chances are the single adults are not staying home Saturday night studying their Sunday school curriculum!
2. Boredom within the group.
3. Poor evangelistic/outreach attitude. Christians are commissioned to carry the Good News to the world they live in. However, when the concern of a group is mainly their own spiritual growth, their concern for the needs of those around them can drop off.
4. Low visitor return.

The group is "too" social. Primary focus is outward. The emphasis is only on the social. *Motto: Party!* The characteristics of this group are:

1. Little spiritual growth in individuals.
2. Lack of a solid foundation in the group.
3. Complaining in the ranks when personal needs are not met.
4. Low visitor return. There's no community being developed when the spiritual is ignored. It is purely superficial.

In summary, both situations fail to insure longevity for the group. Chances are either type of group will die a slow, stagnating death.

Hindrances to Balance

There are certain hindrances to maintaining a balanced ministry. Imbalance is not something a leader decides one day to have. Instead it is usually a gradual slide to one side or the other—a slide that may at times go unnoticed until too late! There are many contributing factors to imbalance:

Demands. It is quite obvious that what people demand may not be all they need. Therefore, it is important for the leaders to keep demands in the proper perspective.

Expectations. Meeting everyone's expectations can be as unhealthy as meeting everyone's demands.

Preoccupation with numbers. This causes a leader to go for the "big number events" in programming. The problem is that often less glamorous needs go without being met. Another problem is that the ministry ends up only "tickling" the single adults' ears and not challenging them to grow.

What has been done in the past, especially if the past includes a ministry way out of balance. The mentality will need to be gradually changed.

Staff pressures/board pressures.

Lack of creativity. The ministry does the same thing year after year. Leaders fail to come up with innovative ideas.

When the leadership allows these factors to control or influence the direction of the group, they run a high risk of imbalance. Any one of these or a combination of several may cause a gradual shifting of weight and eventually a fall off the high wire.

Maintaining a Balanced Ministry

The leader. Balance begins with a balanced leader. It is an essential element to having a balanced ministry! The leader should be an example of balance in his personal life. Participants should see both the spiritual and social needs of the leader being met in an integrated manner.

A leader must not be so quick to lay the blame for the imbalance of the group on the people involved, the church board, or certain circumstances. Often the imbalance may simply be a reflection of the leader's own imbalance!

The group. As with anything else, attitude is of key importance to a group desiring balance. Maintaining balanced attitudes will play a major role in maintaining a balanced ministry.

Understanding. Leaders should understand that people are not exclusively spiritual or social.

Sensitivity. A leader must be sensitive to the changing needs both within the group and in the world around the group. Without sensitivity a leader may attempt to do the same things over and over again even when the program or idea has outlived its usefulness.

Adaptability. Be willing to adapt a program or method to a certain situation or need. Have a structure that is able to shift in one direction if there seems to be some imbalance.

Flexibility. The leader must avoid rigidity in the approach to people and ministry.

Risk-taking. Be willing to try new ideas, new methods, new strategies. A leader who desires a balanced ministry will be a leader who is willing to take some risks in that ministry!

A balanced ministry is a necessity for effective long-term ministry in the single adult community. Therefore, the leaders need to pause from time to time and get a feel for whether or not the ministry is balanced. The high-wire artist contemplates each step because his or her life is on the line. In ministry, leaders need to be equally thorough in thinking through each organizational step because the lives of so many single adults, both in the church, and perhaps more importantly outside the church, are dependent on those balanced steps.

Part 4

Programs for Single Adults

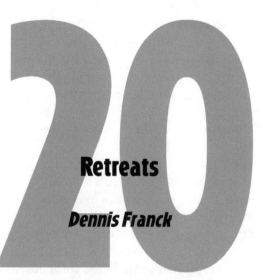

Retreats

Dennis Franck

One of the highlights of the year for adults involved in a singles ministry is the retreat. A retreat is a time for "getting away from it all," a time for refreshing the mind and spirit, a time for renewal of purpose, a time for rekindling of enthusiasm, a time set aside for learning, relating, and growing.

Targeting a Purpose

There are several different types of retreats. Each type requires differences in format, organization, teaching material, and so on. Depending on group size, you may want to target one particular type of adult single.

The purpose of the retreats need to be determined far in advance to ensure direction and the proper planning of every area. The retreat setting easily lends itself to a variety of purposes. Some of these include:

Spiritual growth. Teaching sessions and activities could be planned specifically to affect spiritual growth in individual lives.

Practical instruction. Issues relating to the single life could be addressed in depth.

Personal fellowship. Adult singles do not have a mate with whom they can laugh, cry, pray, make decisions, share, and grow. It is important that they develop genuine, healthy relationships. The retreat provides an atmosphere conducive to the interacting of minds and hearts in a concentrated, intimate setting.

Ministry. Because ministry to adult singles is relatively new to many parts of the country, the majority of churches do not plan retreats for singles. If the retreat is publicized correctly, many people will come whose churches do not have a local ministry to singles.

The development of new ministries. Another purpose of a retreat could be to inspire others to begin a singles ministry. After attending these events, people not having a local singles ministry become extremely excited about the possibility of beginning one.

Leadership training. Leaders need training, motivation, fellowship, and a sense of team spirit. A retreat is an excellent setting in which to establish these basic components of the leadership core.

The purpose of the retreat could be any one or a combination of these. It is important that the purpose(s) be clearly and adequately identified so that people may have an understanding of what to expect. The retreat leader should not try to meet too many different needs. It is possible to aim at too many and hit none.

Location and Facilities

Make the location of the retreat close enough to home so that parents could return in case of an emergency with children but far enough from home so that people are not distracted by work associates, friends, and children whose general interests and demands may tempt them to run home for insignificant things. A distance of one to three hours may be ideal for a "getaway" experience.

Several different types of facilities could be considered.

Motels or hotels. These usually offer comfortable sleeping rooms and meeting rooms equipped with tables, chairs, P.A. system, and visual aids. Many motels and hotels also have restaurants, food services, and recreational facilities. Price may be somewhat of a concern; however, negotiation of prices is often possible. The motel or hotel provides a neutral atmosphere that may attract some who would not attend if the retreat were held in a church.

Retreat center. These can be found in many parts of the country. Benefits of the retreat centers are similar to the motel or hotel with the possible further benefit of additional recreational opportunities.

Camp. The camp setting usually provides a "rougher," more casual setting and may be less expensive than a motel or hotel or retreat center.

Church. A church building or campus might also be considered. The church usually offers a closer location and would be less expensive, if not free, in regard to meeting room expense. Unless the church has a gymnasium, recreational facilities may be limited and might need to be found elsewhere. Sleeping and shower facilities must be considered (remember singles are adults, not teenagers).

Depending on the style of retreat desired and the preferences and interests of those expected to come, one facility may be more appealing than another. Whatever type is chosen, many items will probably prove to be basic needs. Among them are sleeping rooms, rest room facilities, meeting rooms equipped with tables and chairs, P.A. system and microphones, piano, overhead projector, chalkboard, meal facilities, and recreational facilities.

Involving People

Planning the retreat involves a great deal of effort on the part of many people. Planning should begin six to twelve months in advance to ensure selection of the speaker(s) and adequate time for organization.

The first and most important person to secure is the retreat coordinator. This should be someone who is spiritually mature, organizationally competent, and whose leadership abilities are respected and proven. His or her responsibilities will demand that he or she be visible and able to spend many hours working to ensure a successful retreat in every way. The retreat coordinator will need to recruit support leadership to coordinate various aspects of the retreat. These people would direct such ministries as:

publicity	devotions
registration	recreation
emcee	sound/taping
transportation	photography
music	book table
drama	housing

These individuals play a vital role in making the retreat effective, and their work will give them a sense of responsibility, importance, and ownership of the ministry.

Selecting the Speaker(s)

Selecting the speaker(s) is a very important task. He or she will affect the lives of many people. It is important to look for certain qualifications in his or her life that will affect his or her ability to minister to singles. Questions to consider are:

- Does the potential speaker have an understanding of the needs of all types of single adults (college-age, career-oriented, never-married, divorced, widowed, single parent)?
- Does the potential speaker have an understanding of the local church? Most people attending the retreat will be involved in a particular local church. He or she needs to know about the ministries, problems, and opportunities for him or her to relate effectively.
- Does the potential speaker possess good communication skills? Is he or she able to hold people's attention? Is material presented in a logical, thoughtful manner? Is there good eye contact with the listeners?
- Does the potential speaker have a good knowledge of the topic(s) to be covered? Definite interest and teaching experience is needed. Will the speaker present biblical truth?
- Does the potential speaker have a vital, growing relationship with Christ? A person cannot give anything that he or she does not possess. To give lasting spiritual significance to people's lives, the speaker must have a personal relationship with Christ.

It would be very helpful to obtain this information from others who have heard the person speak. Recommendations are usually trustworthy, if the source is. Other means of becoming acquainted with a particular person include books and articles he or she has written. In some instances there may be a problem in even obtaining names of potential speakers. If this is the case, contact others who are currently involved in single adult ministry for suggestions.

Selecting the Topics

Know the needs of your target group. If adult singles of all ages are invited to the retreat, ask the main speaker(s) to use a holistic approach in teaching. By doing so, needs and interests of people of all ages and all single statuses will be touched on, thereby ministering to everyone.

Be mindful also of the unique needs that people may have from the various singles ministries represented at the retreat. Examine these too before deciding on the topic(s).

Scheduling

The length of the retreat can be varied. The most common are:

- one day
- one day and one night
- two days and one night
- two days and two nights

It is even possible to plan a four- or five-day camp experience. For many groups, however, a weekend retreat usually serves the purpose well. Since most adults work weekdays, beginning Friday evening and concluding Sunday noon is a very workable schedule. Whatever length is chosen, make certain that it is agreeable to the speaker(s).

A variety of components could be included in any retreat; however, there are several basics:

main sessions	recreation	refreshment breaks
elective classes	special events	free time
devotional times	meals	rest

These nine components seem to surface as major parts of a retreat. Balancing them is a task for the retreat coordinator and speaker(s).

Special events can be used effectively and become a highlight. There are numerous ideas that can be utilized depending on preference, availability, and cost:

film	drama group	talent show
concert	comedy group	amusement park
tour	shopping	athletics

These, as well as other ideas balance teaching, listening, concentration times that are part of a successful retreat.

Publicity

Publicity for the retreat should begin three to five months in advance. This would allow adequate time for planning and coordination. Announcements about the retreat should begin two to three months in advance to allow for building enthusiasm, momentum, saving money toward the cost, and planning for possible child care. If the retreat is sponsored by a church or group within the church, two major areas of publicity should be considered.

In-house publicity includes:

| brochures | announcements | slides |
| posters | skits | pictures |

Out-of-house publicity includes:

- brochures to other churches, groups, etc.
- posters to other churches, groups, laundromats, shopping centers, apartment buildings
- letters to other churches, groups, organizations
- radio—public service announcements

- newspaper—public service announcements
- cable TV—public service announcements

All advertising should be as specific and clear as possible. The who-what-when-where-why-how needs to be told. Remember, the person who knows absolutely nothing about the retreat needs to be adequately informed and interested.

The General Sessions

The general sessions are the times when everyone comes together for teaching from the main speaker(s). These meetings are the principle times of communication and inspiration to the whole group and consequently need to be planned and coordinated well. Many items could be included in the general session. Following are five major components that I believe are "musts" and several other components that are "mights."

Musts

1. Music. Music of some sort should be playing before the session begins as people are coming in. Taped background music seems to work very well. It can help achieve a mood of excitement, relaxation, inspiration, etc.
2. An icebreaker. An icebreaker is a short activity designed to help people become acquainted. As they participate they will feel comfortable with each other and will be more receptive and responsive to what is to follow.
3. Announcements. There inevitably will be information that needs to be conveyed to the group (schedule times and changes, meal instructions, etc.). These should be given during the general sessions.
4. Prayer. Prayer is the underlying force that causes the retreat to be a success. Prayer should take place not only before the retreat, but also during the retreat. It is exciting to sense God's presence and direction as the whole group prays together for God's blessing.
5. The speaker. The speaker is the main part of the general session and needs adequate time to present his or her material.

Mights

1. Group singing. Singing helps to relax and inspire people as well as to center attention on God and spiritual matters. The words to each song should be displayed for all to see. An overhead projector and transparencies work well.
2. Special music. Try to use the talent of several people who sing or play instruments. This gives people a chance to participate and brings a personal sense of contribution as well as blessing to the group.
3. Drama. Drama is also a very good addition to the retreat. It could be used for emphasizing a particular point in the speaker's teaching, presenting an announcement, or just for entertainment.
4. Testimonies. An individual sharing personal information about his or her life is an effective tool for motivating and challenging others. A testimony also helps to solidify faith and direction in the life of the one who shares.
5. Book reviews. Short book reviews pertaining to the speaker's topic(s) help to further inform and inspire. Check with the speaker for any books he or she may have written as well as for names of other books that would relate.

Additional Ideas

Scholarship money. Some will not be able to afford a retreat. A fund should be set up to assist these people. Offerings, donations, and fund-raising activities are three ways of raising money. It's good to have the person being helped financially pay part of the cost if at all possible. This personal investment is important for self-esteem and encourages appreciation for the retreat.

Child care. Most single parents may not be able to come to the retreat because of either not being able to find child care or not being able to afford it. Helping to provide child care through announcements in the church bulletin and from the pulpit not only assists the single parent but also brings understanding of single parents' needs to people in the church.

Evaluation form. A comprehensive evaluation sheet allows people to respond to the many facets of the retreat and gives the leaders input into the retreat's strengths and weaknesses for the sake of future planning.

Taping. It is helpful to tape both the general and workshop sessions to sell to those at the retreat and those unable to attend who want to buy them. Any profit can help finance the retreat.

The retreat is an effective tool for developing the individual as well as the group. It is usually a highlight of the year for those who attend. The knowledge learned, inspiration received, and friendships formed leave lasting impressions and produce meaningful fruit in people's lives.

The Single Adult Conference

Doug Fagerstrom

A singles conference is single people coming together for personal growth through a short-term, high-intensity Christian experience. The singles conference is often life changing for the conferee. That fact must be remembered when considering to have a conference and during the planning of the conference. Indeed, God uses short-term teaching and training experiences to draw us closer to himself and to motivate us to make significant decisions in our lives.

The Purpose

As in every ministry, there must be a purpose to the conference. The purpose should clearly answer the questions, "Why are we having this conference and what specific needs of singles will be met?" The purpose could be discipleship or spiritual growth, evangelism, leadership or ministry training, divorce recovery or inner healing, building of relationships. Your decision should be based on the needs of the singles in your area. The answer must be very clear to the leaders designing the conference and then should be made into a purpose statement. There must be unity in meeting the purpose statement.

The Theme

It is from the purpose statement that a theme for the conference should be developed. For example, if the purpose is to help singles grow in their personal devotional life, then the theme could be, "Building a Better Body—A Conference for Spiritually Growing Single Adults." The purpose is rather specific, it targets a particular need. The theme however should be broad enough to give freedom within the structure of the conference to meet the need with variety and creative means of ministry.

The Target Audience

The next question is, "Who are and where are all the people we can reach with this conference?" The initial need to have the conference was probably born out of the specific needs of a few singles in the sponsoring group. They represent a large number of singles with the same need in your community. Are there more in your church? Are there singles with that need in other churches? Where are the singles with that need in the community?

Not all singles will want to come to your conference. The reason is because of varying felt needs. If the greatest need is for fellowship, the conference should address relationships and be very relational. If there are many divorced singles in your area, a divorce recovery conference might be the best. The key is to target the conference toward the group of people who have the need addressed by it. Consider the people and where they are before planning. List their characteristics before you line up a place and a speaker. You may discover that the target group cannot financially afford to cover the cost of your favorite speaker or cannot spend the time that you idealized for a three-night or weekend conference. Know your people first. Now you can think about plans.

The Conference Staff

The conference staff is the first and most important element in designing the conference. A wise leader will begin by taking a few potential conference planners and leaders to a singles conference planned by someone else. The group can then see their dreams as reality or gain a vision if one was lacking. They can also learn concepts and procedures to use in your own conference.

The singles leader must then recruit a team of people who want to meet the purpose statement and can formulate as well as expedite a strategy for the conference. The strategy asks, "How can we make this conference a reality in the lives of a certain (maximum potential) number of singles?" Who, what, where, why, when, and how much must be answered. The team must own the conference.

Ideally, the team should represent the felt need and the target group. Some members should also have administrative skills. Some should be willing to work very hard in recruiting others. The expanded conference ministry team (people your staff will recruit) is a key to reaching many more people. The more people who are involved with some task for the conference, the more groups of people outside of the core group will learn about the conference. The conference team should probably include all or a combination of the following staff members:

General Coordinator—makes sure the staff members do their jobs

Conference Administrator—recruits all behind-the-scenes personnel including people to handle food service, to provide child care, and so on

Program Coordinator—recruits speakers, musicians, and emcee and designs the conference schedule

Facilities Coordinator—secures the needed facilities and physical amenities (overheads, tables, chairs, etc.) and works closely with custodial crews for setup and teardown

Registration Coordinator—recruits people to do the conference registration, ushering, signage, and ministry table

Publicity Coordinator—recruits a team of people to publicize to the target audience

Prayer Coordinator—designs a plan and recruits many people to pray for the needs of the conference

Follow-up Coordinator—designs a plan and recruits members of the sponsoring ministry to keep contact with conferees after the conference

Leaders need freedom to design and develop their own areas of responsibility. If you have a registrar, encourage that person to design the registration card, recruit other people to help, and plan the registration event. Remember that your team members are adults, but make sure they know that reporting back to the conference leader is part of their responsibility. Recruit them with both aspects in mind.

The Conference Personnel

Conference personnel are the people who will make the actual conference come alive. These people are the most visible and are responsible to be at the conference itself. The conference staff plan the conference; the conference personnel carry out the plan at the conference. In some cases the two teams can overlap where gifts and abilities apply.

The personnel team will often include:

Conference Keynote Speaker
Emcee
Workshop/Seminar Leaders
Musician(s) and Entertainers
Registration Personnel
Hosts and Hostesses
Food Service Staff
Small Group Leaders
Book/Record/Resource Table Staff
Ministry Booth Representative
Information Host/Hostess
Child Care Coordinator
Sound/Taping/Lighting Coordinator
Counselors
Decoration Coordinator

The conference personnel team must own the conference just as the conference staff do. They all must know and clearly understand the purpose and theme. They are responsible to build the spirit of the conference and to work for the common good. The food service should not run the conference, nor is the keynote speaker the whole conference.

The Conference Speaker

The speaker must be carefully chosen. Dennis Franck has given some excellent guidelines in choosing a speaker in the previous chapter.

It is helpful to have one person assigned to host the speaker. That person should be available to meet the program and personal needs of the speaker.

The conference leaders and the single ministry leaders of your group should concentrate their time on relationships with conferees. The speaker will leave after the conference, but the conferees will still be in your community in need of ministry. It might be good to plan a time for leadership to meet with the keynote speaker at another time outside of the conference program. This can be a special growth time for your leaders and a way to say thank you to them.

The Content of the Conference

The keynote speaker should be able to address the general theme of the conference from a biblical base. He or she lays the foundation for the entire growth experience. The keynote speaker stimulates and challenges the conferees to make some kind of decision for God, for themselves, and for others.

The workshops, seminars, and other small-group experiences are places to learn and discuss specific areas of life that fall under the general theme. They should not be mini-keynote sessions. Interaction is imperative.

Again, the content of the conference should be biblical, otherwise it will accomplish no more than what the community adult education program provides. Lives must be radically changed, not just slightly altered. Finally, the conference should challenge the conferee to evoke a response to either know Christ personally or as a Christian to make a life-changing decision.

The Promoter and the Registrar

To the promoter: You can have the best and most well-known speaker come to your conference, but if the community has no idea who your speaker is and when he is coming, the attempt is futile.

To the registrar: You and your people are the first impression and contact that the conferees will have with your conference. If you do not handle their needs with care and gentleness, the entire conference can be a very negative experience.

The quality of a conference is caught when conferees see their first brochure. What will you give them and show them? Will they see a quality brochure that says, "We care enough about you to put in the extra effort"? The sincerity and spirit of a conference is caught when the conferees enter the front doors. What will their first impressions be? Atmosphere is created by the conference staff; it does not just happen.

The information people received about the conference, and the atmosphere there prepares them for what they are to hear. Will singles be prepared to receive the message that you have to meet the stated purpose? Or are they there for a totally different (misunderstood) reason?

The Many "Extras"

Now that you have established your purpose, staff, personnel, and atmosphere, the following details will help make the conference flow more smoothly. Remember, it is often the little things that make the big difference.

- Facilities: They should be known and accessible to your conferees. Be sure you have the freedom to do in the facility what you need to.

- Schedule: Plan the schedule to be tight. But plan time for relationship-building. Keep to the schedule that you set.
- Communicate: People want to know what is going on. Print schedules and maps. Let your conferees know that you know what is going on. Always have someone at the registration/information table.
- Costs: People will pay for what they receive. However, be sensitive to what your target group can afford. Conferences should not be planned as fund-raisers. That is a weak purpose statement.
- Hospitality: Have a hospitality room or area where conferees can come to relax, meet the staff, meet other singles, etc. Too many come alone and are left to wander the halls looking for someone to talk to, sometimes unsuccessfully.
- Name tags: Everyone should have one!
- Food: Keep the menu light, but use quality as the standard. Buffets and box lunches work well. Allow time for people to eat and to enjoy the fellowship around the tables.
- Dates: Be careful not to stack conferences with other events. Don't give people so many choices during the conference month that they cannot afford the conference or they choose other events instead. If your purpose statement is strong, then you can be single-minded about the conference.

Singles conferences can be used by God to change lives. Decisions will be made. Friendships will be found. God's truths for everyday living will be discovered.

22

Community Service and Outreach Ministry Projects

Carolyn Koons

Service and outreach projects for single adults often are last on the agenda of goals and future programs in single adult ministries. Solid teaching, counseling individuals suffering the pains of a loss due to divorce or death, attempting to build community through fellowship and worship, and developing new leadership are continually needed and demanded in singles ministry. Programs developed around each of these goals are geared to "reach in" to help, heal, give new insight, and bring wholeness to singles. In order to have a well-rounded singles ministry, singles need to be encouraged to "reach out" and help others, whether that means helping other singles in the group, reaching out to others in the church or community, or moving beyond our borders into other countries to share their faith and love. These opportunities not only create a healthy singles program but also a healthier single.

Outreach and service help singles get balance in and a perspective on their own lives as they share in the joy of healing. When one is hurting the most can be the best time for service. Looking outward and seeing a bigger, needier world deepens our walk with God.

Which Project?

There are many service projects from which to choose. You can serve others in your own singles group or church. The community surrounding the church is dotted with dozens of exciting possibilities for ministry. Or there is the opportunity to venture outside the state or country for outreach.

A singles group should begin locally, choosing one community service project. Service can be either a one-time effort, such as special holiday projects for the elderly, poor, or handicapped; or long-term projects, such as weekly or monthly Big Brother or Sister participation or visits to hospitals or convalescent homes. As these ministries progress, service can expand to an outreach trip for a couple of days or weeks into Mexico, Haiti, or the Dominican Republic, for example. The list is unlimited and the needs of the world are big. No dream or vision is too great. If you are not ready to take on the project yourself or sense that the singles groups is too small, join with two or three other churches in a combined effort.

In Southern California seven churches joined forces during the Memorial Day holiday, sending 135 single adults into Ensenada, Mexico for three days of exciting ministries in orphanages and villages. Three years later the excitement and momentum attracted other singles, and the group grew to 650 single adults from 25 different singles ministries for the Memorial Day Ensenada Outreach program. The three-day outreach project had such an impact on the lives of those who participated that most of the participating singles groups have expanded this once-a-year project into monthly trips into Mexico or monthly local community projects.

Reaching out changes lives within and will bring vitality, energy, and commitment to a growing singles ministry.

Planning, Motivation, and Training

The keys to a successful and effective outreach ministry are thoroughly planning the specific service project, motivating the group, and training the team for ministry. Talk it up, advertise, and have singles who have participated in past projects share their testimonies during various meetings. Build an excitement and passion for ministry and service.

Make an application form for the service project that will help eliminate certain individuals who are not ready for the project or who are wanting to participate for the wrong reasons. The application process should also help you discover new leadership and hidden talents. Identifying and utilizing these can enhance the project outcome.

Training is vital for the success of the project. The training program needs to prepare team members for each aspect of the project. This may require a weekly meeting for several weeks in advance or a number of all-day sessions. Develop a leadership team and let them coordinate the various committees responsible for the project. Let the singles be the leaders.

Community Projects

Community projects are found everywhere. The following are people or organizations currently receiving help from singles groups.

Handicapped children. Hospitals are eager to have groups work with the handicapped, taking them on field trips, helping them with their training. One church planned a Zoo Day and took busloads of handicapped children to a special day at the zoo.

Orphanages

Convalescent homes

Homes for abused children

Big Brother/Big Sister programs

Welfare Department. Check your local Welfare Department, a place where there are usually an abundance of programs and projects that need volunteers.

Hospitals

Inner city/urban plunge. Check several agencies for a listing and description of projects and needs.

Latchkey children. This is a valuable program for children and teens and can be conducted throughout several neighborhoods or at the church.

Juvenile facilities.

Homes for developmentally disabled adults.

Monthly or quarterly new becomers (divorce recovery) dinners.

Foreign Projects

Foreign projects usually require a major trip. Leaving one's familiar setting and traveling, often to a deprived Third World culture, can be a life-changing experience. Contact missionary organizations, missionaries of your church, or another singles group that has been on an outreach trip for project ideas. Know what kind of project your group wants to undertake, and remember to plan carefully, train well, and minister.

Projects will vary according to the needs of the culture and missionary organization, so be flexible. Some project ideas include:

Help at orphanages. Deliver food and clothing, clean up, participate in children's programs, provide recreation and crafts, adopt an orphan.

Building. Building projects are in abundance, but the key is finding a contact person attached with the project who will get the project ready and have the supplies available.

Food or clothing distribution. This can generate a lot of enthusiasm. Work closely with the missionaries or sponsoring organization.

Evangelism. Conduct children's programs that consist of Bible stories, crafts, games, and recreation; conduct women's ministries or teen projects; plan churches; even contribute to church or mission services with music, drama, testimonies, and more.

Getting singles involved with reaching out to others is one of the major steps to developing a healthy single adult ministry.

23

Integrating Single Adults into the Life of the Church

Mary Graves

Approximately one half of the adult work force in this country is single. What percentage of the church work force is single? A successful singles ministry helps the church realize that single adults are not just one part of the church to be ministered to (like the youth). They make up an important part of the ministry team, and the church must recognize their part in the body (Rom. 12:4–5).

One single adult leader claimed that if you took all the singles out of his church it would be paralyzed. This is the vision. That is what it looks like when singles ministry comes to full maturity. It isn't just providing a place where singles can learn and grow with other singles; it is connecting them to the larger body of Christ. As Bill Flanagan (Newport Beach, Calif.) put it, "Integrating single adults into the life of your church is an absolutely fundamental principle for doing ministry."

The Attitude of Your Church

When Highland Park Presbyterian Church in Dallas hired a singles pastor, it was spelled out in the job description that this person was to bridge the gap between singles and marrieds and, by a consciousness-raising on both sides, to bring singles into the center of the church's life. But when a large community church in southern California hired a singles pastor, there was no such intention. This pastor was to take care of single people and their needs and keep them "out there" as a separate department, a specialized area of ministry, apart from the whole life of the church, almost like a satellite church—what you might call a "leper colony" mentality. Whether articulated or not, every church has an attitude toward singles and singles ministry, and that attitude is lodged in the leaders of the church. The task of integrating singles into the life of the church begins and ends with their vision. All the creative program planning in the world cannot overstep the boundaries set by the ruling bodies in each church. And that includes the boundaries set by the singles leader.

There seem to be two basic images of singles ministry: singles as a separate colony or as a necessary part of the whole. The first task is to determine the premise that prevails in your church and in the singles leader. If the "leper colony" image prevails, then consciousness-raising will have to happen in the leaders first before integration is even a possibility.

A Problem or an Asset

In conversations about people it is hard to find the word *single* without also hearing words such as *lonely, divorced, depressed, swinging, sleeping around,* etc. Most single adults don't like the title of "single" because of negative connotations. So with that kind of press, it is not surprising that many churches hold singles at arm's length, unable to ignore them and unwilling to draw them in. They are often perceived as people with problems whose lot is contagious; people who demand much more than they can give; people whose only hope and solution is to get married.

But more and more churches are discovering that single adults are not a problem to be solved but a gifted work force to be employed for the work of Christ's church. Singles often ask honest questions and come up with new solutions; they break out of the conventional or make the conventional more practical. Singles are an asset to the church not because they have more time and money (a stereotype that is simply untrue) but because they bring a fresh perspective that allows God to do the new thing that needs doing. Perhaps it's a program for latchkey children, or a support group for abused women, or an adopt-a-grandparent brunch, or a breakfast club for men, or a "Run for Missions," or a Christian concert for the whole church—all of these are ideas that have been spawned and developed by single members who are discovering that they are the church.

The Attitude of Single Adults

Between the why and the how of integrating singles into the church lies one huge assumption that should be addressed: It is necessary to have a church that singles want to go to. Several critical factors will make your church a place where single people want to be involved.

The worship service must be enthusiastic, not lifeless. The preaching must be inclusive of the experiences single adults are facing. The church must express an openness to the wounded—especially to the divorced. Sunday schools must address the needs of single parent homes with a sensitivity to custody arrangements. The church must have a desire to do outreach and a willingness to bring in some "different" people (i.e., those with non-Christian backgrounds).

There are many subtle ways that the church can say to singles, "You do not belong here." The leadership, program, and language of a church can say very loudly, "This is a family church," and singles will be left out. Singles will go where they aren't put on hold until they are married. They will go where they are recognized and counted. And that's where they will want to get involved.

Cultivate a Desire to Serve

Single adults must first have a desire and willingness to serve before they will move into areas of ministry in the church. This grows out of discipleship; it results from people being nurtured and trained to think of themselves as belonging to Jesus Christ, to his family, being his servants.

This desire is cultivated at an academic and experiential level in Bible studies (e.g., studying the "one another" passages in Scripture), in leadership training (e.g., studying Jesus the Servant), and in one-on-one discipling. Teach about Jesus washing the disciples' feet and follow that with your own foot-washing. Talk about serving the needy and follow that with a volunteer assignment to work at a local soup kitchen. Affirm that it is more blessed to give than to receive and then live out that truth with a mission trip to Haiti. With this training and exposure singles will already be thinking ministry and looking for ways to do more.

Orient Your Singles to the Church

Many singles are totally uninformed about activities going on in the life of the church and can easily remain that way. It is not that they don't care; they don't know!

At a deeper level singles need to know where they can serve in the church. It is important to note that different commitment levels are required for the various volunteer opportunities. Low-level commitments might include ushering, greeting, or serving coffee, whereas high-level would include teaching Sunday school or singing in the choir. Look for the commitment level suited for the different singles in your church.

Singles seem to respond well to commitment responsibilities where high demands of energy and attention are required for a short period of time (the task force model). Planning a one-day conference on intimacy or a New Year's Eve party for the whole church family are examples of tasks that have a beginning and an end and much visible reward for invested labor. Other opportunities in this category might include teaching Sunday school just for the summer or organizing a mission trip.

High-level commitments require training and equipping and much encouragement. Perhaps the first high-level commitment for your singles is church membership. Every church has its own requirements, some more rigorous than others. But whatever the requirements, the commitment involves consciously making one particular church their church home. All other major commitments to the church spring from that. Let your singles know when new members' classes are held and what is required for church membership. Encourage your key singles leaders to be members (many churches require leaders to be members). Move your singles into training events and experiences that will prepare them for greater levels of service in the church (e.g., training classes for Sunday school teachers or lay counseling).

Orient Your Church to the Singles

It's not only the singles that are uninformed about the life of the church; often church members are totally uninformed about their singles. Once again, it is not necessarily because they don't care; they don't know!

Single adults and your singles ministry can be made more visible to the whole church in a variety of ways. Starting with the obvious means of publicity, use your church newsletter, featuring articles on the activities of your single adults (e.g., an individual's specific acts of service or group events). Find a way to get your singles on every bulletin board or publicity piece in your church. The more pictures the better.

Search for ways to be creative. The singles at Calvary Community Church in Thousand Oaks, California, have an annual Singles' Day at their church that features a big jamboree with a pastor's dunk booth, a chili cook-off, live music, and all kinds of fun for the whole church family. It is effective for the singles to sponsor events for the whole church, even simply a reception after church with good food and catchy displays of the things that the single adults group is doing.

These events do not always have to be overtly advertising in nature.

Another area of promotion is among your staff and church leaders. The singles leader should keep them aware of the gifted people available and encourage them to invest these leaders in their own ministries. This means that you must be willing to let go of these leaders to let them serve elsewhere.

It is also up to the singles leader to help the church leaders know what's going on in the lives of your single adults. Keep them informed about your program. Give them a copy of your newsletter and the minutes from your leadership meetings.

In the body of Christ we are one family with one Father and "he made known to us the mystery of his will . . . to bring all things in heaven and on earth together." It is in that union that we will attain "to the whole measure of the fullness of Christ," when we are "joined and held together" and each part of the body is working properly and "builds itself up in love" (Eph. 1:9–10; 4:13, 16). That is the vision. That is what it looks like when singles ministry comes to full maturity.

24

Growing a Single Adult Ministry

Rich Hurst

You've got to keep them busy!" said the senior pastor of a large metropolitan church when asked how to grow a single adult ministry. He was of the opinion that a church must offer something every night of the week or singles will go somewhere else to have their needs met.

The Wrong Reasons

When you decide you want a growing single adult ministry, you must start by asking yourself *why*. Paul, speaking to the church at Philippi, said, "Do nothing out of selfish ambition" (Phil. 2:3). There is such a temptation to do a ministry like single adult ministry for the wrong reasons. When you do, the results can be failing or unhealthy ministries.

We should grow single adult ministries to meet needs and to develop a ministry that helps bring about wholeness in each individual's life. We must always check our motives. Before we look at how to grow a single adult ministry it is important to look at wrong reasons to grow a single adult ministry.

Because It Is the Thing to Do

There is always the temptation to try to stay current with the latest in ministry. Staying current has nothing to do with being the church God wants you to be. God never called us to be trendy; he called us to be faithful. Trying to grow a single adult ministry because of its popularity can often hurt all involved once it is no longer trendy.

Because Other Churches Are Growing

The reason others have growing single adult ministries is that they had people who had a heart to see that ministry develop. In Nehemiah 1, we see that Nehemiah became heartbroken when he heard about the conditions of his home city. The Scripture says he wept and mourned for days. Out of that broken heart came a desire to help his people restore the walls of Jerusalem. Out of a broken heart came a desire to do something. This is the same way healthy ministries are grown; they develop from leadership that has a heart for single adults and wants to do something.

When I moved from one city to another several years ago I received a call from a local pastor in the new city asking me to come and talk with him. As I sat in his office he asked me questions about myself and my move, but after a while he got around to his real interest. He said, "I understand you had a very successful singles ministry before you moved here." I replied I had, to which he responded, "We would like to have you help us start one." He told me there were several single adult ministries in the area and that he felt they should also have one. I wish now I had asked him why. We began small, but within six months we had grown to large numbers on Sunday nights. Since this was a church with a Sunday morning attendance of 350, we became a threat to the membership and to the pastor. It became apparent over the next two years that the pastor had only wanted a single adult ministry because he saw that others had one. It was costly for him, for me, and for the ministry that we had not counted the costs before starting. From that experience I learned you must never start a single adult ministry out of competition but from a heartfelt desire to meet needs.

Because There Are Single Adults in Your Church

Need does not always dictate the call to do a ministry. Just because there are single adults in your church does not mean God wants you to have a single adult ministry. Many churches across this country are growing well without formal single adult ministries. If the singles themselves don't feel the need to change the way the church is meeting needs, then your church is probably doing its job.

On the other hand, do not ignore a genuine need in your church. Several years ago the church I attend began to hear murmurings from the single adults that they needed a singles pastor. Not much was done until the church leaders conducted a survey and discovered that over half of their 3,000 members were single! They began at once to look for someone who had a heart for single adult ministry.

To Keep the Single Adults Busy

It's easy to assume, like the pastor mentioned in this chapter, that you must have a ministry that will keep single adults busy or they will go to another church. Single adults do not need to be kept busy; most single adult are busy enough! Instead, they need to be encouraged and trained to be all God has planned for them. They need to be free to become all that they have ever dreamed, and if we keep them so busy that they can't discover this dream, then we have shortchanged them.

The Right Purpose

I want you to understand what can happen when you do decide to grow a single adult ministry. Frank Tillapaugh of Bear Valley Baptist in Denver says, "No target-group ministry holds more potential for the church today than does this one. We have found a special ministry to them has greatly helped our Christian singles grow spiritually and become fully integrated into the church. We have also found that non-Christian singles tend to be responsive to a ministry that is not out to exploit them. The evangelical church has the greatest product in the world to attract today's single—we have the gospel. Our challenge is to find a way to bring together the ministry of the church and [the] single."

John Westfall of University Presbyterian in Seattle says, "The question is not what kind of single adult ministry do we want to have, but what kind of single adults do we want to send out into the world? I believe our goal is not to have a strong single adult ministry but to train single adults to have strong ministry." If our goal is just to have a program, then we are defeated from the beginning. Though it may work for a while, in the end it will be the program that is important to you and not the people. God has not called us just to build strong programs; he has called us to build people who have strong ministries. There is a real but subtle temptation to allow the few to get better at being ministers while the majority become better at watching.

In the church, our first priority should be making sure each member sees himself or herself as a minister. This is especially true for single adults because somewhere along the road single adults have been given the message that life begins at marriage. Having a healthy ministry will depend on each single getting the message that you believe God has a dream for his or her life.

Train Leaders

In growing a healthy ministry it is important how we spend our time. As a pastor and a leader, I see my main responsibility to be training others to be leaders. For example, I limit the time I spend counseling and participating in meetings with those people who are not in leadership. I spend a lot of time with those who are or will someday be in leadership; in turn, it is their ministry to meet with others.

We must operate purposefully to grow a healthy single adult ministry. By purposefully I mean that you make a plan and then choose those in whom you will invest. Paul wrote, "You shine like stars in the universe as you hold out the word of life—in order that I may boast on the day of Christ that I did not run or labor for nothing" (Phil. 2:15–16). It is your role in growing a single adult ministry to train leaders. This means you must commit to invest in individuals, not crowds. It is so easy to find yourself spending time with crowds or doing things that will bring out the crowd. Usually you do this at the expense of the individual. You must make it a priority to train leaders; and, though everyone is a minister, not everyone is a leader. Invest your time in leaders and you will grow a meaningful and vibrant ministry.

Crossroads

When growing a single adult ministry there will be normal crossroads along the way. Here are five that you will encounter.

Why do we exist? It is very important to answer this question before you do anything else. The best way to find the answer is to have a group of single adults get together for a "dream session." A dream session is a time when you list the needs in your church and community as they relate to single adults. Needs can be both felt and unfelt. For example, a felt need is to grow spiritually, and an unfelt need might be to become more emotionally supported by the church. To acknowledge that there is a need does not mean you have to meet it. This is a time to list needs with no expectation as to meeting them.

Who will lead? It is always hard to pick leaders. When you look at the ministry of Jesus you see that even he had ups and downs in the area of his leadership team. His disciples had times of utter confusion and of not getting along. There were times of positioning to be first and then times of betrayal and denial.

It is simply not easy to choose leaders, but there are several guidelines that will help you to have a growing single adult ministry. First, choose people you know and have had a chance to watch for a while. There is always a temptation to choose the people that look good or the ones that seem to have it all together, only to discover they were not ready to be leaders. This is usually a very disappointing experience both for you and for them. Instead, choose people you know to be faithful, responsible, and positive in outlook. Nothing will kill a group quicker than a negative leader. In addition, leaders need to be relational with each other and must understand how to relate to others in a caring, responsible way.

If you find yourself short on leadership, begin to pray (Matt. 9:35–38). In the first singles group I attended, the singles pastor,

Jerry Donaldson, along with the senior pastor, began to pray for more male leadership; there were plenty of women available for leadership but Jerry wanted a balance. Within several months there were enough men and women to move forward.

Ask your leaders for a commitment, and make it reasonable. Remember, we are building people and not programs, so new people need a chance to try their gifts.

What should we do? Pray! A growing single adult ministry begins with a small group of committed people who are willing to pray. Mike Regele, a former singles pastor in California, decided with a group of people to start a singles ministry. They were only a small group, so at first they met together once a week to pray together about when to start this ministry. After a few months there were twenty-five people, and so Mike suggested it was time to start the ministry. The rest of the group did not feel the time had arrived so they prayed for another six months. At the end of this time there were over one hundred people coming together weekly, and everyone agreed it was time to "begin." Never underestimate the power of prayer in growing a single adult ministry.

What should we do when people fail? People will fail in any ministry, and single adult ministry is no exception. The one difference is that single adults are likely to be more open and honest about failure. Failure is never the final word in peoples' lives; it is often the beginning of newness.

What happens when things begin to change? Change is an everyday word in single adult ministry. We must learn that status quo should not be a way of life in a growing single adult ministry. We will encounter the need to change on a regular basis; we never exactly arrive or have a complete program.

There are three possible states of ministry: (1) moving ahead, (2) maintenance, or (3) meltdown. The healthy and growing single adult ministry will always be defined as having an attitude of moving ahead and welcoming change.

All the world is asking for answers: Single adults have a lot of them and are looking for a place to give and serve. When you make a choice to have a growing single adult ministry you are making a choice that will change the whole direction of your life, your church's ministry, and the lives of 50 percent of the people in your community. You will make a difference when you grow a single adult ministry.

A growing and healthy single adult ministry will produce unbelievable results in your church and community. As the ministry begins to meet needs it will dispel the stereotypes some people may have that singles are irresponsible and socially unaware. In our church the Sunday school classes are heavily staffed by single adults. Because the church is located in an urban setting, the singles have begun a street ministry. There are groups of single adults who bake bread monthly for food distribution centers and others who meet downtown for lunchtime Bible studies.

When you have a well-balanced ministry it sends a message that you want to care for and participate in your community. There are plenty of uninterested churches all around the country, but I have yet to see a church with a growing single adult ministry that is not making an impact on its community.

25

Ministry to Single Adults in the Small Church

Jim Smoke

While programs in large churches get even larger, small churches struggle to keep their existing programs functioning. The nagging question in single adult ministries seems to be, "Can a small church have a successful singles ministry?" Fifteen years of ministry in the single adult field prompt me to answer with a resounding yes! But the reality is that a ministry to singles in a small church will be different than in a larger church.

One given in a singles ministry is that single people go where other single people are. The more singles you have, the more seem to come to meet the existing group. Since many singles are looking for relationships, they will attend the larger groups in order to broaden their relational base. That may or may not be the right reason to attend a singles group but it is a reality. Not many wish to travel across town to attend a singles group with eleven members. How does the eleven-member group offer quality programs and ministries that will cause their group to grow? Here are some keys to these questions from observing small but growing ministries across America.

Think outreach. Many singles groups limit their growth by the number of potential members within the walls of their churches.

They feel their task lies solely in getting every available single body in their church into their group and then living happily ever after as they plod through endless potlucks, Bible studies, and retreats. Within shouting distance of most churches there is a vast, unreached population of singles who would happily reach out to a church group rather than a bar group if they only knew the singles groups existed and what they had to offer. Singles groups in most churches are the best-kept secret in the community. If you only have eleven singles, target the ministry toward the needs of the unchurched to reach singles for Christ in your community.

Think interchurch. One difficulty we face in church life is that almost every church wants to be an entity unto itself. Many areas of singles ministry become virtual impossibilities for the small church. But when small churches join together, any dream can be realized. A retreat, a singles conference, a singles rally, or a missions trip can all be better accomplished when churches unite. I know that the impasse often lies in the pastor who is fearful his singles will leave and go to another church if churches cooperate. If a single has a strong tie to his home church and has received personal ministry, that will seldom happen.

Think community network. In some areas, smaller churches have united to form a city-wide singles network with each church having representation on the council. Large events are planned by the network, where all share equally in leadership and responsibility. Problems are openly shared and resolutions sought. The goal needs to be to win singles to Christ and help them with their spiritual walk through ministries that all can share in creating.

Think through your own church's distinctives. People go to different churches for different reasons. What is there about your church that would make singles want to become a part of its life? The reason for a single being in a church singles group should reach far beyond the group itself and into what that particular church is all about. Learn to highlight your church when building your group. Churches have their own unique personalities. The entryway to your church may be through the singles group, but your singles should not hit a wall after they walk in!

Think ministry. Most singles groups think PROGRAM AND CALENDAR. They believe their job is to fill all the open dates in any month with activities. It is true that we all need things to do, but more than that we all need to be spiritually ministered to by the things we attend. *Ministry comes from knowing the needs of your people.* Plan the things you do with a purpose. Ask yourself why you are doing what you are doing.

Think team, think leadership. The question in a small church is usually, Who are the leaders and who are the followers? The lingering singles malady across America seems to be lack of good leaders. This is always true and this will never end. Leaders must be challenged, built into a team, and allowed to lead. People seldom go where they have no vested leadership interest. Leaders should be selected, not elected. If your group is so small that all you have is leaders, train them and then go find some followers. You need both kinds of people to have a group. People only support what they help create.

Think lay leadership. In a small church, you will never have the luxury of a full-time singles pastor. That type of role will need to be filled by some layperson who does other things to make a living but has a heart for singles ministries. I have met hundreds of those special people across America, and they are doing a great job. Somebody must be in charge of the ministry or it will fail. God calls people to those responsibilities.

Think about the things you can offer your own group. There is a time to come together with other singles groups and a time to do things with your own group. Community is seldom built in a crowd unless there is a shipwreck that draws people together. The Sunday morning singles class is a must in every church. Sunday night afterglows are important fellowship times. Weekly prayer, share, and care groups can be times of real closeness in your small church ministry. Retreats with your own group are important for growing close. Learn to do what you need to do for just your own people. Learn what you need to invite others to share in.

And finally—don't worry about what others are doing. Ministry takes place in the heart and is never evaluated numerically. Whether you have six or six hundred makes no difference in God's measurement scale. What you put into the hearts of the six or six hundred does!

26

Ministry to Single Adults in the Large Church

Bill Flanagan

Church planners and demographers who analyze the development of the church in the last years of this century see a continuing growth in the number of large congregations. At the same time, the need for fellowship and intimacy in a neighborhood context also has brought an increase in the number of smaller churches. In the middle are the congregations of medium size (two hundred to six hundred), which may suffer from the growth of both larger and smaller churches.

Not every congregation will have a single adult ministry, but every church needs to minister to single adults. Studies of larger congregations reveal that churches that have well-established singles ministries have one or more of the following ingredients present:

- A vacuum in the community creating a large felt need that the church as a whole and the singles ministry in particular could answer
- A strong leader with a clear vision, focused goals, and plans for what needs to be done

- The use of solid ministry skills, good management techniques, and excellent support leadership

The following are some principles and guidelines to follow in order to develop an ongoing ministry in the total program of a large multiple-staff congregation.

Know why you exist. In the midst of large numbers and personal diversity, it is fundamental to know why you exist. A clear statement of the ministry's purpose and its goals is crucial in order not to get sidetracked into peripheral issues. A constant reference point as to *who* you are and *what* you are about saves a lot of energy and time as the ministry matures.

Understand differences. It is important to understand the differences between single adults as a group and the rest of the church. Singles tend to be fickle and mobile. They like large groups with lots of relational possibilities and yet, at the same time, small groups where there is relational intimacy and close fellowship. Single adult ministries have a greater turnover than the church as a whole. It is axiomatic in most singles fellowships that the turnover is 50 percent every six months. This necessitates rapid growth just to stay even. Single adult ministries must be set up and organized to grow, or very quickly they will die. Also, females tend to outnumber males, particularly in groups where the average age is over thirty. Because of this, ongoing programs of welcoming newcomers and developing leaders are crucial not just for growth but for continued existence.

Realize the ecumenical spirit. Single adult ministries are always ecumenical in spirit. Even in denominational churches, a singles ministry is a smorgasbord of humanity and a melting pot of various denominations, traditions, and sectarian backgrounds. Teaching and structure that does not recognize this is bound to get in trouble and will have to overcome some severe difficulties.

Invite smaller churches to activities. Large church ministries are wise to invite to and include in their special activities adults who are involved in smaller congregations in the community, without expecting them to sever their roots. Many adults have strong emotional ties to a smaller church where their children may be involved, and they find it difficult to sever those ties. Yet, they also have needs that may be met by a singles ministry in the larger church. For a season, at least, it is possible for an adult, to join the programs of two churches as long as geographical and scheduling conflicts can be worked out. Time tends to take care of any tensions and pressures that are created.

Integrate singles into church life. The integration of singles into the whole life of the church is important for the ongoing nature of the ministry. The singles pastor or professional leader needs to be patient and persistent to get single adults to join the larger life of the church. Over a period of time most single adults who are not there just for superficial reasons will be ready and willing to do this.

Make use of church facilities. Use the church plant or campus, if possible, for most of the main events of the singles ministry. Single adults need to gather in the church facilities to feel included and accepted by the larger church as well as to feel a part of its life and fellowship. Churches that use off-campus facilities for main events very soon have the problem of the single adult ministry feeling totally independent and disconnected from the body of believers. It is also significant for the senior pastor and other staff to participate, at times, in the singles ministry.

Divide into age groups. Singles groups in large churches need to be broken down into age-groups rather than the status of the participants' singleness. In other words, it's not a good idea to organize groups for divorced, never-marrieds, or widows, but rather to divide singles in terms of their ages, usually within about a fifteen-year span, denoting the age limits of each group. This is often easier to project than it is to actually make happen. The attempt to put single adults of all ages into one fellowship to form an ongoing program is not realistic. It is important that each of these various groups has its own name, identity, leadership team, and place to meet as well as a calendar for its events and activities week to week.

Understand the true meaning of family. Most large congregations that develop a singles ministry need to come to a new understanding of the term "family." Many married adults understand their congregation as a "family church," which whether consciously or unconsciously does not include single people. In beginning a singles ministry, churches need to decide whether they will be inclusive or exclusive of singles. Many congregations are unaware of the singles phenomenon in America in the past few decades that has brought the number of single people in this country to almost the same as of those who are married. The singles pastor or professional leader should be invited to speak to the various couples groups in the church to raise their vision and overcome the stereotypes of singles that are in the church. The married portion of the congregation needs to understand clearly that singleness is not a disease for which the only known cure is marriage. There are many myths to be shattered in order for a congregation to become a real family.

Maintain communication between staff members. It is important to maintain the communication and unity of purpose within the pastoral or program staff. Churches with large staffs should have single adults on staff in proportion to the singles in the congregation. This leadership team needs to have a clear understanding together of what each department and area of ministry is doing and be able to pull together. A large congregational program staff is no place for lone rangers, solo artists, or the building of exclusive, autonomous little churches within the larger one.

Team unity is primarily built by the head of staff, or senior pastor. It is the responsibility of that person to be the primary interpreter of the singles ministry to the church at large. The singles pastor needs the total support and consistent encouragement of the senior pastor.

Benefit from singles. Single adults need to see themselves and be seen with the church as a whole, not only as a target group that needs a special outreach ministry. Rather than simply viewing singles as people who "need our help," churches need to understand how much they have to benefit and receive from single adults. Single people can teach the larger congregation much about coping with living alone, handling pain, living without a spouse, and turning loneliness into an opportunity for focusing on one's own inner strength. A congregation needs to be ready not only to minister *to* singles, but also to celebrate ministry *from* singles. They have something very valuable to offer the whole body of Christ.

Reach out to the community. A single adult ministry in a congregational setting needs to have a vision and strategy to reach the broader community. The size and influence of a large congregation is a valuable asset in developing programs of community outreach that are significant and measurable. It is important that the ministry is seen not just as an aspect of the church's program, but rather as a service to the community. If your singles group is meeting felt needs in a quality way, advertising such programs and special events through the local media will attract people who normally wouldn't darken the church's doorway. Single adult ministry assists a congregation in getting into the marketplace in a way that many churches never really experience.

Prepare for additional ministries. A growing program needs to prepare for additional ministries. It is also an axiom that the more a congregation does and the more ministries it develops to meet felt needs, the more needs will be felt. The more you do, the more you realize you need to do. A door opening to a new ministry opportunity will usually open three or four related doors to other possibilities to meet the needs of people. A divorce recovery ministry will raise the issue of working with remarried couples, single parents, and teenage youth of divorcing parents. It will also raise questions about the quality of your premarital counseling and opportunities for marriage enrichment.

Generally, as the doors open, there will be people there with the vision, energy, and commitment to assist the staff in providing for such opportunities. Workshops, small groups, classes, and special seminars will present themselves in great diversity. Program people are constantly faced with the pressures of time and priority as to which needs are greatest and how to respond to them. All of this leads to a visionary church that is constantly following the leading of Jesus Christ into new avenues of evangelism, caring, and mission.

27

The Role of the Single-Adult Minister in the Church

Jim Smoke

The role of today's singles minister is not an easy one. He or she must be involved in interpreting and communicating an often unknown, misinterpreted, and in some places controversial ministry in the local church.

The reality of a single adult ministry is that it will not exist and thrive unless the senior pastor endorses it, the church board approves it, the body encourages it, and the finance committee budgets money to insure its implementation. The singles minister is a key to gaining these endorsements. There are several things a singles minister can do once a church starts a single adult ministry.

Present the ministry to the congregation. It is the responsibility of the singles minister to present the ministry and those who work with it to the congregation. This is not a "once a year, let's cheer for our singles" event. It is weaving information and blessing from the singles ministry into the fabric of daily church life. If this is not done, the ministry will be largely misunderstood and filed under "not important" in the annals of church life.

Define family. It is the responsibility of the singles minister to help redefine the word *family* in a broad sense so as to include single parents and their children. Too many single parents are hammered into the ground each week when they are treated as less than family by church interpretation. The word *family* as once defined in American life now only represents about one half of our population. It is up to the singles minister to update congregational understanding of the word *family* as well as the word *single.*

Be available. It is the responsibility of the singles minister to be actively available to the singles of the church. Beyond speaking to them, it is always special just to be physically present in their homes, workplaces, and at their functions. Simply sitting behind a desk will disintegrate the ministry. The shepherd must actively meet the sheep's needs of nourishment and healing. Most mature singles ministers are able to cover a lot of ground in a week without camping in any one place. Human presence means to the adult single, "You are important."

Interpret the ministry. It is the responsibility of the singles minister to interpret single adult ministry to the rest of the church staff and the church boards if necessary. Because a single adult ministry deals with divorced people, a church staff should have a solid understanding of what this means in other ministry areas, such as youth and Christian education. It could also have implications theologically, and this needs to be talked out and understood on staff levels. The remarriage issue looms large in this respect as well. Some churches will marry the divorced, others will not. There is even a division on some church staffs. This can cause great disharmony on a staff if not properly and biblically addressed.

Inform the community. It is the responsibility of the singles minister to let the community at large know that his or her church welcomes singles and will minister lovingly and positively to their many needs.

Stop discrimination. It is the responsibility of the singles minister to make sure that singles of all ages and stations of singleness are not discriminated against in positions of church leadership. Prejudice is a subtle thing and often masquerades as godliness. If singles cannot serve in your church because of their divorces, it is unlikely they will come to your singles group. If an unmarried thirty-five-year-old single cannot serve on a church board simply because he or she is not married, we are saying, "We love you, but . . ."

I realize that churches have had policies on many things long before singles arrived in quantity on the scene. Some policies need to be reexamined and some need to be changed.

Have correct motives. It is the responsibility of the singles minister not to start a singles ministry because he or she was put in the position to do it. He must support its inception as a ministry born of need in our time that will continue on in the church even if the leadership changes. It is too easy to approve a ministry, then ignore it until it evaporates and the voices promoting it disappear.

Do research to understand the ministry. It is the responsibility of the singles minister to do research, reading, interviews, and homework in the area of singleness to understand the ministry directed toward singles. Taking the time to talk with singles can in itself be a learning experience. Visiting another singles ministry or a divorce recovery seminar can give a new understanding of singles ministry and hurting people. Four years of Bible college or three years of seminary cannot be enough training and preparation.

Share the vision and the burden. It is the responsibility of the singles minister to share with the senior pastor the vision and burden for a singles ministry. Most senior pastors I know have very full agendas. It takes time to get behind a new vision. Most ministers are willing to be lovingly brought along in any new dream. It is only when they are pushed and shoved into something that they look for a side exit. Present your vision and burden honestly to your senior pastor and pray about it. Remember, the ministry is the Lord's, not the singles pastor's or the senior pastor's!

28

Traits of Single-Adult Leaders

Harold Ivan Smith

What does it mean to be a single-adult leader, particularly a professional one? Clearly the definition of *professional* is open to discussion, perhaps debate. F. E. Bullett has defined it as "a field of human endeavor with a well-defined body of knowledge, containing basic principles common to all application and techniques unique to the field, with practitioners skilled and experienced in applying these techniques, dedicated to the public interest."[1]

W. E. Sheer suggests that a profession has eight essential characteristics: (1) a code of ethics; (2) an organized and accepted body of knowledge; (3) specialized skills; (4) minimum educational requirements for membership; (5) certification of proficiency before a member can achieve professional status; (6) an orderly process in the fulfillment of responsibilities; (7) opportunities for the promulgation and interchange of ideas among its members; and (8) requirements for acceptance of the disciplines of the profession, realizing that the price of failure or malpractice is being "out" of the profession.[2]

In establishing a new vocation—single-adult leader—it will take time and effort to formulate a commonly held set of characteristics of the profession. We will start with common traits all singles leaders should have.

Expectations

The expectations of singles determine the qualities their leaders should possess. A single-adult leader must realize that single adults have these expectations:

1. that they can learn the extent of their ignorance and misinformation
2. that the Christian community will replace misinformation with facts
3. that they may ask uncomfortable questions and get biblically sound answers or responses
4. that they will be more moral when adequately enlightened than when they are un- or underinformed
5. that, even when faced with impossible circumstances, they can be victorious through faith in Christ

The singles leader needs to make sure these expectations are realized. Certain traits in the leader will help him or her do so.

Competence

There are two routes to becoming a single-adult leader or minister. One, a staff professional, often with a background in youth ministry or Christian education, takes a personal interest in single adults and gradually assumes formal responsibility, either full time or part time, until "someone can be found."

The volunteer leader, the second route, is common because of budget considerations. Sometimes, single adult ministry has been "forced" on a most reluctant (and often already overworked) staff minister or leader with the instruction, "Do something with those single adults!"

In light of such a selection process, to say nothing of the "whosoever may . . ." approach in other churches, how are we to develop competence in leadership?

The American Association of Marriage and Family Therapy offers some guidance. Single-adult leaders must be "dedicated to maintaining high standards of competence, recognizing appropriate limitations to [our] competence and services and using consultation and referral to/from other professionals." Realistically, in working with single adults, one finds every sort of mental, social, and theological disability. In some settings, simplistic solutions border on quackery, though disguised in religious jargon: "Take three Scriptures and you'll feel better in the morning."

What about those fellowships that offer immediate "deliverance" to persons wandering through the emotional wilderness of singleness? Has there not been theological and psychological abuse, even if well intended? Such abuse is from lack of competence.

Problems arise when the leader wants to be a messiah or deliverer and so will not consider sending someone elsewhere for help. Have you developed a network of resources to which you can confidently and appropriately make referrals? Single-adult leaders must not attempt to diagnose, treat, or advise on problems beyond the boundaries of their competence.

Integrity

Paul warned Timothy, "Do your best to present yourself to God as one approved, a workman who does not need to be ashamed and who correctly handles the word of truth" (2 Tim. 2:15) and, "Watch your life and doctrine closely" (1 Tim. 4:16). Dr. James Brown, a Christian psychologist offers four reasons why people don't initiate counseling with a single-adult minister or leader—all of which strike at the heart of integrity:

- "I don't trust him/her!"
- "He/she is unable to handle my inner secrets and sins."
- "I am afraid to reveal my 'dirty little sins' to a minister."
- "I am really afraid he/she will reject me when he/she knows how I really am."[3]

Integrity is the trait of adhering to a code of ethics. Once a church has determined its ethics, the single-adult minister must adhere to them.

A Commitment to Confidentiality

Confidentiality is an ethic that is universally required of pastors and church leaders. Scripture admonishes all Christians not to gossip or slander. The single-adult leader must respect the rights and reputations of single adults who participate in his or her programs. In the helping professions, confidentiality is a significant concern. Any individual who counsels with a single-adult leader or minister has a right to expect that his or her privacy will be respected. However, a single-adult leader serves in a church and community that wants to be informed about certain acts and intentions. That inevitably creates tension in the church and group.

The single-adult leader is privy to much more information about the lives of single adults than many other professionals. You can expect more legal involvement in questions of practicing ministry and leadership in a church setting. Two major precedent-setting court cases involved single adults: *Nally v. McArthur* and *Quinn v. Elders of the Church of Christ of Collinsville* (Oklahoma).

Situations can create conflict between the single-adult leader and other church leaders. Suppose your pastor or deacons want information about a certain counseling case, i.e., an adultery that leads to a divorce. Suppose there are third parties involved who happen to be key church leaders. Through your counseling (or through rumor), you discover the relationship. What do you do with that data?

One single-adult minister discovered that his senior minister was sexually involved with a single adult in the singles group. If he confronted the senior pastor with the allegation, word would get out in the singles group that he had violated confidence. His effectiveness would be jeopardized, perhaps destroyed.

The single-adult minister in this case chose not to confront but tried to persuade the woman to terminate the affair. That suggestion, however, angered the senior pastor. Eventually, the counselee shared the story with another single adult in the group who, in turn, quickly made the relationship common knowledge throughout the church. The senior pastor resigned. Still, some single adults believe that the single-adult minister blew the whistle and breached confidentiality.

Frequently, in working with the separated or divorced the single-adult minister or leader gains information that is troublesome. Moreover, in a church setting, he is to minister to all concerned. Therefore, a single-adult minister or leader must be slow to take sides or jump to conclusions, particularly in emotion-laden issues such as incest, homosexuality, child custody, date rape, or child abuse. Divorce stimulates curiosity, especially in small groups or congregations, particularly when things "don't add up." Moreover, there can be a significant difference between the public reasons for a divorce and the *real* reasons. You must remember that in the adversarial nature of many divorces, events can be staged or taken out of context. You should carefully weigh active participation in any litigation.

Dr. James Brown presents four facts about confidentiality: (1) Without assurance of confidentiality, many singles adults will *not* seek help for their problems or their secret sins; (2) without assurance confidentiality, many single adults will delay their entry into counseling for fear of being exposed; (3) without assurance of confidentiality, many single adults will be reluctant to divulge essential information during the course of counseling; and (4) without assurance of confidentiality, many single adults who have needs for counseling will end up terminating their counseling prematurely and not receive the help that they so desperately need and that you can give.

Brown concluded, "We must take our promises [stated or implied] seriously when dealing with the injured, tortured souls of God's people. If you truly wish people to seek out your wisdom and guidance, then you must learn to listen *and* to keep their faith by maintaining confidentiality."[4]

Simply, a single-adult minister or leader must be cautious in sharing in prayer groups, committees, or private conversations material that is confidential or unsubstantiated. If the cat's out of the bag, it doesn't matter how "spiritual" the setting in which it escaped.

Finally, confidentiality raises a significant question in lay leadership selection and development. Suppose a committee nominates a person for leadership. However, in counseling, that individual has confessed to a struggle with an issue that would cloud or compromise his leadership. What are you to do both to guard the group and maintain confidentiality? What is your responsibility should that person move to another group? Is your problem solved?

One single-adult minister asked a man to leave his group for "hitting up" sexually on female members. Imagine his surprise when he received a newsletter from another single adult group and found this individual actively involved in a position of leadership.

The problem is not new in single adult ministry. Paul warned about those "who worm their way into homes [groups] and gain control over weak-willed women [and men], who are loaded down with sins and are swayed by all kinds of evil desires" (2 Tim. 3:6). The vulnerable, fragile emotions of single adults must be protected, particularly within the body of believers.

Conclusion

Paul offered good advice to Titus, "In *everything* set them an example by doing what is good. In your teaching [counseling] show integrity, seriousness and soundness of speech that cannot be condemned" (2:7, italics added). Every single-adult leader needs a desk copy of *Clergy Malpractice* by Malony, Needham, and Southard as a guidebook for referral.

Paul warned, "Give the enemy *no opportunity for slander*" (1 Tim. 5:14, italics added). That is still sound advice for those who wish to provide leadership with America's fastest-growing subculture.

29
The Importance of Prayer

Mary Graves

If my people, who are called by my name, will humble themselves and pray and seek my face and turn from their wicked ways, then will I hear from heaven and will forgive their sin and will heal their land" (2 Chron. 7:14).

Paul Cho, pastor of the world's largest and fastest-growing church, traces the success of that Korean ministry to its beginnings in prayer. The Christians in Korea have learned how to live their lives in prayer, and because of that, a revival is happening in that country.

The late Keith Green, who made contemporary Christian music big in the '70s, addressed a concert crowd of college-age Christians in Chico, California, with this question, "How many of you would like to see a revival happen in Chico?" to which the crowd cheered their enthusiastic approval. Then he asked, "How many of you are praying for it?" Silence.

Singles could easily be considered an unreached people that need to be touched and revived with the grace of God given in Jesus Christ. We can do our best to make that happen, but no one can program a response to God's grace. A handbook can give information, but only the Spirit of God can bring faith. A handbook can put flesh and bones to the whole idea of singles ministry, but only the Spirit of God can give life to it. And prayer helps breathe that Spirit of life and faith into our ministries.

This book depends on people kneeling before God in prayer before its ideas and suggestions can come to life. God commands our prayers (Luke 18:1), and he has made his work contingent on them.

Obstacles to Prayer

"Prayer is a problem," says David Hubbard in the opening line of *The Practice of Prayer*. Christian leaders can teach it, advocate it, believe in it, and yet national surveys show that very few Christians spend much time doing it, including those Christian leaders. Why is it a problem? Because there seem to be so many good reasons not to pray.

In light of the sovereignty of God, prayer can seem a bit presumptuous. If God knows our every need before we even utter it, and if God rules over all things in power and nothing falls outside of his control, why pray? To miss a prayer time here and there doesn't feel all that tragic because God is still on his throne doing business as usual.

With our tendency to champion "human potential" it is easy for us to let work become a substitute for prayer. After all, God does expect us to do our best; and we must not use prayer as an excuse to dump on God the work that needs to be done by us; and "God helps those who help themselves." So, fueled with that kind of logic, we busy ourselves with the tasks of ministry and end up with no time or energy to pray.

There may be a myriad of other obstacles that trip up the prayer life of eager singles leaders. Perhaps God's silence at a critical time of need provided convincing proof that prayer is ineffective. Perhaps our sin and pride have convinced us that we cannot pray right, and so we don't try. Many times, in many ways, and for many reasons, we just don't feel like praying.

But praying is too important to depend on our feelings. According to Jesus, by far the most important thing about praying is to keep at it. Prayer is a response, it is an answering speech and presence to what God has said and done, and the call to pray transcends our own ability and desire to do it.

Prayer in Your Singles Ministry

Prayer can be built into your ministry as an activity that engages you, your leaders, and your singles. And there are several treasures that time in prayer will bring. First we will explore the treasures and then we will look at intentional ways of grabbing those treasures and making prayer a priority in your singles ministry.

The Treasures

Singles ministry brings an overwhelming variety of life situations under one umbrella and often an overwhelming assortment of needs. As one singles leader described it, "There are more problems per square inch than anywhere else in the church." If the church is a hospital for sinners, then singles ministry is the intensive care unit. Not all singles are hurting, but the hurts that singles bring are critical and often beyond human healing. Singles ministry can be overwhelming.

But with all the promise of a treasure hunt, Scripture declares that "the prayer of a righteous man is powerful and effective" (James 5:16). Indeed, we already affirmed that truth at the outset with the words of the writer of Chronicles. Prayer brings forgiveness of sin and healing to our land and far greater things than we could possibly ask or think. There are unnamed treasures in store for the men and women poised in a posture of prayer. And no problem is too overwhelming for our God.

We are humbled by our own neediness and lifted up by the only one who is able to save. That is a treasure and a necessary assurance for anyone who hopes to do singles ministry.

Another jewel from the treasure chest of prayer is compassion. To pray for others is to affirm our concern for them. There are many singles in the category of "unlovely" and "socially inept" people who are not easy to care for. But when we quietly lift the names and needs of these people before God's throne, their hurts become our hurts, their burdens rest on our hearts too. And through the ministry of prayer, a love and compassion develops where there was none before.

One more gem from the wealth of prayer's treasures is intimacy. As one seminary professor said, "If you want to get to know someone, pray together." Prayer brings an honesty and openness that can only occur before the throne of God. It brings a bonding, a spiritual unity, that cannot be manufactured by human engineering and cannot be easily severed by human weakness. Singles have a hunger for honesty. Singles do not want to be alone, and many are starved for intimacy. Prayer speaks to their deepest longings and brings them to the only one who can fulfill all of their needs.

Where to Start

As far as building prayer into your ministry, the most appropriate place to begin is with the leader and the utter necessity of a predictable, consistent, structured time in daily prayer. Many end up praying for the needs of their singles as they happen to come to mind. Instead of that random method, try putting the various people and programs on a weekly calendar. For example, on Monday you might pray for divorce recovery and the people giving leadership there (by name), Tuesday pray for single parents—and on through the week, making sure that all your key people and need areas are covered regularly in prayer.

Then look at the day's schedule—the counseling appointments, the leadership meetings, the programmed events—and lift them, one by one, to the Lord, expressing your greatest fear and asking for your wildest dream. And look back with a thankful heart. Praise God for what He is doing, for the lives that are being touched and the prayers that have been answered.

But you are not the only one called to pray. Cultivate prayer as a priority agenda item for your leaders. In your leadership meetings, pray not only at the beginning and end (popularly known as the "Oreo prayer"), but also make a major time commitment to a prayer session together. Teach the necessity, the urgency, and the power of prayer—and then pray. One minister takes his leaders through the singles mailing list, praying regularly for each one by name. Other leaders gather together before an event to pray for it. Program prayer into your leadership training.

And program it into your singles gatherings. The fear is that prayer times will exclude the non-Christians at your outreach events. But some have found that prayer for the whole group at the end of a meeting can be very nonthreatening and offer great love and support to everyone there. Perhaps some of your small groups can explore the topic of prayer. What a great way to build closeness and disciples at the same time!

"If my people, who are called by my name, will humble themselves and pray," then they will see ministry happen, they will see lives transformed, they will experience the reviving and saving power of God in and through Jesus Christ. Talking about prayer, writing about prayer, reading about prayer accomplishes nothing unless it causes God's people to pray.

Part 5

Developing Leadership

30

Developing a Ministry Vision

David Savage

Recent magazine and newspaper articles are declaring that the traditional family is dead, that the American people have become a nation of friendless adults, and that marriage is an outdated institution. While some journalists have exaggerated the state of affairs regarding family and friendship in America, they have captured the spirit of likely changes in the next decade.

George Barna, president of Barna Research Group, believes that the reported disintegration of the family is not an accurate portrayal. What has happened is that the traditional family unit—the working father and a mother who stays home to care for the two children—has been replaced by a different type of household. In 1960, this stereotypical family represented 60 percent of all households; by 1990, it reflected just 7 percent of our households.[1]

The average American family in 1990 consists of a married couple with one child; both parents are employed. At least one of the parents is likely to have been divorced, or it is likely that the couple will divorce. Parents are having fewer children and having them later in life. Increasing numbers of households are "blended families"—homes in which the children from two or more marriages are combined as a result of remarriage. There is also a growing trend for partners to have children without being married. In 1990, it was estimated that one out of every fifteen children would be born out of wedlock.[2]

In his book *The Baby Boomerang*, Doug Murren states that the single population in the United States may exceed 50 percent of all adults over age 18 before the year 2000. Such figures mean that the church is faced with the "singling" of its communities.[3]

The attitude of society toward marriage and the traditional family and the rising divorce rate affect the growing singles population. The church for the 1990s will have to redefine its role to single adults if it intends to minister to them. The new realities of the single life must force the church to be fresh and creative when planning outreach and overall ministry.[4]

An Inward Look

Divorce, a largely unthought-of and unplanned-for event in the lives of over a million Americans every year, can drastically affect children, in-laws, families, social networks, and communities.[5]

In the late 1960s and early 1970s, as the divorce rate among Christians skyrocketed and as disillusioned wives left the house to find work and greater fulfillment, concerned Christians began to look for a solution. Linda Raney Wright in *A Cord of Three Strands* stated that the church could have entertained a number of options at that time. It could have examined the root problems of dissatisfaction in marriage and their solutions; it might have seen each marriage as unique unto itself and dealt with each accordingly; it might have assessed total needs and considerations before drawing a conclusion; it might have encouraged communication between husbands and wives; or it might have observed what was happening between secular couples to determine whether Christian couples could learn anything constructive.[6]

Many churches took the challenge and began to develop ministries to meet the needs of the family and bring healing to marriages, while not neglecting the single adults and their multiple needs. However, the majority of churches did little or nothing in either area.

The recent growth of the single adult population in America has shocked many in church leadership. In many churches couples with children no longer dominate membership rolls. The boomer generation is so large that any statistical slant reflects its size. Its size carries large ramifications for those seeking to serve it.[7]

Not to be forgotten is the "Buster" generation. These post-boomers have been referred to as the "postponed generation." Our ministries will need to adjust and adapt in the present and for the future to this issues-oriented, conservative subculture.

The church must be aware that the singles population in America will impact the function of the church. When a church programs, staffs, preaches, shares illustrations or anecdotes, and addresses needs from the pulpit, leaders should keep in mind that possibly half of the congregation is single.

Therefore, the church cannot be blind to the fact that singleness is a very complex and difficult issue because it represents numerous age categories and life situations: teenagers who have moved out of their parents' homes; never married, young, single moms; divorcées with children; a growing number of single fathers; the never-marrieds of various ages; the elderly—both widows and widowers; and a generation of single-parent children.

This reality of singleness is forcing the church to face new issues when planning outreach and ministry. Each age group and life situation copes with different concerns and challenges. Each one requires a different setting for fellowship and pastoral care.[8] Before a church starts a ministry to single adults, it must have an inward look into two basic issues—divorce and remarriage, and single bias.

Divorce and Remarriage

Possibly the most difficult issue the church faces is divorce and remarriage. Since there is so much controversy over this issue, it will be dealt with as a relationship issue first.

Jack and Judith Balswick in *The Family—A Christian Perspective on the Contemporary Home* deal with divorce and remarriage from a relational position. They state that wherever Jesus talks about divorce (Matt. 5:31–32; 19:3–9; Mark 10:2–12; Luke 16:18), the thrust is that marriage is of the Lord and is not to be broken. Christ calls couples to a lifelong commitment. However, he does not have in view a marriage of legalism and law that involves a commitment only to the institution and not to the relationship. The Balswicks state:

This perspective that the well-being of the people involved is more important than the structure of marriage has shaped our view of simple parenthood and remarriage. The Christian message is that out of brokenness can come forgiveness and restoration.

Some divorced persons with children will choose to remain single and shoulder the responsibility of being the head of a one-parent family. We must not deny them or their families the encouragement and support that are necessary for them to thrive. These members of the church body are to be accepted and welcomed into the church as legitimate parts of God's family.

Some divorced persons will find restoration through remarriage. The church must resist the temptation to develop a legalistic rationale which would deny them the opportunity to find wholeness and hope through remarriage. Remarried persons who live in reconstituted families have much to offer to our community in Christ. When our theology of relationships is practical, the restoration and renewal of the remarried will be a blessing and strength to the whole community of believers.[9]

Many church groups do not accept the Balswicks' position on divorce and remarriage. They believe that the doctrinal position is the only way to deal with the divorce and remarriage issue.

Since the issue of divorce and remarriage will continue to be a doctrinal issue for the church in the 1990s, a book, *Divorce and Remarriage—Four Christian Views*, is helpful. This book includes four standard views of divorce and remarriage as well as refutations from each of the other three. The four standard views are

no divorce and no remarriage;
divorce, but no remarriage;
divorce and remarriage for adultery or desertion;
divorce and remarriage under a variety of circumstances.

There is considerable controversy over the meaning of certain Hebrew and Greek words, and often the meaning of a Scripture passage will turn on the correct understanding of these words. The contributors to this book come to different conclusions because of the different weight they give to the various passages.

To develop a ministry, bold questions need to be asked and answers need to be sought. What is the meaning of one flesh? Does it refer to blood relation? What is the meaning of marriage? Is it inherently indissoluble? How does one explain the divorcing of foreign wives in Ezra and Malachi? Is Jesus speaking of fornication in the betrothal period in Matthew 19:9, or is this a reference to an incestuous act? Does Jesus offer new teaching that sets aside the teaching of Moses in Deuteronomy? Is only divorce in view of Matthew 19:9 and not remarriage? Or is remarriage inherent in the understanding of divorce? If fornication includes adultery as well as other sexual sins, does it refer to a single act, or does it refer to a continual state? Does Paul introduce another exception besides fornication or sexual immorality in 1 Corinthians 7, namely, desertion by an unbelieving spouse? Does this require the believing spouse to remain remarried or does it allow a new marriage to be contracted?[10]

Although there are varying interpretations of the divorce and remarriage issue, church leaders need to reflect on this statement: "While the church must uphold the importance of marriage, the church cannot reject people who are divorced, or who struggle with the need to extricate themselves from a destructive marriage."[11] The church that ministers to singles will be able to love the divorced and the remarried and truly care for the needs of their families without feeling that this ministry contradicts their doctrinal views of divorce and remarriage.

Biases

The second major area where the church needs godly wisdom is in dealing with the biases it may have against single adults. For some time the church has looked at singleness as an oddity, or seen singles as "swingers." Leaders need to dispel these images.

An Upward Look

The church has a vital role in relation to the family structure designed by God. The church needs to educate people about the benefits of permanent monogamy and intense family relations. It also needs to provide more extensive premarital counseling.[12] The church ought to consider celebrating successful marriages instead of just wailing over the demise of relationships. Americans learn best by behavioral modeling. Showing that marriage can work is part of persuading people to rethink divorce and "serial monogamy."

While the church must uphold the importance of marriage, people who are divorced or who battle with the need to extricate themselves from a destructive marriage cannot be rejected. Postmarital counseling must be available to help people through the rocky times. Churches must offer counseling programs, support groups, and recreational opportunities for single parents and for their children; it is important to help them become the kind of people they want to be.[13]

Some churches are providing counseling and support groups for single adults. Jim Smoke in *Growing in Remarriage* states that many churches have classes for those entering first marriages, covering the various facets of building a healthy marriage; but few churches have classes for those entering a second marriage. Generally, these couples are left to fend for themselves when, in truth, they need far more help and instruction than those entering first marriages.[14]

A marriage preparation manual prepared by Wes Roberts and H. Norman Wright, *Before You Say I Do*, should be considered a requirement in counseling a couple planning remarriage. This manual can help any couple to understand that "marriage is a refining process that God will use to have us become the man or woman He wants us to be."[15] If children are involved in this newly formed family, Wright suggests that counseling is essential.

> Can the person who may never have been married before accept the experience of the other's love life with someone else in years gone by? If there are children still in the home can the new partner accept and love them? Will the children accept someone else in Mother's or Father's place? If one has never married before, can he or she suddenly take on a ready-made family and adjust to them?[16]

The new parent may fail to understand the psychological problems of the stepchild and retaliate by rejecting the child or showing favoritism, if that parent's own children are involved. Older children can oppose the marriage and even from the beginning of courtship show hostility toward the new partner.

David and Bonnie Juroe in *Successful Stepparenting* emphasize that church leaders and Christian counselors need to see the importance of reaching out to children of the divorced. The number of people waiting for help because of the staggering problems encountered in step families is rising. Many parents really do care about their children's needs and sincerely want to help them through the pain of a divorce or remarriage, but they do not know how. As church leaders become familiar with the reasons behind the stresses these parents have to cope with, the quality and durability of the new step relationships will be greatly enhanced.[17]

The Juroes also suggest that churches desiring to have an effective ministry to blended families need to consider having Stepparents Day. "The neighborhood church that celebrates Stepparents Day builds a bridge of friendship and acceptance to families who need support and love but have not been sure that their participation is welcome." A special day would give recognition to a growing host of people in the church and society who rightly should be honored for their great sacrifices of caring. A Stepparents Day would allow stepchildren a special opportunity to express appreciation without feeling a divided loyalty between a stepparent and the absent, natural parent.[18]

Church leaders can train teachers to include in their lessons illustrations and Bible stories about one-parent homes. Leaders can visit single-parent homes to express a more caring, empathetic relationship with members of these families.

Church leaders must make sure that children of divorce are not excluded from church activities just because parental visitation schedules keep them from achieving perfect attendance, because they lack transportation or funds, or because the "right" parent is unavailable (as in a father/son dinner). Every teacher in the church should make a commitment to unconditionally love and accept each single-parent family in their church and community.

It is also essential that the church exercise the belief that God can heal the hurt of divorce, by focusing on the wholeness of families in crisis rather than treating them as second-class citizens or emotional "basket cases." The emphasis in ministry should be to lead children of divorce and their parents to adapt positively to the changes they face.[19]

If a church serves a number of teens from broken homes, it may wish to form an ongoing support group for them. However, the teens should also be encouraged to stay with the established youth group.

A support group led by a youth worker with counseling experience can be valuable for teenage divorce victims on the road to recovery.

Such groups will not work if the church leadership does not have genuine love. The "don't touch" syndrome is a part of a Victorian attitude about sex and the human body. However, not all the blame can be placed there, for among men, this rule about not touching is related to deep fears of possible homosexual tendencies. Is it not interesting that in our society the bumper sticker appeared, "Have you hugged your kid today?" Why should such a question ever be asked? Because there is a hang-up about hugging on the part of many parents.[20] Churches that reach the single adult population will express love in a genuine, healthy, and caring way. That includes hugs.

One of the most important ministries to the single adult community is the divorce recovery support group. A divorce recovery program must integrate the truth of the Gospel into a program mix that meets the felt needs of the participants. Such a mix will include crisis intervention and grief management within a framework designed to understand the past, cope with the present, and prepare for the future. Divorce recovery provides an excellent opportunity for outreach and evangelism, since participants are attracted to fellowship within the singles ministry of the sponsoring church.[21]

Harold Ivan Smith, in *I Wish Someone Understood My Divorce*, gives three reasons why a divorce support group is essential for a church. First, such groups are emergency rooms for the newly separated or divorced, providing the care needed to heal hurts and help to reenter the world of singleness. Many people attribute their survival to the nurture of a support group.

Second, these groups are stabilizers because they provide structure, friendship, social activities, and leadership opportunities. Third, the groups help the newly divorced to learn the ropes of their singlehood. They serve a valuable cultural role because divorce has not been recognized as a rite of passage. Such support groups are not pity parties but rather cheerleaders who help individuals to function more effectively.[22]

Support groups, seminars, and retreats can be used to educate or reeducate the single in enhancing communication skills, restoring self-esteem, and learning personality traits.

An Outward Look

The church of the 1990s needs to meet single adults where they are. This means presenting them in a positive light. The church that is effectively reaching single adults knows that the secret of successful single living is not self-sufficiency, but sufficiency in Christ Jesus. The season of singleness must be understood as an opportunity to discover and become all that God dreams for one to be.

Single adults must come to realize that they can lead productive lives, contradictory to the stereotype of the swinging single. Single adults generally have more time to invest in careers, and business rewards such commitment with raises, bonuses, and promotions. Single adults must be taught to alert themselves to the danger of "unproductive spiritual lives."[23] The church that teaches that God calls all of his children, married or single, to ministry and endows all of his children with ministry gifts, will be a church with the outward look.

The church with the outward look is the church that has a goal to minister salvation to all. The word *salvation* in its broadest sense means "to bring to wholeness," and is interchangeable with the word *healing*. In James 5:15 we read, "And the prayer of faith shall save the sick" (KJV). The same Greek word rendered "save" here is translated "heal" elsewhere; the NIV version says, "will make the sick person well."

Within the community of the gathered church, married and single adults need to be saved, healed, and brought to wholeness in every sense of their lives. But before there can be a coming to wholeness, certain guarantees must be made to people. Otherwise, they will not risk themselves to be open with the church leadership to receive this healing.

The first guarantee the church must make to people is to always love them, under every circumstance, with no exception. The second guarantee is to totally accept them, without reservation. The third guarantee is that the church will reach out to them, no matter how miserably they fail or how blatantly they sin. Unreserved forgiveness is theirs for the asking, without a bitter taste left in anybody's mouth. The final guarantee is the absolute faithfulness of God and truthfulness of the Bible. If singles are not given these guarantees, they will never allow the church the marvelous privilege of bringing wholeness to them.[24]

The aggressive outreaching church of the 1990s will also look for alternative church service times. The Barna Research Group has found many reasons why single adults do not attend church. According to this research, Murren believes that the most common reasons for not attending church are problems of time and priority. Most single adults say they have to work on Sunday or that it is their only day off. They also say that other issues in their lives take precedence over church attendance. The typical all-American single adult claims she or he also needs Sunday for doing other activities to keep life and limb together.[25] New paradigms for ministry are needed.

The aggressive outreaching church will present singleness in a positive light, will recognize the potential spiritual leadership single adults can provide, will give themselves to the challenge to guarantee to love, accept, and forgive, and will provide alternative worship times and new ministries appropriate for single adults.

Conclusion

In a survey of unchurched single adults, Barna Research Group found that almost four out of ten said they had a positive disposition toward attending church in the future. This finding may mean that at least four out of every ten single people in your community would be happy to attend the church if someone would reach out to them in a friendly, accommodating manner.[26]

The role of the successful church in the 1990s will be in relationship—friendly and single-sensitive. Once this church has had an inward look and is truly prepared to minister to the single community, then an upward look will give that church a vision as to what they can do to reach out to and meet the multiple needs of the single adult community. Then their focused outward look will be followed by an aggressive mission to bring in the harvest.

Developing Spiritual Leadership

Robert Duffet

The term "spiritual leadership" has been much discussed and debated during the last several decades. Books, sermons, and seminars on the subject have tried to define it and encourage its development. All agree that effectiveness in ministry and world evangelization will be determined by the quality of spiritual leadership in the church.

All institutions in our society are searching for ways to raise the quality of leadership. It is almost a universal principle that the success and effectiveness of any endeavor will depend on the quality of leadership. In a general way, leadership may be defined as influencing people in a certain direction. President Dwight Eisenhower defined leadership as the ability to get people to do what you want them to do. In his excellent book *Leadership*, James Burns calls leadership "the ability to induce followers to act toward certain goals that are important to both the leader and followers."

These definitions are applicable to almost any leadership situation—politics, educational administration, business management. But at issue for ministry is the similarity and difference between the above definitions and spiritual leadership. At first glance, single adult leaders would affirm these definitions. They certainly are influencing people, at times getting others to do what they don't want to do, and they firmly believe followers in single adult ministry need to be committed to the goals of the ministry. However, the difference between leadership in general and spiritual leadership is the means and ends. Spiritual leadership is concerned with influencing followers by the *right* means toward the *right* ends (goal). The Christian single-adult leader demands a more comprehensive definition of leadership that emphasizes means and ends. To find such a definition of leadership, we need to consult the Bible.

A Biblical Definition

Spiritual leadership may be defined as the increasing personal acquisition of world vision, ministry skills, and character development, all grounded in a commitment of faith and obedience to the gospel of Jesus Christ.

World vision is the ability to see the world in all its complexity and diversity. It is the opposite of ethnocentrism, racism, and provincialism. It encompasses the whole world in response to Christ's mandate to preach the gospel to every person and to the recognition that God loves all people. Specifically, world vision means a personal grasp of the principle of spiritual multiplication, personal involvement in world need, and an understanding of the infinite worth of the individual.

Ministry skills are required to be an effective servant of Jesus Christ. The single-adult leader recognizes the priesthood of all believers and the fact that the Holy Spirit gives ministerial gifts to all. These skills include the abilities to share one's faith, to encourage other people, to apply the results of Bible study to one's life and behavior, to work with those who disagree with one's point of view, to practice the spiritual disciplines, to be flexible, and to understand one's spiritual gifts.

Character development is the cultivating and evidencing of the fruit of the Spirit (Gal. 5:22–23). This includes love, honesty, obedience, faithfulness, a servant heart, generosity, openness, humility, patience, confidence, hospitality, gentleness, stability, kindness, and self-control.

The definition of spiritual leadership, with its emphasis on world vision, ministry skills, and character development, attempts to balance the *being* and *doing* of the Christian life. Balance is important. In her book *Journey Inward, Journey Outward,* Elizabeth O'Connor observed that those who overemphasize the outward journey (doing) of spiritual leadership (social change, evangelism) often run out of the necessary spiritual power to make the desired and needed changes. Similarly, those who overemphasize the inward journey (being) discover that their spiritual experience is stunted, self-centered, and devoid of meaning.

Without the other, each is shallow and lacks substance. Being (inward journey) without doing (outward journey) is idolatrous and the worst sort of putrid piety. Doing (outward journey) without being (inward journey) will ultimately collapse under its own weight, since being provides the spiritual strength and power to persevere. Unless the inward journey is cultivated, individuals and the Christian community will not be able to stand up to the oppressive powers of the world and, hence, will either capitulate or become status quo. The inward journey will provide the motivation, discipline, and staying power needed to love, care for, and heal those who are broken. The goal, then, of spiritual leadership is to open our lives to God in such a way (inward journey) that we may be used to help heal a world of pain (outward journey).

The Theology

Any discussion of spiritual leadership must begin with the gospel, the Good News. By definition the gospel is the proclamation or announcement of a new reality of living for individuals and communities that has come to pass because of the death and resurrection of Jesus Christ. This is not just a new possibility but a new reality of living. The apostle Paul speaks about this new way of living as being "in Christ." Being "in Christ" gives individuals and communities the inclination toward responsibility and obedience. This inclination comes from a moral transformation of life through faith. Hence, the gospel is both indicative and imperative—we personally experience the power of Christ through faith (what

God does for us) and then live out a moral and obedient lifestyle based on our experience of faith (what God expects from us). Through this gospel, salvation is experienced by the people of God.

Salvation implies a twofold commitment of faith: to God through Jesus and to the community of believers. True spirituality manifests itself in community. Spiritual leadership must go beyond the privatization of faith to a growing demonstration of the presence of God's kingdom in our midst. The power of the kingdom is demonstrated by relationships based on humility, responsible living, forgiveness, compassion, bearing each other's burdens, and obedience.

At the heart of spiritual leadership for single-adult leaders is the need to provide programmatic and personal means to encourage other single adults to choose—in every event of life—to act obediently and responsibly before God. As this happens, both individuals and ministry will experience the power of Christ. In our life together, the gospel calls us to do for others what God has done for us. Since God is giving, merciful, and forgiving, we must be giving, merciful, and forgiving to each other based on Christ's acceptance of us (Rom. 15:7).

The Necessity

Why is spiritual leadership important? Why should single-adult leaders aspire to spiritual leadership or bother to train others to be spiritual leaders? The answers to these questions come from the Bible and also from contemporary needs. The first book of the Bible clearly explains the problem of humanity; the present brokenness of our society cries out for some type of leadership to heal our land (2 Chron. 7:14).

The story of Adam and Eve (Gen. 1–3) is fodder for advertisements, jokes, and sermons. But the event itself describes humanity's problem in such clarity that it sounds like it occurred yesterday. Through Adam and Eve's choice to disobey God (3:1–7), the harmony and joy of creation were shattered. Adam and Eve experienced fragmentation of their lives in four ways.

First, there was relational fragmentation between them. They were created to have open and trusting relationships with each other. Once they were "naked and not ashamed" (2:25); now they were naked, ashamed, and they hid from each other (3:7). The perfect relationship was now shame-based and fractured.

Second, the relationship between God and humanity was fractured. Not only did Adam and Eve hide from each other, but they also hid from God (3:8). After experiencing all of God's gifts in an astonishing environment, they chose to overstep their bounds and jeopardize their relationship with the one who gave them beauty and happiness.

Third, the story of Adam and Eve demonstrates intrapersonal fragmentation. Both explained their actions to God by blaming. Eve blamed the snake and Adam blamed Eve (3:12–13). Blaming another for one's actions indicates the presence of an inner war—the essence of intrapersonal fragmentation.

Fourth, the removal of the first couple from the Garden produced the world's first ecological disaster and environmental fragmentation (3:20–24). Gone were the beautiful surroundings, and basic life functions (work, childbearing) were painfully altered (3:16–19).

The first three chapters of the Bible offer perspective on the pain and brokenness of our lives. Humanity *did not* and *does not* accept the limitations placed on us by God. As a result, we live in the midst of fragmentation and brokenness. Although all ministries attempt to deal with human brokenness, few see that more clearly than the single adult ministry. Much of the single adult leader's time is given to personal and programmatic ministries dealing with broken relationships.

Stan and Debby promised to live together and love each other ". . . till death us do part." But one day Stan walked out for another woman. Devastated, Debby turned to the single adult ministry in her church. Many other women there had gone through a similar experience. For several months, members of the group and single adult leaders helped pick up the shattered pieces of Debby's life. The betrayal still hurts, but by her own admission life is getting better.

Bill wanted to marry and have children, but the right woman never appeared, and he is lonely. Now in his mid-forties, he sees some of his college friends' children having children, and he often feels left out. He loves his nieces and nephews, but his family takes little interest in his life. Everyone is so preoccupied—his parents with the grandchildren and his brothers and sisters with their homes, children, and lives. Bill often wonders who loves and cares about him.

A few years ago a single adult-leader took an interest in Bill. A bit shy at first, Bill wanted no part of a single adult ministry. But now he feels a sense of belonging. His sense of fragmentation due to loneliness is lessened through the single adult ministry in his church.

Susan and Ray were the perfect couple. Two years ago Ray went out for a morning jog and never returned. He was found on a running path in a nearby woods. While running he suffered a massive heart attack and died within minutes. Susan's grief was unbearable, but a single-adult leader encouraged her to participate in a grief recovery group. She still misses Ray, and her life at times feels broken, but she is growing stronger and more confident each day. Her radiant smile, so much a part of her demeanor but missing since Ray's death, is now back. She tells all who will listen how the single adult group was there when her world fell apart.

Why is spiritual leadership important? Only spiritual leaders put in place ministries that enable people to hear and respond to a God who will put the shattered fragments of their lives together through faith in Jesus Christ.

Criteria for Spiritual Leadership

The Bible offers five criteria for spiritual leaders.

1. *Personal integrity.* Single adult ministry is rooted in the ministry of Jesus. As Jesus sought those whom society at times shunted aside, so single adult ministry works with those who often feel marginalized by the church. Jesus demanded followers to "follow him." Single-adult leaders must hear the call of the Master as well. The call to follow Jesus demands obedience and an ethical lifestyle.

Let it be said firmly and clearly that there is no spiritual leadership where there is no personal integrity! First Timothy 3:1–7 and Titus 1:5–9 not only spell out the moral criteria for spiritual leadership but also define the nature of personal integrity. Based on these passages, a spiritual leader must be reliable; an effective mother/father, wife/husband; an able teacher, competent, experienced, and blameless from scandal. In a day when the juiciest scandals and stories come not from Hollywood but from high-profile ministries, personal integrity for spiritual leadership must be reemphasized. Moral words without a moral life are hypocritical and hollow.

2. *Self-awareness.* American culture and high-power ministries encourage and thrive on action. Some ministries are so fast-paced there is hardly time to catch a breath. If their leaders do slow down to reflect on life, ministry, interpersonal pain, or the future, they can feel bewildered about their motivations.

It is essential that spiritual leaders periodically set aside time to think about why and how ministry is done and about the impact the spiritual single-adult leader has on his or her followers. The result of this exercise is increased self-awareness.

They not only need to reflect on their impact, behavior, and ministry, but also to develop a small group of trusted peers who will honestly provide feedback on their strengths, weaknesses, gifts, limitations, and on how they are being perceived by others. Without an accountability group, a single-adult leader's ministry will be limited, if not hampered. The individuals who constitute this group must be "safe." That is, they must be individuals outside the ministry with whom single-adult leaders feel free to open their hearts without fear of condemnation or job reprisal.

There is a link between personal integrity and self-awareness. No one is so spiritual that he or she no longer possesses character defects that could undermine ministry. However, awareness of these defects and a small group of supporters who allow the leader to talk about them will enable him or her to gain an increasing sense of victory over the problems. Defects, sins, and temptations named and discussed with others often cease to have power to harm.

Bob was the recognized spiritual leader of one of America's largest single adult ministries. A gifted communicator and able minister, he was asked to speak all over the country. When he traveled, the urge was overwhelming—he simply could not resist adult bookstores and X-rated pay-per-view films in his hotel room. What started as merely sensual curiosity led to a literary, pictorial, and video obsession. He even paid in cash for his pay-per-view movies so they would not appear on his hotel bill. Bob confessed to the Lord time after time in city after city that he would never look at that material again but simply could not stop.

Healing came when Bob told his small support group about his behavior. As he talked through his feelings of guilt, pain, and disappointment, he began to feel healed. They did not judge but prayed for and encouraged him. Although still tempted, the craving within subsided. In Bob's case, his honesty and confession and the support of his group gave him freedom.

3. *Building on strengths and seeking balance.* Single adult ministry is a high-touch, people-oriented concern for individuals. Single adult ministries start with the needs of people, but they do not end there. The biblical goal (or task) is to develop ministries that enable some single adults to come to faith in Jesus, some to grow in faith, and others to become spiritual leaders. However, a tension exists between concern for human need and programmatic ministry. If the single-adult leader becomes so preoccupied with needs, the numerical growth of ministry will be stunted. One person is able to effectively minister to about eighty people. In time a ministry fixated on interpersonal need will become little more than a therapy group. Key biblical mandates—outreach, inclusion, expansion of ministry—will be subverted.

On the other hand, a single-adult minister who is a great programmer, visionary leader, first-class marketer, and inspiring teacher may be perceived as aloof, cold, or uncaring. The programs and attendance may be great, but the commitment to the task may thwart other biblical mandates like compassion, joy, and peace. Often ministries like this subtly reinforce the notion that single adults must look good and appear successful.

A ministry takes on the characteristics of its spiritual leader. No one is so perfect as to consistently balance what leadership theorists call task orientation and people orientation. Both task and people orientation are needed in single adult ministry. One is not better than the other, and effective spiritual leadership may be either task or people oriented. Most people lean to one side or the other. Self-awareness and feedback from those who observe one's leadership are the best sources to determine one's leadership style.

Since few of us are both task and people oriented, and since single adult ministry needs both styles to be effective, the goal of spiritual leadership development is to surround yourself with people of a different style. For instance, a hard-charging task oriented person should build a leadership team of those who are people oriented. Likewise, a warm, loving, caring person, one who is able to "key into" individual hurt, should build a leadership team from task-oriented people.

The apostle Paul's teaching on spiritual gifts is helpful (1 Cor. 12–14). All have some gifts, but no one has all the gifts. When all use their gifts, ministry is dynamic and effective. One key criterion of single adult spiritual leadership is to follow Paul's pattern of understanding the gifts, allowing the utilization of the gifts and building a leadership team that balances task and people orientation.

4. *Bouncing back from failure.* How happy it would be if God never let us fail, if all efforts ended in success. The Bible offers no such guarantees. We will fail—sometimes miserably, despite our best efforts!

Single adult ministry is often about failure. Death, divorce, bankruptcy, job termination, and sickness make us *feel* like failures. Even if they are not our fault, our goals are thwarted and the future seems bleak. To be a spiritual leader means dealing with failure—either in the past, present, or future. For most, the real question is not failure, but whether they will bounce back.

I live in Chicago. Michael Jordan, a player for the Chicago Bulls, is considered by many to be *the* best basketball player ever. But Jordan was cut from his high school basketball team. Only he knows his feelings and how he dealt with this setback. It must have been difficult. I am sure he felt like a failure; nevertheless, he continued to play and today he is at the top.

There is no easy way to get cut or fail. It is not a pleasant experience to be dismissed from a church staff. There is no medicine for the emotional pain and no road map leading to success. However, if the world's best basketball player gets cut and bounces back, there is hope for you.

The apostle Peter had a similar experience of failure. During Jesus' most difficult days, Peter promised to stand by him, regardless of the consequences. But when Jesus was seized and taken to Pontius Pilate and Peter was recognized several times as one of the groupies, in a fit of anger, cursing and swearing, he insisted to an inquirer he did not even know Jesus (Mark 14:71–72). Is there a more egregious example of failure in all history? A close confidant of Jesus denied even knowing him when Jesus was being falsely accused!

There is an interesting twist to this story. When the women went to Jesus' tomb on Easter morning and found he had risen, the angel told them to tell the disciples *and Peter* that he would see them later (Mark 16:7). Peter was singled out because Jesus wanted to make sure that he was not cast aside. He was not washed up. He had a future with Jesus.

On the surface spiritual leadership can appear to be risky business. All will not go smoothly. However, in the midst of failure, the promises of God shine brighter. Peter's life, ministry, and failure show that Jesus grants all a second chance, a new beginning, another opportunity.

Spiritual single-adult leaders will fail. However, the story of Peter is a reminder that failure is not the last word. We have a God of the second chance.

5. *Hanging tough when times are tough.* The biblical word for this is steadfastness, or perseverance. Some would call it guts. It is the ability to hang in there when times are tough. The single-adult spiritual leader knows how tough it gets—people's needs, demands, and crises never end. Add to this the constant complaints, and it is no mystery why the single-adult leader wants to quit. Wanting to quit is a natural and logical feeling. Other spiritual leaders have wanted to throw in the towel too. Since perseverance, or steadfastness, is such an important quality in the New Testament, it would seem that many spiritual leaders of the first century were tempted to quit as well. Scripture gives three reasons not to quit.

First, God is with you, particularly when times are tough. At low points God is especially close to you. Throughout Scripture, God delighted to work in and through those who were at the end of their rope.

Second, spiritual leaders face a spiritual adversary. It should come as no surprise that the spiritual nature of leadership will come into conflict with the demonic. Ministry today follows in the same pattern. As spiritual leaders seek to heal the brokenness of people's lives, they should expect conflict from the source of the brokenness! Conflict is never easy. Warfare is always taxing.

In the midst of spiritual warfare it is easy to become discouraged. However, the conflict and pain may in actuality be a sign that you and your ministry are successfully causing Satan to fall.

Third, quitting now may foreclose on a future victory. No one quits at half-time, regardless of the score. With time left to play, anything may happen. Often dramatic events and unforeseen happenings occur, and all of a sudden the losing team wins!

The moral of the story is—don't quit! There yet may be a dramatic turnaround from the Lord.

32

Developing Volunteers

Rob McCleland

My first recruiting experience as a minister with single adults was a dismal failure. I asked ten gifted and capable young adults if they would consider serving on our leadership team. Eight of them said yes, so I took them on our first leadership retreat. During our first session, I had each of them write down what role they desired to fulfill. A few of them had specific answers, but most said, "I'll do whatever you want me to do." There was only one problem—I didn't know what I wanted them to do. I had no vision, no direction, and no goals for our ministry. Since I didn't know where we were going, I couldn't tell our volunteers how to get there. By God's grace and hard work, I've come a long way since then. I want to share with you a few of the things I've learned along the way.

Your success in singles ministry will be directly proportional to your ability to recruit, equip, and encourage volunteers. That's a strong statement. You may be a paid singles ministry professional, or you may be a layperson who desires to lead. Either way, in singles ministry volunteers are everything.

The goal of this chapter is not to enable you to double your group in the next year or even to lessen your workload. The goal is to help you to build people. No singles ministry will fulfill its potential unless lay volunteers are actively involved in meeting the group's objectives. Therefore it is essential to continually find new volunteers, train them in ministry skills, and encourage them to continue developing in their effectiveness for the kingdom of God.

I've worked with many people who feel competent in completing assigned tasks but feel very uncomfortable trying to involve other people in the completion of the tasks. Don't get me wrong; they have great excuses—"I'm not a people person," "It's easier just to do it myself," "I don't have the time to train other people." They need to be reminded that training lay leaders is top priority. Recruiting and equipping volunteers is challenging, but without them our ministry cannot reach its full potential. I believe our work with volunteers is the most important work we do.

Recruiting

Many single-adult leaders recruit and work with more volunteers in their first year of service than most people do in a lifetime. It is essential to recruit well if you want to have a solid leadership team. There are several prerequisites to actual recruitment. Applying these four biblical principles will give you a head start in recruiting volunteers.

Pray (Luke 6:12–13). Our tendency is to say, "Of course I would pray," and go on to step two. I'm not talking about the kind of prayer that says, "God, please bless our recruiting efforts." The text cited records the only instance where Jesus stayed up all night praying. Why? "When morning came, he called his disciples to him and chose twelve of them, whom he also designated apostles." Earnestly pray. Ask your pastor and your elders to pray for your selection process. Ask the single adult group to seek God's guidance for the group's leadership. Put your request on the church prayer chain or ask that it be noted in the Sunday morning worship folder. Please don't overlook this step. Prayer is your first priority in the recruiting process.

Seek advice from people you trust (Prov. 12:15; 15:22). You may be tempted to choose your friends to serve with you on the ministry team. Friendship is a very poor recruiting criterion. If you recruit only your friends, you will have a difficult time reaching those with whom you do not have a natural affinity. Ask for advice from a well-balanced group of people whom you respect. Be certain to include many opinions from the opposite sex. I've had the privilege of working with many outstanding individuals whom I personally would never have chosen for a position of leadership. Their service on our leadership team is due to answered prayer and wise counsel.

Recruit to specific tasks (Acts 6:2–4). After reading my earlier comments, you can tell I've learned this lesson from experience. It is fine to give a new leader options for his or her leadership role, but the options must be defined by those areas you see as essential to your group's purpose. It is paramount that your group have an overall vision and that you know how each role contributes toward that goal.

Set standards (Titus 1:7–8). A call to leadership is a call to a high standard. This theme runs throughout the Bible. As I develop standards with each new Core Team at the beginning of their term, I have found that they tend to set higher standards for themselves than if I made up the standards. The requirements are fairly consistent from one core group to the next. Our current leaders adhere to the following:

1. They attend all weekly meetings when they are in town.
2. They attend church on Sundays.
3. They tithe.
4. They attend at least half of our group's social events.
5. They meet half an hour before the weekly meeting for prayer.
6. They attend one core group meeting per month.
7. They greet new people before socializing with their friends.

The issue here is not the above seven criteria of a leadership team in one church, but the development of biblically based standards for commitment, modeling, and growth.

Now you are ready for the actual recruitment contact. I personally meet with each person we invite to be on our leadership team. The meeting usually takes place over a meal. I say that we have been praying and seeking guidance for selecting our new leaders, that their name has come up on several occasions, and that I would like to discuss the possibility of their making a commitment to our group. I talk to them about the specific options available and do my best to listen well.

Two common fears I hear during a recruiting contact are fear of failure and fear of time constraints. These two reservations might be stated in any number of ways. When I hear people say they are not sure that they could do a good job or that they lack experience in singles ministry, I realize that they probably have a fear of failure. To counteract this, I take two steps. First, I assure them they will be given every opportunity to use the strengths and abilities God has given them. I also commit to assisting them in acquiring any needed skills. (See "Equipping" section.) The second step is to inform them that they will have significant input in their job description. They will be encouraged to use their personal gifts and creativity to accomplish established goals.

The fear of time constraints seems to be an ever-increasing burden to single adults. During my recruiting contact, I show people a copy of the current standards set by our Core Team. I point out that they are meeting most of the criteria already. I don't belittle the fact that I will be asking them to invest about three additional hours per week in the ministry. Most individuals with leadership capabilities understand this necessity.

Volunteers should always be recruited for a specific time period; they must be given an ending date. Your recruiting efforts will be more successful if you say, "Will you organize our greeters from January until July?" instead of, "Will you lead our greeting ministry?" We have found seven months to be a very effective leadership term. These seven-month periods begin in January and July. The first period begins January 1 and ends August 1. The second period begins July 1 and ends January 31. These overlapping terms allow new leaders to learn their jobs for one month, perform their job for five months, and teach their job to the next leader for one month. We have found it necessary to have two leadership meetings during the transitional months of January and July. This system has enabled many individuals to serve in leadership capacity for one term, while most serve two terms (one year), and several serve three terms or more. This system also allows leaders to take a term off and then return to leadership, often in a different role.

Before leaving the subject of recruiting, let's note one more principle for finding volunteers. What if a visitor comes along who has great potential to hold a future leadership position? I believe these highly motivated individuals are going to plug in somewhere, and I would prefer it to be in our singles ministry. People with great leadership capability need to be challenged as quickly as possible. I have three suggestions that have worked well in the past. First, meet them as soon as possible for a meal or a cup of coffee. Taking this personal interest means a great deal. Second, inform them of a ministry area that needs assistance and ask if they would consider helping out. Third, invite them to come to your meetings for three to five weeks and to note what they observe. Is your group friendly? Do they see areas that could use improvement? Tell them that you would like their fresh perspective. By making simple observations they will assist your group a great deal. Involving capable people early will greatly enhance the retention rate.

Each time we recruit a new Core Team there is a great sense of excitement about the possibilities that lie ahead. New personalities, high energy, fresh creativity, and renewed commitment are wonderful, but the most challenging work lies just ahead. It's one thing to talk about what you are going to do, but now it's time to do it. Equipping your volunteers for service is where the rubber meets the road. In addition to being the most challenging area, it also holds the greatest potential rewards.

Equipping

I've never had a problem getting people to volunteer. My first years in ministry, I recruited dozens of volunteers, and I needed every single one because I lost them as fast as I found them. They were not enjoying completing tasks that brought no rewards or fulfillment. I had not considered how personalities, gifts, and abilities fit into the picture. Now I find *equipping* volunteers to be most challenging and most essential.

Believe it or not, there are still some who say, "Why are you getting others to do all the work? That's why we hired you!" That statement is unbiblical and also disregards sound management principles. We are told in Ephesians 4:12 that we have a responsibility to "prepare God's people for works of service." But why? The rest of the verse holds the answer, "so that the body of Christ may be built up." John MacArthur's commentary on this verse expands this line of thinking:

> No pastor [singles leader], or even a large group of pastors can do everything a church [singles ministries] needs to do. No matter how gifted, talented and dedicated a pastor may be, the work to be done where he is called to minister will always vastly exceed his time and abilities. His purpose in God's plan is not to try to meet all those needs himself but to equip the people given into his care to meet those needs. Obviously the leaders share in serving, and many of the congregation share in equipping, but God's basic design for the church is for the equipping to be done so that the saints can serve each other effectively. The entire church [singles ministry] is to be aggressively involved in the work of the Lord.[1] [Additions mine]

Your group's vision or purpose statement should point the direction that you want to take. Then you equip your people for the journey.

Just prior to some practical application steps for equipping, I want to share two foundational principles. First, we do not do all the work just so others can come to a singles club. Second, we do not try to meet everyone's needs. What we do try to meet is the single's need to serve God in a tangible way. This necessitates our being willing to make new contacts and continually include nonleaders.

The second principle is that if we don't have the leadership, we don't have the ministry. I learned this from Don Cousins, Administration Pastor at Willow Creek Community Church, who writes:

> Ask most leaders on what basis they start a ministry and they'll say, "We see a need, and we try to meet it."
>
> That need is undoubtedly the seed that plants a ministry idea, but we found need alone is an insufficient foundation upon which to build a ministry. We need to start with leadership. Any endeavor that works seems to require a strong leader.
>
> Yet what do we often do in our churches? Well, we have a need, so we round up a committee and . . .
>
> We went four years without a junior high ministry—no youth meetings, no Sunday school, nothing. Parents asked us what we

were doing for junior high kids and we had to gulp and say, "We're looking for a leader, but right now we can't meet your needs."

We looked high and low for qualified junior high leaders—volunteer or paid. The man who eventually became our key leader had proven himself as a lay leader in a high school ministry. Eventually he developed such a zeal for junior highers that he quit his job and joined our staff. He has since built a tremendous junior high ministry.

We could have begun with three or four untried volunteers. But we're convinced it was worth the wait to find the right person and build the ministry properly. It's a lot harder to undo and redo a weak program than to build a quality program from scratch.[2]

In our ministry we stopped having a praise time when we couldn't locate a new leader. Our music had been one of our highlights each week. After the first meeting without music, I got home late and had several messages on my answering machine. Two of them were "volunteering to lead the worship team." It's amazing how God supplies!

To practically equip leaders, we must insure that they have the opportunity to gain skills necessary to accomplish their task. Since people enjoy participating in things they do well, we help our leaders discover their spiritual gifts and then allow them to minister accordingly. One of my favorite Bible passages on this subject is from Exodus.

> Then the LORD said to Moses, "See, I have chosen Bezalel son of Uri, the son of Hur, of the tribe of Judah, and I have filled him with the Spirit of God, with skill, ability and knowledge in all kinds of crafts—to make artistic designs for work in gold, silver and bronze, to cut and set stones, to work in wood, and to engage in all kinds of craftsmanship." . . .
>
> And he [God] has given both him [Bezalel] and Oholiab son of Ahisamach, of the tribe of Dan, the ability to teach others. He has filled them with skill to do all kinds of work as craftsmen, designers, embroiderers in blue, purple and scarlet yarn and fine linen, and weavers—all of them master craftsmen and designers (31:1–5; 35:34–35).

God blesses every group with uniquely talented individuals, but none of us has the ability to equip every volunteer. God has gifted me with leadership skills and the ability to communicate effectively.

I attempt to prepare our volunteers in those areas, but I can't equip them to lead our small groups. You might have to locate someone in your church or in the larger Christian community, but God will supply a person, a resource seminar, or another means to guide someone in their gift and skills development. Another practical step is to have each person on your current leadership team equip a leader for his or her position. As you read earlier, we have a one-month overlap between leadership teams specifically designed for this purpose.

Another way I equip volunteers is to prepare a practical lesson for each month's Core Group meeting. I got this idea from Pastor John Maxwell at Skyline Wesleyan Church in San Diego. Each month he records a teaching lesson from his staff meeting and makes it available to leaders throughout the country.[3] I'll use one of his *Injoy* lessons or one that I develop on my own to teach a ministry principle to our leaders each month. The past few months I have concentrated on teaching them how to reach out to new people in our group. Other topics have included mentoring, giving, and teaching someone to pray.

Encouraging

Recruiting and equipping have us well on the way, but encouraging volunteers is what keeps them there for the long haul.

By nature, I'm a self-starter. While there are probably some strengths to this personality trait, I've discovered several weaknesses. Primarily, I don't tend to include others in what I'm doing. Since I don't need others to come along and give me a pat on the back, I don't naturally encourage others. But I've found volunteers respond more to encouragement than to any other form of motivation. I believe encouragement deals with attitude. Pastors, leaders, volunteers, janitors, and garbage collectors who have a good attitude greatly enhance their work environment. Each of us should do everything possible to see that good attitudes abound in our ministries. A leadership team characterized by many encouragers, and therefore much encouragement, will be infectious to the entire group.

There is too little encouragement in the world. To encourage simply means to give courage. Single adults have fewer possible sources of encouragement than married people, and we have the opportunity to play a very positive and important role in their lives. Be an encourager; give courage to your volunteers!

I challenge you to come up with many creative ways to involve your volunteer leaders in the encouraging process. Your goal is not to have everyone think what a wonderful encourager you are. Your goal is to have encouraged leaders. Practical ways in which our volunteer team encourages each other include:

- Celebrating volunteers' birthdays. Surveys continue to show that a person's birthday is their most important day of the year. Yet most singles go home to an empty house and no presents. Do everything you can to encourage your group to make this a special day.
- Core group date night. One night per month our Core Team goes out on a group date. We've gone out to fancy restaurants, to baseball games, or to someone's home for pizza and a video. On our date night we don't discuss any group business, we just enjoy each other's company. We plan all of our date nights at the beginning of the leadership term so everyone will be able to attend.
- Handwritten notes. When you get your mail, what's the first thing you look for? . . . an envelope that is not computer generated. Personal mail always brightens the day. Each week, jot a note to a different person on your volunteer team.
- Meeting for lunch or breakfast. If possible, meet your volunteers where they work. This will enable you to better understand their work culture, and it will communicate your personal interest in their well-being.
- Publicly acknowledging their efforts. Express your thankfulness in front of the rest of your group. Cite specific instances in which a volunteer has gone "above and beyond."
- Appreciation time. Before a meeting, challenge each leader to talk to at least two people and say, "I appreciate you because . . ." and let him or her fill in the blanks. Encourage them to approach individuals who might not have received much encouragement lately. Note the effect this simple step will seem to have on the rest of your group. People respond to encouragement.

- Rewarding faithful servants. At the end of each leadership term, make sure to recognize those who are leaving your volunteer staff. Give them a token of your appreciation (we give a gift worth about $10 for every six months of leadership service). Prepare some personal comments as you recognize each person.

Recruiting, equipping, and encouraging volunteers is extremely challenging but worth every ounce of effort. Volunteers will look forward to working with those they believe have their best interest at heart. The most gratifying experience I have is to see our volunteers' spiritual gifts and ministry skills blossoming. I'm thrilled when they realize they are being used by God in the lives of other people. Yes, it takes a lot of time, but it's top priority. If you are effective in developing volunteers, you will be effective in ministry. Working with volunteers does not *prepare* for real ministry; working with volunteers *is* real ministry.

Developing Ministry through Spiritual Gifts

Paul R. Ford

The orchestration of the Body is something beautiful to behold. Christ himself selects who will play each instrument. As the conductor, he determines the sections and then decides which parts each will play. Because he is also the composer, the music he writes is perfectly designed to impact the world as well as encourage the members of the orchestra. It's a phenomenon duplicated nowhere else.[1]

Singles who claim to be followers of Jesus Christ are part of a grand scheme that stretches from the whole of the universe down to every individual Christian. "And God placed all things under his [Jesus'] feet and appointed him to be head over everything for the church, which is his body, the fullness of him who fills everything in every way" (Eph. 1:22–23). We are a part of the church, an organic body that is being built together as a place where God lives by his Spirit (Eph. 2:22). Single Christians are instrumental to God's purpose—not because they are single but because they are Christians, crucial players in this phenomenon called the church!

There is more. God is in the process of reconciling the world to himself through Jesus Christ and granting the forgiveness of sins in him (2 Cor. 5:19). Who carries out this incredible ministry of reconciliation? He has chosen Christians. "All this is from God, who reconciled us to himself through Christ and gave us the ministry of reconciliation. . . . We are therefore Christ's ambassadors, as though God were making his appeal through us" (2 Cor. 5:18, 20). Christian single adults, are you ready for your role of reconciliation?

There is still more. Single adults are very much a part of the church, *the body of Christ, where God lives by his Spirit.* They are his ambassadors, those carrying the responsibility to bring Christ to the world. How can this plan involve every Christian on earth? It comes back to that remarkable phrase—the body of Christ. "The body is a unit, though it is made up of many parts; and though all its parts are many, they form one body. So it is with Christ. . . . Now you are the body of Christ, and each one of you is a part of it" (1 Cor. 12:12, 27). There are no exceptions. Single adults have no special exemption!

How do you and I play our parts in this body, in this ministry of reconciliation, in this world scheme where everything will be filled up with the fullness of Jesus Christ? It is through the gifts of the Holy Spirit, spiritual gifts exercised by each Christian. Listen to God's grand strategy as expressed in these words of the apostle Peter: "Each one should use whatever gift [charisma] he [she] has received to serve others, faithfully administering God's grace [charis] in its various forms" (1 Peter 4:10). In his amazing design, the Lord of the universe has chosen to manifest his free gift of grace by empowering us with supernatural gifts of grace.

It is time that we take seriously the task of enabling Christian single adults to discover and use these supernatural gifts of grace. What a broad and forceful impact these Spirit-empowered gifts would have in maturing, building up, and unifying the body of Christ in its mission of reconciliation to the world!

A Biblical Background

God has done a marvelous work in our lives. By his free grace we have been saved: "For it is by grace you have been saved, through faith—and this not from yourselves, it is the gift of God— not by works, so that no one can boast" (Eph. 2:8–9). We not only have been saved, but also creatively prepared to do God's work. "For we are God's workmanship, created in Christ Jesus to do good works" (v. 10). As God's workmanship, we have been equipped with Holy Spirit-empowered spiritual gifts. God calls us out, saves us, and then equips us—all with his grace! "Grace comes from God, [and] takes hold in humans. . . ."[2]

What, then, is a spiritual gift? Basically, a spiritual gift is a supernatural endowment of God's grace given to every member of the body of Christ to glorify Jesus Christ, to equip the body for ministry, and to build the body to unity and maturity in Christ.

Jesus established a plan on how the world would be reached. His followers were empowered and gifted by the Holy Spirit to be part of an organism, the body of Christ; with each part of the body doing its work, that body would multiply throughout the world. Thus Paul commends us, "We have different gifts, according to the grace given us. . . . *let him [her] use it* . . . prophesying . . . serving . . . teaching . . . encouraging . . . contributing . . . leadership . . . showing mercy" (Rom. 12:6–8, emphasis mine). The issue is clear: Get moving, body of Christ! Every Christian single adult: Go after it! Spiritual gifts are already in place to be used by each and every Christian.

It seems that service was always on Paul's heart when talking about spiritual gifts, and for good reason. "Every service . . . finds its meaning in the organic unity of the body of Christ."[3] A spiritual gift for the individual Christian "sets him in a concrete place and equips him for specific service."[4] Do you know any Christian singles who are searching for identity and meaning in the midst of life's crises? The process of discovering and using spiritual gifts will bring meaning to the life of the Christian single adult. A new sense of place and a purpose will invade any person who gets serious about the use of spiritual gifts.

Christian church "body life" now has opportunity to develop itself organically:

> Gifts are awakened, identified, and channeled as believers are intimately tied into the community life of the church. Further, as the range of gifts is awakened and begins to function, these gifts quicken other aspects of the church's life and mission . . .

The functioning of gifts provides much of the dynamism of the church's witness and worship, as well as building community. If we trust God and His working in the body, we will find that the Spirit raises up people with the necessary gifts to make the full ecology of the church function.[5]

Discovering one's spiritual gift focuses each Christian on his or her task in the larger body and initiates the expression of the gift. Everyone ends up fitting in and playing a crucial role designed by God with God's best interests in mind!

When I came to the realization that my primary gifts were exhortation and leadership, I suddenly found myself able to focus in ministry as never before. It helped to clarify what areas of service I could be most effective in, and I found that I bore much more fruit there as well. Ministry was most certainly still a challenge, but my joy in doing God's work grew tremendously. I was playing my part in the ministry of the body of Christ! I did and do have personalized equipment for ministry, given to me by the Spirit of God himself.

If all members of the body of Christ began to experience what I have in spiritual gift discovery and usage, a remarkable thing would begin to happen in the church. "Many people [would] begin to demonstrate the multiplicity of ministries which He [Christ] longs to perform through their united efforts."[6] We would indeed begin to understand that each of us has an instrumental role to play in the ministry of the body of Christ—created, motivated, and empowered by God himself!

Do not overlook one critical element in the giving of gifts by God: Spiritual gifts were given to the individual for the common good. The sum of the individuals makes up the church. If you have any question about this, try going to a symphony concert and listening to a bassoon solo for two hours! It is the total of all parts of the orchestra that produces a unified, joyful sound. It is teamwork all the way, rather than a bunch of individuals doing their own thing.

This interdependent functioning of the members of the body of Christ is the way God orchestrates it: "The body is a unit, though it is made up of many parts; and though all its parts are many, they form one body. So it is with Christ" (1 Cor. 12:12).

Do We Use Our Spiritual Gifts?

> The identifying of gifts brings to the fore . . . the issue of commitment. Somehow if I name my gift, I cannot "hang loose" in the same way. I would much rather be committed to God in the abstract than be committed to Him at the point of my gifts. . . . Life is not the smorgasbord I have made it, sampling and tasting here and there. My commitment will give me an identity.[7]

Many Christian singles simply do not exercise their spiritual gifts, for a variety of reasons. Some do not recognize they have gifts, and most often their leadership does not encourage them to discover their gifts. Others refuse to recognize that they are called to the work of ministry. Still others are lazy in carrying out their Christian body life responsibility. But after the overview we have just been through, what options are there for empowered Christian single adults who have been purposefully gifted by their Maker to play their part? The call is clear. It is now our choice—our chance—to act!

Shall we get serious about body life, the context for a ministry of spiritual gifts? "An active congregation, given the liberty to do so, readily develops the necessary gifts among her members."[8] Single adults using their spiritual gifts are an important segment of natural growth in the larger church.

George Patterson gives us a glimpse of just exactly what this reality looks like. Feel free to substitute the words *Christian* or *single adult* for *elder* or *deacon* in the following text:

> An elder with the gift of teaching interests himself in the details of biblical doctrine. Another with the gift of prophecy is more concerned about the long range implications of theological truth for men [and women] in today's world. . . . Another with the gift of exhortation just wants to get the job done. . . . A deacon with the gift of serving wants better worship facilities. . . . God's Spirit coordinates different people, interests and truths in the one combined ministry of the body of Christ.[9]

Preparing for a Gift-Based Ministry

How are people prepared to play their part? Go back briefly to Ephesians 4:11–12 to again catch God's strategy for every member ministry preparation. "It was he [Christ] who gave some to be apostles, some to be prophets, some to be evangelists, and some to be pastors and teachers, to prepare God's people for works of service." Certain Christians in the body have been empowered to function as primary equippers. They have been prepared by God to prepare the rest of the church to fulfill their ministry roles.

It is important, then, that those in church leadership, both paid staff persons and laypersons, have at least one equipping gift. Scripture acknowledges that the gift to equip is the key ingredient in church leadership. The preparation for using gifts starts with those whom God has designed to equip and train the rest of us!

Step One: Develop Leadership That Releases Authority with Responsibility

Those in primary leadership, often paid staff persons, are the start to a gifts-based ministry for single adults. They must do more than just say they support single adults in ministry. Such leaders must be willing to free single adults to do ministry, without seeking to overly control their actions.

Approaching leadership as a parent rather than an equipper—the more dominant model practiced in the American church—will greatly limit the ministry of singles in the local church in fulfilling its discipling objectives. Equipping leaders are compelled to lead by calling out, training, and releasing adults for their God-anointed ministry. Singles' gifts will not be found and exercised unless equippers allow enough freedom in ministry for gifts to be confirmed and used.

A gifts-based ministry means growth. In a living organism there will be spontaneous movement, change, growth, and multiplication. "Under His [Jesus'] sole command, the Church grows and multiplies in a manner natural to herself."[10] This is not a church growth principle pulled from some marketing manual. Listen again to Paul on growth:

Instead, speaking the truth in love, we will in all things grow up into him who is the Head, that is, Christ. From him the whole body, joined and held together by every supporting ligament, *grows and builds itself up* in love, as each part does its work (Eph. 4:15–16, emphasis mine).

Some Christian leaders fear that if the body of Christ did indeed begin to expand in amazing ways spiritually and numerically, they could not handle it. But it is the Lord who established a ministry of spiritual giftedness, so that the Holy Spirit can provide a balance of shared ministry in the body expressed through spiritual gifts.

Yes, leaders still lead, and submission to that leadership is still essential in any local church ministry. Teachers still teach truth, and pastors protect and guide. But we must acknowledge that the organic process going on is much more complex than any Christian leader can control and direct. God has created an order that grows out of the ministry of the body, as each part does its work. Many are called to equip and lead, thereby enabling others to play their God-ordained part in the serving, administration, leadership, teaching, and discipline of the local church. Consider what could happen in your ministry to and through single adults with such a biblical mind-set!

We are seized with terror, as Roland Allen says, for fear of disorder.[11] But body life is not so called for nothing! With Christ the Head, we will in all things grow up [together] into him, *as each part does its work*, and as *each supporting ligament strengthens the church* (Eph. 4:15–16). When you consider the number of spiritually active, growing single adults available for such grace-empowered work of the Lord, the potential is staggering.

Step Two: Develop Lay Ministry Job Descriptions

If everyone is supposed to play a part, how do we begin to work out that "casting" process? As part of the local body, each active participant is responsible for his or her part of the work of that local ministry. Every single adult has a place to fit in the carrying out of God's call in the church. Perhaps a "ministry prospectus" showing possible ministry opportunities would help people prayerfully determine how they might fit into body life. Make special note in the following suggestions to see whether they can be best carried out just within your single adult ministry or as an overall ministry to the church, where adult singles would be active. Neither is better; wisdom on which direction to take is the issue.

What better way to provide specific information about specific ministry roles in the church than to develop a lay ministry job description notebook! On a half or full page, develop basic information on every church ministry position presently available. Include these particular aspects of the role:

1. Area of ministry (if needed)
2. Job title
3. Three or four sentence summary of the position
4. Time commitment (weekly)
5. Length of service desired or required
6. Whom responsible to (ministry leader)
7. Whom responsible for (group, individuals, if anyone)
8. Special qualifications
9. Helpful spiritual gifts

How does one determine the helpful spiritual gifts for any one particular ministry role? It takes a great deal of study on the individual spiritual gifts, for which many resources are available.[12] Put together a team from your church, including spiritually gifted teachers, to study the gifts and determine several qualities about the function of each gift in action.

Secondly, go over each ministry role and list from two to five gifts that could be very helpful in carrying out the responsibilities for the position. Anticipate some margin of error, since this is not intended to be a scientific procedure. The intent of providing *potentially* helpful gifts will have been met.

As new ministry positions are created according to need, a new job description should be provided and immediately put into the lay ministry job description notebook. New ministries and positions will indeed begin to appear, especially as a process is provided for people to learn to discover and use their spiritual gifts.

After the job descriptions have been assembled into the notebook by category, the gifts can be presented in a simple fashion. In addition to listing gifts as a part of the job description, develop a comprehensive list of ministries by spiritual gift categories. Each ministry would be listed in as many places as gifts listed for that position. For example:

Ministries Suitable for Helping Gifts

Administration
Senior High Youth Coordinator
Vacation Bible School Coordinator

Helps
Information Booth Worker
Youth Club Cook

Leadership
Director of Youth Choirs
Singles Lay Coordinator

Pastoring
Small Group Leader
Stephen Minister (lay pastoral counselor)

Notice one very important factor in the ministry possibilities listed: Many of them are in areas other than single adult ministry. It is absolutely essential that single adults be encouraged to use their gifts beyond the area of single adult ministry! The larger church body needs the vision, the understanding, the availability, and the perspective that single adults can bring to various ministries. If you want your single adult ministry to truly impact your church, then infiltrate the trenches from every angle!

Once the lay ministry job description notebook is done, who will oversee its use and updating? Equally important, what process can be established to assist people to find out their potential gifts and then gain access to the notebook?

Step Three: Develop a Gifts Discovery Class

As you develop several program tools to assist single adults in gift discovery and usage, make certain that you know what you are really helping them to do. Two elements of identity are central in the gift discovery process.

The first is obvious: *spiritual gifts,* as God himself has given (1 Cor. 12:18). Who we are determines what we do. Our identity as Christians is who we are in Christ, and our gifts are clearly a part of our spiritual identity.

The second important area of identity is *burden for ministry*. This is the "where" and "who" that God so often places on your heart with great conviction. You might also call this spiritual want-to. A burden is not just something you ought to do, but something or someone that you really have a desire to pursue or encourage. Though this is not always clearly discernable at first, through prayer, the counsel of godly friends, and your own sense from Scripture, it is clarified. This calling may be to:

1. A certain group of people or an individual:
   a. Muslims in Egypt
   b. Young Christians in the first few months of their spiritual growth
   c. Unwed mothers
   d. Other single-again men and women in the workplace
2. A particular or timely need:
   a. Responding to a crisis situation: i.e., flood, etc.
   b. Caring for persons with AIDS
   c. Assisting children with learning disabilities
   d. Sharing Christ with anyone in crisis
   e. Helping a newly divorced single get through the "crazies" period
3. A specific type of situation or interest:
   a. Teaching church history
   b. Discipling someone on a one-to-one basis
   c. Assisting single moms with child care needs
   d. Serving through medical missions in poor countries

Throughout one's lifetime, the particular burden for ministry or service can change a number of times, but to identify one's burden now can be strategically helpful to ministry focus.

What happens when we clearly define our gifts and our burden? We become organic! That is the fancy way of saying that we become fully available to the Holy Spirit in our ministry focus so he has free reign to work mightily in and through us. We stop doing Christian things and start being Christians, living in the Spirit. Beyond conversion, there is no more important discovery than clarifying these identity issues.

I am free to be me, to find tremendous joy exercising my gifts in the primary contexts for which God has burdened me! I am functioning *as* God wants, *where, and/or with whom* God wants. The apostle Paul did suggest staying single to more freely serve the Lord. What could be more exciting than sold-out, focused, Christian single adults with a clear sense of ministry identity?

One of the easiest and most effective ways to help individuals discover and use their spiritual gifts is to provide a learning context that has concrete points of application in ministry placement. People may be drawn to the process to learn about their gifts, when in reality the true result will be the actual testing of gifts in a ministry setting.

With a team of laypersons I have had the opportunity of developing a spiritual gifts process effective for use in a classroom setting or in small groups. Hundreds of people have gone through the process over the past five years, and the results are fascinating:

- 35 percent of the people found confirmation of ministries in which they were already involved.
- 35 percent either got out of ministries in which they did not fit and into new areas by gifts or entered ministry roles for the first time through the gifts process.
- 30 percent took no action following their spiritual gifts interview.

The two biggest pluses of the process were first, the discovery that no is a spiritual word, that people do not have to participate in every ministry role they are asked to consider; and second, a discovery of greater joy, fulfillment, and fruit with the accurate ministry placements.[13]

The purpose of such a class is to move individual Christians from a basic understanding of the Holy Spirit into a biblical rationale for discovering and using one's spiritual gifts. The six weeks of spiritual gifts presentations are done by students to model body life in the very process of the class. The class is taught by both pastoral staff and laypersons—again for the purpose of modeling body life in the process. Pastors are not the only gifted ones.

Although the class can be taught in fewer than twelve weeks, one value of a ten- or twelve-week class is that it demands high commitment over an extended period of time. Commitment to a gifts discovery process may lead to commitment in a future ministry role for confirmation of those gifts.

Each of the nine assignments included in this gift discovery process is personally focused on an individual's spiritual background, ministry experience, potential gifts, and burdens for ministry, among other tools. The nine tools are invaluable resources both in preparation for and during the actual interview with the adviser. No student may go through the class without an interview with an adviser at the end of the process, nor can anyone be interviewed without completion of all the assignments.[14]

Step Four: Develop a Gifts Discovery Small Group

While the classroom process is aimed at helping the individual find his or her role in the larger body, the small group context provides a totally different dynamic for spiritual gift discovery. In fact, the small group context may well be the most powerful setting for spiritual gifts discovery. The established group has its own dynamics:

- The group is a place where one studies God's Word and functions in accountable relationships with others (two-thirds of discipleship triangle).
- Because of the already established relationships, the small group is a "safe" place for testing gifts.
- Who would be better qualified to affirm potential gifts than a small group leader with whom a solid relationship has already been established?
- The small group is a living unit of the larger body of Christ. People not only have a safe, natural context in which to discover their gifts, but they also have the dynamic of the Holy Spirit already present in the group, seeking to bring unity and build the body. Want to get into a prime context to discover your gifts? Get into a small group.

The small group can establish its own gifts discovery process in its group context or can go through the classroom process as a group and focus on class issues at their meetings. When it comes to confirming gifts, the small group may use its own structure to enable some to find their gifts. Here are some sample ministry roles that provide contexts in which giftedness could be discerned:

1. Assistant leader (potential gifts of leadership, pastoring, exhortation)
2. Prayer logkeeper (intercession, service, helps)
3. Teacher (teaching, knowledge)
4. Hospitality host (hospitality, service)
5. Pastoral supports (pastoring, mercy)

The small group leader may function as an enabler for placing people in ministries in the group itself (with counsel from the group), in the larger church body, or beyond.

Step Five: Develop a Spiritual Gifts Ministry Team

Spiritual gifts and specific ministries need to be brought together. The spiritual gifts ministry team helps coordinate the job description notebook and an understanding of the ministries of the local church. They serve individual Christians who are searching for their ministry identity out of the gifts discovery class or small group process.

Team members are the specialists: the consultants for small groups, the class facilitators for discussions on the individual spiritual gifts, and the interviewers for those involved with either type of gift discovery ministry (classroom or small group). Note that different advisers need varying gifts to effectively function in one or more of the potential advising roles.

Since your team may need training, I want to suggest some resources for this. Both *Networking* and *Spiritual Gifts Implementation* by Robert and Janet Logan provide solid models for training spiritual gift advisers or consultants. I also suggest *The Spiritual Gifts Data Base*, an invaluable resource for both ministry leaders and spiritual gift advisers. It makes available to ministry leaders and advisers the following:

- Information on individual's giftedness, ministry interests, and history of involvement

- Information on all church lay ministry job descriptions
- Ease of entering data and maintaining information by laypersons, through menu-driven software
- Timely processing and printing of sorts and searches
- A design for matching individual giftedness with gifts associated with lay ministry job descriptions

Data gathered has shown that people who are asked to consider a ministry because of giftedness respond positively at twice the rate of those asked through arbitrary contact. Since gifts are a part of ministry identity, such high results make sense. This gifts approach to ministry lets church leaders invite people to serve out of giftedness rather than from guilt or pressure. This means that body life can function from healthy motivation.

Using a Gifts-Based Ministry

Put the newly found gifts to use in different areas.

Educational ministries. The class can be a core class in your singles educational curriculum or a part of the larger church. Other classes that can be developed along this same focus include a series called "A Deeper Look at . . . " that would cover definition, key biblical passages, characteristics, liabilities, and context for use of each gift.

Another course to consider is a follow-up course to the gifts discovery class, honing in on burden for ministry issues, continuing education on all the gifts, and having an in-depth interview with a spiritual gifts adviser.

Small groups. Group ministry projects designed by each group would represent how the Lord had burdened them as a whole for ministry or service. The spiritual gifts adviser could come alongside in a consultant role.

General ministry possibilities. Specific ministries could be developed from some people's spiritual gifts. For example, a ministry of evangelism could grow up in a singles ministry where several had the gift of preaching or teaching. The discipling of new adult education teachers would most certainly be done by teachers and exhorters presently involved in that ministry. Our church is developing a specialized ministry for those with the gift of discernment of spirits. The possibilities are endless!

New ministries. When singles have the chance and freedom to respond to the burden and gifts that God has laid on their hearts, a door to new opportunities opens wide. One can expect that new ministry ideas will come out of spiritual gifts interviews, out of the ministry identity that the Lord has placed in some individuals. In our church, over a five-year period with over 400 people interviewed, four new ministries were developed by people with distinctly different burdens and gifts.

Outreach possibilities. Here are some ways to allow the Great Commission to affect your thinking and actions while people seek to discover and use their spiritual gifts.

1. Be particularly sensitive to those who have a burden to develop a program that has tremendous evangelistic implications.
2. Encourage the development of ministries targeted to reach unbelievers and new Christians, such as a specialized ministry to mothers with young children or a Christian Big Brother/Big Sister program, especially considering the overwhelming needs of children from single-parent families today.
3. Team up a gifted evangelist with a person who has the gift of hospitality for a short-term evangelistic Bible study. The combination will bear fruit in conversions.
4. Effectively train gifted exhorters to share their faith as they invest in the lives of unbelievers. Exhorters are proving to be particularly effective witnesses for Christ in their verbal sharing.
5. Help people whose dominant gifts are more service-oriented to realize that their most effective investment in unbelievers will often be with serving, rather than with a verbal witness. Finding who they are in Christ by ministry identity will make their nonverbal witness be filled with the Holy Spirit. They will indeed *be* witnesses!

"A church that faithfully uses its gifts in the Spirit's power experiences the joy of great unity, love and fellowship in ways that no amount of human ability, planning or effort can produce."[15] This sounds like a plan of action for single adult ministries today!

34

Developing Ministry with Women

Pamela Dodge

Because many churches all across the country are now aware of the great need to reach out and minister to single adults, such ministries are increasingly a part of church life. Pastors, elders, deacons, and church members are increasingly sensitive to single adults. But many churches have failed to take into account the lives of single adult women and their changing roles in our society. Therefore, they have been slow in adapting ministries and programs to include this large segment of our society.

Insensitivity will also lead to a disregard of a large segment of the church's own human resources—women who can meet the many needs within the church community as well as fulfill the Great Commission. This task is large enough in itself to involve every member of the church for a lifetime.

While the church's message should never change, its methods and strategies must consider societal needs. Many women are justifiably becoming frustrated because many churches ignore the ministry of women at any level.

Stephanie has never married and is in her early thirties. After attending a church for almost a year, she decided it was time to get involved. A corporate executive in a large company and holding a Ph.D. in business administration, she is a gifted manager and possesses people skills. But when she approached one of her pastors about her becoming involved in the church, he directed her to the church nursery. She served there for about six months but found that she was not especially suited to this task and so she quietly resigned. She never volunteered to serve again.

Mary was a young Christian and divorced mother of two small children who was forced to work in order to provide for her family. She desired very much to grow in her relationship to Christ and to enjoy the fellowship of other young mothers. But when she tried to get involved in a small group study within her church, she found that all such events were held during the day while she was working. As a result, Mary was never able to get involved.

Churches must stop ignoring the spiritual giftedness of women. Today's highly educated, working, single woman wants to serve in ways that offer her the chance to make a significant contribution.

Women represent a valuable resource for ministry and should be given greater opportunities to serve within the church. No issue in the church seems to raise more questions and tempers than that of women in Christian ministry. It is not my purpose to argue a particular theological viewpoint. Questions concerning the ordination of women and limitations on women in the area of teaching are beyond the scope of this chapter. My purpose is to show that the church must increase its sensitivity and adapt its programming in order to meet the changing needs of today's woman. Churches need to actively explore ways to involve women, particularly single women, on a more meaningful level.

Three Points of Agreement

If the church as a whole is to progress in this area of women in ministry, it must acknowledge that differences do exist and will continue to exist and then help people to respect one another in those differences. The church also needs to look for solutions at common points of agreement. What are some of these common points? It seems appropriate to highlight briefly three common biblical teachings on which most churches do agree.

1. *Men and women are of equal value to God.* Galatians 3:28 says, "There is neither Jew nor Greek, slave nor free, male nor

female, for you are all one in Christ Jesus." When we make single adult women feel that they are misfits in the church, we have failed to accept them as created in God's image. Genesis 1:27 tells us: "God created man in his own image, in the image of God he created him; male and female he created them." Applying this passage practically means that there is a sense in which both the male and the female working together as a team reflect God's image completely. A church that encourages only male involvement in specific areas does not fully reflect his image.

2. *Men and women are interdependent.* First Corinthians 11:11 states: "In the Lord, however, woman is not independent of man, nor is man independent of woman." That means we need each other. Studies have shown that men and women often think and view situations differently. Neither is right or wrong in itself, just different. But when both perspectives are brought together, a more complete picture is likely to appear. Men and women need to minister together in order to achieve a truly balanced perspective.

3. *God has equipped every believer with spiritual gifts,* according to 1 Corinthians 12:7–11 and Ephesians 4:11–16. In 1 Peter 4:10 we read: "Each one should use whatever gift he has received to serve others, faithfully administering God's grace in its various forms." Spiritual gifts are not given just to men. The use of spiritual gifts is essential to one's completion in Christ. When women are not allowed to use their gifts, they fail to grow as they should. In the past, being denied opportunities to serve, many women sought to use their gifts outside of the local church. Also, women have been drawn to the mission field to be able to serve the Lord with their unique capacities.

Meeting the Ministry Needs

Many churches today have tried diligently to understand and develop new marketing strategies in order to meet the needs of people within their communities. Yet often these same churches have failed to understand the feelings, needs, and strengths of single women who are within their ministries.

What are the needs of single women? First of all, they have a strong need to feel significant. They need to understand their identity as Christians and to see how they fit into the body of Christ. The lack of a family is not going to keep a single woman from a promotion in her profession. When the church offers few opportunities for women to be involved, it is not uncommon for the career-oriented single woman to seek that feeling of significance and value in the workplace rather than the church.

Single women also have the need to discover and utilize their spiritual gifts and God-given abilities. Understanding and using their gifts helps them answer the question of who they are and how they fit into the body of Christ. Gifts are given to be used, and when these gifts lie dormant, whether in men or women, the entire church suffers. We dare not ignore the immense potential of the spiritual gifts that women possess; we must encourage them to exercise these gifts and abilities. As a result, the church as a whole will profit.

What are some practical suggestions and possibilities for single women to be more involved in the church? There are many creative ways they may serve. Ephesians 4:11–13 reveals God's purpose for the church: "It was he who gave some to be apostles, some to be prophets, some to be evangelists, and some to be pastors and teachers, to prepare God's people for works of service, so that the body of Christ may be built up until we all reach unity in the faith and in the knowledge of the Son of God and become mature, attaining to the whole measure of the fullness of Christ." When we understand that God designed the church to be an equipping agency, as opposed to a programming agency, we will be more likely to include women in all aspects of service within the church. In fact, it will be hard to exclude them, because all gifts will be needed in order to complete the tasks.

Women are able to serve effectively in any area within the church. Often women are quicker to volunteer and are more willing to serve than men. Those with administrative gifts and people skills will be an asset to any committee or ministry. Women often have a different perspective, and this allows for a greater insight and perhaps new approaches to tasks.

Many women have the gift of teaching, and there are varied ways of allowing them to exercise this gift. They can lead or co-lead small group studies. They can teach Sunday school classes. Workshops and seminars that utilize their own particular background and strengths are other ways to involve them. For example, if a woman works as a personnel manager in a business, she could teach a seminar on writing résumés or how to interview for a job. Training and skills seminars for various jobs within the church also allow women to use their gift of teaching. A woman who is a schoolteacher by profession might be willing to lead a one-day training seminar for potential Sunday school teachers. (Many people do not volunteer to take on a task because they feel that they are not adequately trained.)

Many women have the gift of hospitality. They enjoy entertaining and reaching out to others, including strangers. They would love to be asked to greet newcomers at the door or to host a dinner during the week for these people. Holidays can be lonely times for many, and some women enjoy overseeing holiday programs such as Christmas or Thanksgiving dinners. Fellowship activities within most churches are usually delegated to women. Many women are very relational and love to be involved in this capacity. But they also need encouragement; their hard work should be acknowledged and not taken for granted. They are part of the larger ministry—not just hosting a dinner, but reaching out and ministering to newcomers.

For those who have writing skills, writing Sunday school curricula, plays, dramas, and so forth uses this gift. Many churches put out newsletters or bulletins, and women can find satisfaction helping out in these areas.

For those with the gift of evangelism, opportunities abound. Women in the work force can reach out to their fellow employees by inviting them to Bible studies, seminars, or concerts in the church.

Mission opportunities are another way women may be involved. Many churches send out summer mission teams. In many urban centers of the world, as well as in most Muslim and other patriarchal cultures, women and men live in separate worlds. The only way the women of that culture will be reached is by other women.

Every area of the church needs to use women who possess the gift of leadership. They should be present on long-range planning committees, heading up task forces, giving overall direction to any number of programs based on their particular gifts. A woman manager who gives direction to a group of employees at her job could also lead people within the church, perhaps on the single adult council or in taking charge of a retreat.

Counseling is another area where women are gifted and can be included in ministry opportunities. Many churches are not large enough to support their own counseling center, but they can use those with a degree and background in counseling to help meet individual crisis needs. Many churches offer telephone ministries where people may call day or night. Single women could help in this area.

A number of women today have financial and accounting skills and gifts. They should be included in this area of ministry as well.

This list of ways to utilize the gifts of women is by no means complete. We could add prayer ministries, community service opportunities, discipleship, driving the church bus, and many others. I hope it has stimulated your thinking on creative ways to involve women more meaningfully within the life of the church.

Women are greatly needed now in these crucial days when our world cries out for every believer to participate in the great harvest. Jesus illustrates this truth in the parable of the vineyard (Matt. 20:1–16). In this parable a landowner went out five different times to hire workers for the vineyard. He asked those in the last group, "Why have you been standing there all day long doing nothing?"

They responded, "Because no one has hired us." They were then invited to join in the harvest, and they were given the same wages as all those who had worked all day. We are not told why these workers had not been hired. Some have speculated that perhaps they were women.

For women, the hour is indeed late and the Lord is calling them to serve. Jesus' concern is reaping the harvest. And the time is now for women to join the work.

35

Developing a Leadership Team

Jeffrey R. King

In his book *Holy Sweat*, Tim Hansel begins his chapter on teamwork with a terrific anecdote from the life of Jimmy Durante, one of the great entertainers of a generation ago. As the story goes, Durante was asked to be a part of a show for World War II veterans, and he agreed on one condition: Since his schedule was so busy he would be able to do only a short monologue, after which he would need to leave for his next engagement. The show's director happily agreed.

When Jimmy appeared on stage, he went through his monologue, but then stayed on. As the applause grew louder with each succeeding joke, he stayed longer and longer. After thirty minutes he took a last bow and left the stage. The director stopped him and said, "I thought you had to leave after a few minutes. What happened?"

Jimmy replied, "Yes, I did need to leave, but let me show you the reason that I stayed. You can see for yourself. Look down there." In the front row there were two men, each of whom had lost an arm in the war—one his right arm and the other his left. But together they were able to clap, and that's exactly what they were doing, as they were thrilled to see and hear Jimmy Durante perform.

That's teamwork! By definition it only takes two to make a team! The principle that two people effectively working together can achieve greater results is emphasized in Ecclesiastes, "Two can accomplish more than twice as much as one, for the results can be much better. If one falls, the other pulls him up; but if a man falls when he is alone, he's in trouble . . . three is even better, for a triple-braided cord is not easily broken" (4:9–12, TLB).

The creative genius Buckminister Fuller explains in his book *Synergetics* that it is very possible for "one plus one to equal four if we put our efforts together in the same direction." The word *synergy* means "the sum total is greater than the total of the separate parts." It is derived from the two Greek words *erg* and *syn* meaning "work" and "together" and implies that a team can be far more powerful and effective than any of the separate members working individually. It has been estimated that if we could get all the muscles in our bodies to pull in one direction, we could lift over twenty-five tons!

The business sector has also caught on to the team concept. Although many people think the use of self-directed workteams is a recent import from Japan, the fact is, teams were pioneered in Britain and Sweden during the 1950s. Volvo is now so advanced that in their new Uddevala plant, work teams assemble entire cars. In the United States, Procter & Gamble, along with other forward-thinking companies, implemented workteams in the early 1960s with very profitable results. The list of major companies using self-directed work teams includes Boeing, Caterpillar, Champion International, Cummins Engine, Digital Equipment, Ford, General Electric, General Motors, LTV Steel, and Tektronix, to name just a few.[1]

When we turn to the Bible for examples of team leadership, we find no shortage. In Exodus 3 God told Moses to talk to the elders of Israel. These men were a team set apart by God for judicial and governing purposes, to rule his people in the context of a body. Hundreds of years later Boaz, in his action as the kinsman redeemer, went to the elders in order to have them witness a land transaction.

Jesus Christ clearly believed in the principles of teamwork when he chose twelve men to follow him closely in a Rabbi-disciple relationship. He subsequently divided that twelve-member team into six two-member teams for a specific task (Mark 6:7–13). And then James, John, and Peter emerged as a kind of executive team within that apostolic band.

This same theme of team leadership permeates the pages of the Book of Acts—the apostles in Jerusalem, the various missionary teams consisting of Paul, Barnabas, Mark, Silas, Timothy, and Luke, the appointment of elder teams with the establishment of every new church. Throughout the Old and New Testaments, we repeatedly find models of team leadership. They are the norm, not the exception.

The Benefits of Team Leadership

Rod Wilson of Ontario Theological Seminary has outlined five key reasons for a team leadership approach in ministry endeavors.

1. *Team leadership allows for the contribution of varied individual gifts.* Every team has players of differing traits, strengths, talents, and abilities. When the team is working well together, there is a certain chemistry and magic about it. Each member knows where he or she fits and why. But this presupposes team members who complement each other's strengths. One of the most subtle dangers is a leadership team comprised of similarly gifted people who are merely echoes of each other. They may double their strengths, but they also double their weaknesses. Leadership teams must be very careful to round out and complete their team, rather than simply extend themselves.

2. *Team leadership allows for sharing wisdom.* Our contemporary culture tends to exalt individuals, isolated and autonomous, who have expertise and skill in a certain field. This is a different notion than we see in the Scriptures. The Bible places more emphasis on the principle given in Proverbs 11:14: "For lack of guidance a nation falls, but many advisers make victory sure." Team leadership allows for the blending of unique backgrounds, experience, and approaches to creative problem-solving.

3. *Team leadership allows for mutuality.* Much has been written about the inherent faults of pyramidal management structures. In this system, power resides at the top in one person. The sense of mutuality and reciprocity is lost since one person has control. This style of leadership risks arrogance, power, pride, and poor decision-making. In team leadership, however, mutual decision-making allows for a solid base of unity. Group decisions arise out of respect and a shared struggle for truth as the best course of action instead of domination and power.

4. *Team leadership allows for representation.* A team approach to leadership creates a healthy environment for the representation of many ideas and concerns. Team members will undoubtedly have different circles of constituents. As each listens carefully and reports back to the leadership team, a free flow of open communication is encouraged. People will feel that their needs are heard, and the leadership team will be able to respond to those legitimate needs.

5. *Team leadership allows for accountability.* Almost without exception, the Christian leaders who have fallen in recent years had no real accountability to a team nor challenge from someone close. Many people do not like or understand the concept of accountability and seek to avoid it. However, individuals, and consequently teams, do their best work under clear terms of accountability. A team built on mutual trust, respect, and a passion for the mission at hand will hold each other accountable for group and individual achievement. They will interrelate in such a way so as to sharpen and encourage one another to greater heights. Teams that take accountability seriously are always winners![2]

The Principles of Team Building

Like most things in life, leadership teams don't just happen. They are the direct result of people who believe in the values of the team concept and deliberately organize their leadership structures this way. Team building is an ongoing process and is never really completed. Healthy teams keep on changing, maturing, and adapting. While the process is fluid and dynamic, it is based on certain principles.

The Selection Principle

By far the most common question about teams is, "How do we form a team and then replace its members over time?" Leadership teams can be put together many different ways, and some are better than others.

First, single adult ministries need gender-balanced leadership; male *and* female representation brings greater insight, integrity, and complementarity. An even balance of men and women is the optimum.

Second, it's a maxim that leaders are the ones most capable of choosing other leaders. Although this idea flies in the face of our culturally created democratic bias, sheep never choose their shepherds. Current leaders need to be on the constant lookout for potential new leaders. They need to be assessing the gifts and leadership abilities of others, evaluating the team's weaknesses and needs, and nudging people toward leadership responsibilities on a regular basis. Whatever the selection methodology chosen, current leaders need significant input. In a very true sense the future of any ministry depends directly on the leadership selection process, whether it be a formal nominating committee or an informal network. The success or failure of the group rides on its leadership.

Third, leadership selection must be based on qualification, not simply on availability or personality. Unfortunately, many churches create leadership "committees" with a certain number of "slots" to fill. Then, one of two things happens: Either the ballot becomes a popularity contest with a winner and loser for each open seat; or worse, the first person to volunteer is offered the position, regardless of qualification. Both compromise the integrity of a true leadership team. The New Testament sets high standards for those who seek to lead (see 1 Tim. 3; Titus 1). Leaders must be chosen thoughtfully and deliberately. Their Christian character, conduct, and abilities need to be evaluated. Only after careful examination should a person be asked to serve in a leadership capacity.

Fourth, we must recognize that most single adult ministries are fast moving and rapidly changing, with a high turnover of people. Instead of despairing, we need to accept this phenomenon and capitalize on its strengths. This means a constant flow of potential leaders. In some ministries, leadership may change as often as every six months by design or natural movement, and that's OK. The challenge is to continually discover and develop new leadership.

The Niche Principle

Great teams are made up of players who understand themselves and their own unique role on the team and also understand the functions and roles of their teammates. Teams break down when team members misunderstand roles and responsibilities. Teams are comprised of individuals who occupy a special place and perform in a special way, in a kind of niche. Each is in the right "spot" for the benefit of the enterprise. It is like saying, "You do what nobody else could do." Members are neither independent nor codependent, but *interdependent!* Understanding those personal niches humanizes the work and makes participants feel special. People need to feel needed, and a philosophy of team leadership capitalizes on that basic need.

Teams are different, but roles are similar. Here are some of the more common team roles:

- The Sparkplug—the one who makes things happen
- The Analyst—the rational deliberator
- The Dreamer—the optimistic idealist
- The Peacemaker—the conflict resolver
- The Engineer—the project organizer
- The Traffic Cop—the project controller
- The Friend—the developer of social interactions
- The Helper—the cooperative supporter
- The Maverick—the nontraditionalist
- The Bridge-Builder—the one who reaches out to other team members

This is not to say that every team must have each niche, but that people tend to fill these general roles. Perhaps you identified your basic role or immediately placed names beside each niche as you read the list. That's fine. The purpose is not to create a psychological personality test, but for everyone to be aware of, accept, and affirm each member's unique and valuable contribution.

The Mission Principle

What transforms a group of people into a team is *a sustained commitment to a common goal with a purpose.* This is usually called a mission, a dream, a vision, or a master plan. It needs to be simple, memorable, inspirational, biblical, and profound and must be capable of energizing and motivating because it is the flag around which the troops rally. Each person on the leadership team must know, understand, and embrace the mission statement since it sets the overall direction and tone for the ministry. The formation of this statement should be the first order of business of a newly formed ministry or leadership team; later, it becomes the baton that is handed off to each succeeding leadership team.

Specific and measurable objectives grow out of the vision at regular intervals, but the controlling mission rarely changes. It is the stabilizing, unifying factor characteristic of successful long-term ministries. The statement must be repeated often, both verbally and in print, so as to be indelibly impressed on the minds of all. Recently, at a very large community church in the Southwest, the senior pastor asked the members at a congregational meeting, "What is the mission of our church?" With no prompting whatsoever, 500 people responded in unison, "To bring people to maturity in Christ." That's a clear, concise, memorable mission statement.

The Ownership Principle

Closely associated to the mission principle is the ownership principle. The more team members participate in setting the practical objectives that operate the mission, the more they will personally own and commit to the dream and its goals. Team members feel a sense of accomplishment when they participate in the goal-setting process and become firmly cemented as a goal-sharing team.

The Coach Principle

Who can imagine a team without a coach? Actually, every team has someone who functions as the coach or player-coach, whether recognized or not. In single adult ministries that person may be the president of the singles group, the director of singles ministries, the pastor to singles, an associate pastor, or even the senior pastor.

What do coaches do? Well, they don't usually play in the game now, but they have played the game before. Their purpose is to teach others to play. Coaches demonstrate skills, develop team spirit, recruit team personnel, design team strategy, motivate, discipline, and do whatever is necessary to prepare the team to play the game. Coaches discover hidden potential and put it to use, create a winning environment, and deploy the team to the field in order to win the battle! In short, coaches teach the basics, are the keepers of the vision, give inspiring pep talks, encourage team-work, develop talent, give credit for success, and take responsi-bility for failure.

Elton Trueblood, one of the foremost evangelical theologians and intellectuals of this century, in commenting about the anal-ogy of coaching and the equipping ministry of the pastor in Eph-esians 4:11–13, wrote: "The glory of the coach is that of being the discoverer, the developer, and the trainer of the powers of other men. But this is exactly what we mean when we use the biblical terminology about the equipping ministry."[3]

Tom Landry, the coach of the Dallas Cowboys football team for twenty-nine years, is often quoted as saying, "I have a job to do that is not very complicated but is often difficult: to get a group of men to do what they don't want to do so they can achieve the one thing they have wanted all their lives."

Another legendary coach, Paul "Bear" Bryant, of the University of Alabama, reportedly said:

> I'm just a plowhand from Arkansas, but I have learned how to hold a team together, how to lift some men up, how to calm down others, until finally they've got one heartbeat together, as a team. There's just three things I'd ever say:
> "If anything goes bad, I did it.
> If anything goes semi-good, then we did it.
> If anything goes real good, then you did it."
> That's all it takes to get people to win football games for you.

A successful single adult leadership team must have a coach who knows how to coach.

The Trust Principle

Team members who share a common vision, who personalize the ministry process through ownership, and who accept one another in biblical agape love come to deeply trust one another. Trust is the glue that binds the team through thick and thin. A member cannot effectively contribute, even in a small way, if ani-mosity and distrust prevail, for it will create further rifts and the formation of cliques. Each team member must come to trust the role abilities of fellow teammates.

The Interaction Principle

Teams have all the characteristics and interpersonal dynamics of a small group. They move through predictable phases and cycles from formation to dissolution. The same team, with virtually the same personnel, may be extremely effective at one time and in disarray later. Much of the success or failure of a team can be attributed to the quantity and quality of interaction between team members. Teams just can't function well when they don't meet to practice. There must be regular face-to-face exposure between team members. The more they see and get to know one another, the more they bond. Bonded people share deep needs and dream great dreams together.

Bonding is one of the most important and yet least stressed needs of solid team building. Some single adult ministries devote up to 60 percent of their operational budget to leadership development retreats and seminars. Getting the leadership team away for an intensive half day, day, weekend, or even week is not only one of the greatest experiences they will ever have, but also is one that will yield the greatest long-term return in the ministry.

The Submission Principle

People who submit to one another in a servant-leadership style elevate the goals and good of the team above the individual. This puts the ministry's vision and goals at the forefront, where it can capture the team's attention and energy. Deep loyalty to the team fosters respect and appreciation for the other team members, confidence in the team and its abilities as a whole, and also personal fulfillment and enjoyment. Team members enthusiastically claim, "I get to play on the greatest team in the world and play the position I want to play!"

Teams are very fragile and can break apart for minor reasons. Petty rivalries can grow to immense proportion if left unchecked. Although there may be a communication problem, more often the root issue is a lack of genuine humility. An attitude of mutual submission keeps one person from taking the credit when the *team* deserves recognition.

The Spirit Principle

Up to this point in our discussion nearly everything that's been said could be true of a leadership team in almost any setting. The social sciences have done extensive research into these leadership issues and have provided us with a solid base of understanding. But Christian ministry adds another dimension—a spiritual one. Leadership teams engaged in ministry endeavors to God's glory are supernaturally empowered by the Holy Spirit. His power generates a new level of vision, unity, and sacrifice.

The Third Person of the Trinity not only indwells each team member but also offers divine guidance. We have to realize that God is more concerned about the success of the single adult ministry in our location than we are! It's his glory and reputation that are at stake! When leadership team members get hold of this principle, they are both freed to minister effectively and are filled with the power necessary to accomplish the task at hand. Then love flows, giving testimony to the world of Christ's love as they love one another (John 13:34–35).

Gauging Team Health

In *The Well-Managed Ministry: Discovering and Developing the Strengths of Your Team*, Philip Van Auken offers some insightful observations about the health of teams. Health is much more than merely the absence of sickness; team health rarely stagnates— it is either improving or deteriorating over time. Teamwork is based on interpersonal relationships—the ability of people to interact productively and harmoniously. Therefore, when interpersonal relationships deteriorate, so does team health. Team coaches and leaders must constantly be sensitive to the warning signals or "handwriting on the wall" of interpersonal problems developing on a team. The five most common warning signals are:

1. Poor communication—team members fail to understand one another; focus is on talking rather than listening: verbal hostility, etc.
2. Sloppy implementation—"the right hand doesn't know what the left hand is doing" syndrome.

3. Avoidance—members show a pattern of avoiding disagreement, avoiding accountability, or avoiding one another.
4. Chronic dissatisfaction—certain members acquire a negative, pessimistic, or critical spirit that casts a shadow of gloom over team activities.
5. Loss of trust—team members doubt one another's motives, submerge agendas, and begin to question the ministry vision.

These five items do not actually cause team problems; they are merely the symptoms of the disease at work: spiritual immaturity. "Spiritually immature people inevitably encounter difficulties working together, because they often act and move out of self-interest and pride."[4] This, of course, brings us back to the principle of submission.

Van Auken's penetrating analysis continues as he suggests seven key ingredients of team health that move in unison, either undergirding teamwork or unraveling it. He says that team health may be gauged by the team's capacity to

- set and internalize goals. When team vision excites members, they readily "buy into" ministry goals they help set.
- make decisions. Consensus in the decision-making process is easily reached because the goals are so firmly shared.
- implement decisions. Smooth implementation of goals results from their ownership.
- resolve conflict. Because trust runs high on healthy teams, conflict is easily resolved.
- change. Change is seen as an opportunity for progress, since members want what is best.
- maintain accountability. Accountability is seen as positive.
- satisfy team members. Healthy teams have satisfied members who feel needed, unique, productive, and appreciated.[5]

Team Renewal

By this point you may be greatly encouraged about the strength of your leadership team, mildly upset, or just plain "blown away."

Assuming that you have some kind of leadership team currently in place, let's turn our attention to practical suggestions for its renewal.

Recruit and recognize the team coach. If the coach of your single adult ministry leadership team is not yet identified or recognized, start there. Use the proper channels and decision-making processes of your particular church. It may mean going to a pastor, a board, or the singles themselves. If *you* are the recognized coach already, then begin coaching!

Go back to basics. Have the leadership team spend a great deal of time defining and clarifying the team mission and operating goals. Current research indicates that *unity of purpose* is the chief distinguishing feature of an outstanding team. Try a one-day strategic planning retreat at a nice location in order to spur creative juices. Encourage leaders to dream great dreams; nothing is too big for God! Ask yourselves:

> If God absolutely assured us of success in this singles ministry, what would it look like?
>
> What hinders us from seeing that success come true?
>
> What do we need to do this month, this year, the next three years to bring this about?

Seek unity and pray about your vision. Word the mission in concise terms, put it in print for everyone to see, and keep it in front of you at all times. It is your biblically based purpose; treat it as such.

Clarify roles within your leadership team. Find and use some good role clarification exercises. Have each person think through and then verbally answer, Who am I in this team? Each person could draw a personal lifeline (history, background, spiritual pilgrimage—perhaps charted in decades), marking significant peaks and valleys. Take plenty of time to hear, interpret, and affirm these autobiographies. The important questions are: How did I get here? What do I bring to this team? What are my strengths—personal, skills, styles? What are my weaknesses—where do I need to develop; where could I potentially block the work of this leadership team?

Enhance the bonding process of the team. Plan annual retreats together, if finances permit. Schedule regular recreation or eat a weekly meal together. Have more frequent but less lengthy work meetings and pray in twos or threes. Whatever the method, increase the time spent together. Emotional bonding is directly proportional to time. Don't expect team bonding to just occur naturally at business meetings. Plan for it!

Mutually decide on a leadership development plan for the year. Find a good book on leadership—there are scores of them available—and read it together, taking the first half-hour of your regular meeting to discuss a chapter and its implications for your team. Try keeping personal leadership journals with insights about yourself and the team. Have an outside consultant objectively evaluate your single adult ministry, but be prepared to receive the report. Attend leadership conferences together or begin a single adult leadership breakfast on a monthly basis with other churches in your locale. Take leadership responsibilities seriously and seek to develop skills just as you would for your career.

Renew your regular business meetings. Arrange the agenda items in order of importance; listen to all the strong points of a new idea before discussing any of its drawbacks; establish a written list of criteria by which to evaluate new ideas or proposals; provide team members with adequate information before meetings to facilitate preparation for the meeting; compose the minutes of the meetings around what was beneficially accomplished rather than around what agenda items were discussed.[6]

Part **6**

Developing the Ministry

36

Let's Begin at Church

Paul M. Petersen

The tip-offs are everywhere, from the grocery store to the news-stand. Stouffer's alone makes eighty-six different foods designed to feed just one person. Want ads in search of relationships are so pervasive they have reached the august *New York Times Book Review*, and dating services have proliferated to the point that some are targeted to such subgroups as the physically handicapped and the astrologically inclined.

Are Singles Welcome?

In the book *Lost in the Land of Oz: The Search for Identity and Community in American Life*, Madonna Kolbenschlag says:

> The Celtic myth of Macha is an awesome metaphor for the wound in our contemporary civilization: a divided conscious-ness that abuses power and breathes all sorts of social ills, while denying the life-giving "feminine" experience and values in human society. This wound in our consciousness, in our cul-ture, has made orphans of us all . . . and is it not easy to see in the story of Macha and her children . . . the *divorced single parent* struggling to work, support, and raise her children in a soci-ety that is hostile to her in the role of provider?[1] (italics added)

Kolbenschlag's observation of hostility is a valid one concerning the oppression not only of divorced single parents but indeed of single adults in general in Western and American culture.

This seems to be a case where what is true of American culture is many times more true of the American church. The instances of alienation of single adults in the church are rife. The church is known to be a couple-oriented society where memberships are measured in families. High stress is laid on nurseries and child care. A common question is, When are you going to get married? The underlying thought is that you are not complete, not whole, until you have a spouse. "A recent study of parish life in the United States indicates several groups who might be perceived as not really included: traditionalists, *singles*, newcomers, cliques that formerly dominated church life but no longer do, *those alienated by church response to divorce*, and ethnic or racial minorities."[2] (italics added)

This reaction is probably encouraged in the Roman Catholic Church by the Pope's own teaching and dictums. "The affectivity of the young Christian must be molded by a process of primary socialization such as occurs, ideally, in the family. Following several texts of Vatican II, Pope John Paul II has expatriated on the family as 'church in miniature.'"[3] Such teaching as this is bound to have an effect on the church's lack of acceptance and encouragement of single adults.

Another author has observed, "Ironically, . . . singles may feel alienated because they are surrounded by a church that constantly uses family metaphors in both theology and parish life; are located in parishes that often list membership family units; worship in liturgies whose hymns, responses, and sermons reinforce family images; and observe that great disproportion in parish programs and activities directed to people in some state of family life rather than to singles."[4]

Even as society has begun to take note of the boom in the unmarried population, so also there is a crack in the door of the church as some local congregations take seriously Christ's admonition to care for all with a cup of cold water. However, even as these ministries begin to flourish and attract large numbers of single adults of all ages, so also are questions raised as to why single adults should be set apart from other adults in the church, how single adults can be ministered to, and what the dangers are to be avoided.

As I talked with a senior minister at a medium-sized church, he asked what area of specialization I was involved in. When I responded, "Single adult ministry" and asked if his church had such a ministry, his response was, "No way! Those single people only take and never give. They don't go to church and they don't pledge. Besides, they're all promiscuous and will cause our counseling load to increase too much."

Such unsubstantiated rumors are circulating widely throughout churches and denominations. I have received calls from singles ministers in despair as churches obscure and famous have reconsidered their commitment to single adult ministry.

As the single adult population flourishes, many questions are raised concerning proper ministry methods and programming ideas. This is due to the relative newness of single adult ministry as a valid and needed area of ministry.

Why Aren't Singles Welcome?

At a Christian Education conference held by one denomination, two singles-related workshops were offered to participants. One workshop was designed for those in positions of pastoral care to assist them in helping adults suffering through a divorce. The second workshop had to do with developing a lay team of single adults to minister to single adults in the church. The first workshop had to be canceled even though over 200 churches were in attendance and in excess of 800 people were registered. The second workshop was held with four attendees. Apparently, the crack in the door of the church is a mere sliver!

Why are our churches "asleep at the wheel"? To some churches single adults are either the lepers or the Samaritans, or both! There are probably as many reasons for this oppressive mentality as there are churches. A brief survey might reveal theological discomfort with divorce and remarriage or a sense that those who are not married must be socially inept, unable to make commitments, or emotionally unstable (not the sort of persons we want in our church).

However, being single does not presuppose irresponsibility; and Christ wants us to accept even those who have suffered and do suffer through physical, cultural, and personal disabilities. Other reasons may hinge on the conservatism of the local church: "We've never done it that way." There may be fears of various unknowns—change in status quo, threat to those "in power," the singles' reputed promiscuity, financial and time drains.

Widows are the "safest" of single adults, and even they are seen as dangerous. A widowed single adult in her fifties (widowed four years) is extremely thankful for the opportunity that a single adult ministry has given her to find friends on equal footing, as well as to offer her a safe harbor from which she can then branch out to the rest of the church and her married friends. In her four years of singleness, only four married couples have invited her to their homes for dinner. One of those four couples was the singles minister and his wife and so (in her words) not necessarily to be counted. Her experience was that when she was widowed, she immediately became a threat to her female married friends.

Why Do We Need Single Adult Ministries?

The above illustration verifies the validity of single adult ministry. Single adults are a group of people whose needs can be met by the church, the same as families, retirees, and youth, to name a few that do receive attention.

Acts 6 tells us that widows in particular are to be cared for. However, a larger principle of the church is found in Matthew 25:35–36: "For I was hungry and you gave me something to eat, I was thirsty and you gave me something to drink, I was a stranger and you invited me in, I needed clothes and you clothed me, I was sick and you looked after me, I was in prison and you came to visit me." The church should look for opportunities to minister to those in need bodily, socially, culturally, and spiritually. This certainly fits the description of many single adults. However, this is not to say that every church ought to have a single adult ministry but rather that every church ought to minister to single adults.

Several months ago eight recent "graduates" and three current members of the Highland Park Presbyterian Church Singles Ministry in Dallas went away together for a weekend. The eight "graduates" consisted of four couples that had met in a young singles Sunday school class, had fallen in love, and married. The response of the three single adults throughout the weekend was that they felt they did not fit. In the words of one of the single adults, "The couples did their 'couples' thing and the single adults felt very much out of place and odd." This is in spite of the fact that all eleven adults were longtime close friends. Single adults need a place in the church that does not apply pressure toward marriage but accepts them for who they are.

I spoke with a singles pastor in the Pacific Northwest whose church has subsumed single adult ministry under the larger department of Adult Ministry. Highland Park has toyed with this idea as a means of integration, and so I asked him about the results. He stated that placing single adult ministry under Adult Ministry had dried up the single adult ministry visibility and decreased their friendliness to the single adult community. If a church is going to expand its ministry program to single adults, then it should be made clear and identifiable.

What Do Single Adults Need?

There are some needs that are shared and some that are different, between single and married adults. Differences include a married's need to consciously work on "family" and intimacy and a single's desire for a more active social calendar. They must deal with their sexuality in different ways. Marrieds and singles must overcome societal and familial biases against single adults.

Hope. Single adults need hope that in spite of the failures in their lives, life has meaning. Many single adults have been let down in relationships, family, and work. This is true of single adults of all ages, as older adults realize their life is passing them by and they may not have reached goals that they have set. In younger singles, this lack of hope is often the result of the realization that they may not attain the status or wealth that their parents had. Single adults first need hope in God—that they have not been abandoned; second, in others—that they can have fruitful and productive relationships; and third, in the future—that all is not lost and that tomorrow holds new opportunities (Isa. 40:29–31; 1 Thess. 1:3).

Understanding. Most of the unique needs of single adults result from their marital status. They have no spouse with whom to share ideas and troubles. Single adults need someone who will listen. True listening gives value to the person being listened to. It helps to rebuild the self-worth of the single adult. Many single adults are suffering from a lack of understanding because of broken relationships (whether from a divorce, broken engagement, or bad social dynamics), as well as societal and family pressure—"Why aren't you married yet? Are you going to let life pass you by?" Single adults need to know that the sign of adult passage is not marriage but assuming responsibility for their own lives. Single adults also need understanding regarding the opposite sex. Society teaches that anyone still single at age thirty must dislike the opposite sex or that "something must be wrong with them." All of this can bring a great deal of confusion. Understanding can be offered concerning problems, temptations, and trials. All people need to know that they are not alone in their struggles (1 Cor. 10:13).

Belonging. Perhaps the greatest need of single adults is to feel a sense of belonging. Our society teaches that two is the "whole" number and that if you are not whole you do not belong. Single adults need to recognize their own singular completeness and wholeness. They need to belong—to others, to the church, to society. Along with this need for belonging is the need for family and intimacy. Family brings much needed stability to individuals. It ideally provides rituals, loyalty, and a nonjudgmental, accepting environment. Single adults need to have their isolation broken down. They need proper and healthy contact with people. A few years ago the rage was that everyone needed between five and forty hugs a day to stay healthy. All people need vital human contact. For a single adult this is difficult, especially in a society such as ours that promotes sex rather than healthy contact through handshakes, hugs, and a slap on the back. Ann Landers conducted a survey asking if women preferred hugs or sex; the overwhelming majority voted for hugs.

Role models. Single adults need to see healthy dating and marriage relationships. Most often single adults see divorce and broken relationships. This leads to a cynical and frustrated view of relationships. Yet God has made each one of us to live in relationship with one another. Single adults also need to observe healthy Christianity. In a world that seems to revolve around broken promises, broken hopes, and fleeting fantasies, the love that Christ has for each of us can appear to be a myth.

Information. For a number of reasons, single adults often lack basic social skills. They may not know how to make friends, especially with the opposite sex, and the harder they try the more they seem to drive a wedge between themselves and others. Single adults need information about themselves: who they are and how they are perceived. They need information concerning proper dating skills, sexuality, finances, and their personal spirituality and relationship with God.

Companionship. Single adults need multiple friendships to take the place of that one spouse so that their needs are met by a variety of individuals. Then when one individual moves on or lets them down, they are not devastated. Companionship allows for a sharing of ideas, feedback, social activities, belonging, and family.

A biblical base. It is critical that a single adult ministry establish a biblical foundation for itself. The Scriptures show a deep concern for widows and the fatherless (James 1:27). Even in biblical times there were those who in their singleness were struggling with broken relationships, pain, and grief. And yet the apostle Paul (Phil. 4:11–13) said that whatever state we are in, we ought to be content. This is what singles need to hear.

If the church is to meet the needs of *all* its members, including single adults, then these needs must be addressed through all the major ministry areas of the church—preaching, administration, pastoral care, and education.

What Can the Church Give?

One of the primary helps that the church can provide to single adults is to feel comfortable with their singleness. We should not be challenging people to make do until marriage but to excel in who they are, whether single or not. The church needs to provide family in a non-nuclear sense to single adults.

Raymond Brown says, "Today, many people seem to be seeking quality and meaning in life. They want a sense of inner direction and forms of community that are inclusive. For the single adults, this means a community that does not put a premium upon being married so much as being whole. To choose the direction that helps persons, whether single or married, to deal with the quality of life is a prime opportunity for the church."[5]

Mark Lee suggests that the church needs to:

1. recognize that the single status is the appropriate available option to being married
2. relate to the interests of singles
3. provide full opportunity for singles to act responsibly in the life of the church
4. call upon Christians to keep fidelity with biblical principles relative to personal conduct
5. adjust the focus of the church's ministry on the nuclear family
6. activate programs that will meet the needs of singles
7. build the church on Jesus Christ.[6]

The church needs to emphasize to married and single adults that marriage, though valuable, is not the measure of one's worth in the eyes of God or the church. The title of a video series produced by Gospel Films with Harold Ivan Smith as presenter sums up this idea very well: *One Is a Whole Number.*

It is important for the church to rethink its theology of singleness in light of changing cultural norms as well as in light of Scripture. We need to recognize that the Scriptures are inclusive of people, regardless of their marital status. The church needs to develop a theology that affirms singleness as a valid lifestyle. The Scriptures are full of examples of single adults other than Paul and Jesus. The attitude toward divorce and remarriage, as well as forgiveness in these situations, needs to be strengthened and better understood. A concise picture of a successful ministry can be found in Acts 2:41–47:

Those who accepted his message were baptized, and about three thousand were added to their number that day. They devoted themselves to the apostles' teaching and to the fellowship, to the breaking of bread and to prayer. Everyone was filled with awe, and many wonders and miraculous signs were done by the apostles. All the believers were together and had everything in common. Selling their possessions and goods, they gave to anyone as he had need. Every day they continued to meet together in the temple courts. They broke bread in their homes and ate together with glad and sincere hearts, praising God and enjoying the favor of all the people. And the Lord added to their number daily those who were being saved.

Revitalizing Your Single Adult Ministry

G. Jerry Martin

Environments exert a strong influence on us. When we visit a group, we quickly size up its environment. We sense the organization (or lack thereof), the plan for inclusion of new people (or that it will be hard to break into), and whether or not we can be included. *Environment* is defined by *Webster's New World Dictionary* as "all the conditions, circumstances, influences surrounding, and affecting the development of, an organism or group of organisms."

As leaders in single adult ministry, we must expose people to a dynamic, caring ministry environment in which they can develop as disciples of Jesus Christ. This means we begin by meeting their felt needs of friendship, resolving conflicts, and then bringing them along in personal discipleship.

Author and pastor Dr. Bruce Larson, made a striking comment about developing the environment of acceptance and community: "We must develop a strong sense of acceptance and warmth in our ministry that goes beyond anything a person can get by frequenting the neighborhood bar."

Jesus dealt with people at different levels of commitment to him. He asked a great deal of the disciples he selected. In fact he asked them to leave their homes and vocations to go with him everywhere he went. Those who called upon him with specific problems were asked to trust him for specific answers. Of course, Christ had a commitment to help his disciples grow spiritually. He took time to teach them, exhort and correct them, and be a model to them.

Christ created the environment for them to grow spiritually so that they, in turn, would be equipped to train others. Single adults need an environment of love and acceptance where needs can be met within a solid biblically based ministry. Therefore, we need to structure ministry to provide for several levels of commitment to assist people in finding their entry point.

For the past several years as an associate pastor in three different churches, I had as one of my responsibilities the single adult ministry. I was involved in the revitalization of three single adult groups: college-career, young single adults, and middle single adults.

In each of these churches there was a need to revitalize the ministry to single adults. We needed to refocus, add new structure, breathe some new life into the ministry—or let the present ministry die and begin a new one altogether.

All too often we treat a sick and dying ministry by placing it on life support and treating the symptoms rather than the problems. We may increase the advertising, add new programs, or plan big events in order to boost the program, and yet the ministry continues to be ineffective. We miss the goal of developing ministry and building a community of believers.

There are those in single adult ministry who advocate that single adults should not stay in a singles ministry for a long period of time. They believe a singles ministry should be looked upon as a transition place, a place to stop off on the way to another stage of life—essentially, a place to find someone and get married.

I believe that being single is a viable lifestyle, one that is acceptable and, in fact, modeled in Scripture. When we take that stand on singleness, we will build the ministry by emphasizing quality relationships and personal growth. For many single adults the people in this ministry may become their "extended family."

We build community by design. It does not happen by chance. Community building tends to happen better in smaller groups and well-planned events. Community happens as you travel to retreats, attend conferences, and participate in "talk-it-over" groups, planning teams, and small group ministries in homes.

Select a Task Force

Every singles group I've worked with had some common problems. The leaders of the group were tired, burned out, or their circumstances in life changed (job, relationships, marriage). Therefore, they were in need of new leaders to get a new perspective on the ministry.

To begin the process of revitalizing your ministry, develop a task force. A task force is a group commissioned for a specific purpose. To establish a task force, select a cross section of people that represent long-time attenders, new members, various spiritual growth levels, and a balance of men and women. Ten to twelve people is a good group size.

It's essential to focus the ministry on God, since effective ministry must be based on a devotional life. Then we can have a more effective evaluation of our ministry. The following steps create simple objectives for the task force to relaunch the ministry.

Evaluate the Ministry

In my first single adult ministry experience, I didn't know the right questions to ask. Since then I have used the following questions to keep a ministry on track.

1. *Where are the leaders?* Have they moved, gotten married, or are they just not available for leadership? In many single adult ministries there will be a significant turnover every six months. In one church ministry we had a significant turnover in the older singles group due to several marriages. The key leaders of the young singles group had career relocations. Some of them had led for over two years. We came to the realization that new leaders were not adequately developed to take their places in time. Leadership development must be an ongoing process.

2. *Have the leaders fallen away from their purpose statement (if they had one)?* In one singles group, we reestablished the purpose statement three times in five years because of the turnover in leadership. When there's a significant change in leadership, the new leaders have to "own" the purpose statement.

3. *Have leaders served too long, and are new ones needed?* In my first singles ministry experience, I came into a group that had

become tired and stale in their leadership. They needed a new vision for ministry and new leaders.

4. *Have the leaders evaluated their ministry recently?* Because of the turnover of people, it's essential to have a major evaluation at least every six months.

5. *Have the leaders tried to be all things to all people?* Select five to seven emphases of ministry and decide to do them well. In one situation, upon my arrival I found a group of singles from twenty to eighty years old. The planning meeting was spent trying to plan events appropriate to meet the needs of the wide age span. It was necessary to break down the events to meet specific needs of the younger and older adults.

6. *Are we more program-oriented than people-oriented?* Certainly schedules and programs and plans are essential to organizing a ministry, but we need to make sure that the programs are meeting people's needs rather than just perpetuating the program. If a group is more concerned with programming than building relationships, the single adults will stagnate socially as well as spiritually.

Identify Needs

Christ identified people as being "like sheep without a shepherd" (Mark 6:34). You and your leadership team need to discover the needs of your sheep so you can shepherd them. "The effectiveness of our ministry is tied to a clear understanding of the needs of those to whom we are called to minister."[1] A single adult ministry needs to focus on the needs of single adults in four areas.

1. *A place to belong.* Many single adults are active in a variety of social, church, and community activities. Christian singles desire an alternative to the singles bar and night clubs. A ministry that desires to attract a large number of single adults will need to schedule a diverse number of events. If your church is not large enough to organize many events, find a few other churches in your community to share in the events.

2. *A place to be known.* One of the big challenges of being single is loneliness. Andrew Greeley says: "There are two kinds of loneliness that afflict human life. The first is the loneliness that comes from the human condition. It can be mitigated and allevi-

ated but it cannot be eliminated. The other is the loneliness that we choose freely. It can always be conquered if we choose to do so."[2] Building a single adult "family" of believers will help the development of good friendships. We need to find fellow believers who are in the spiritual life journey and travel together.

With each structured meeting or planned activity, there should be some "mixer" time for the development of relationships. A variety of icebreaker activities or discussion starters can be used as a group gathers to help people get acquainted with each other. When you have your Bible study, plan time for discussion and interaction as well as for content delivery.

Many single adults will be dealing with some deep emotional challenges related to difficult decisions they have made or are presently facing. There may be issues of vocation, education, separation, divorce, alimony, single parenthood, financial stress, or the struggle of being single.

3. *A place to learn.* There is indeed an intellectual concern among single adults. Specially focused seminars for six to seven sessions once a week, or special Friday nights and all day Saturdays, are appealing. Some of the seminar topics used in single adult ministries are Divorce Recovery (for adults, youth, children), Blended Families, Single Parents, Being Single Is OK, Grief Recovery, Intimacy, and Single Adult Sexuality.

4. *A place to grow spiritually.* It is the spiritual dimension to our ministry that gives what we do an eternal, God-centered focus. God designed us as spiritual beings who desire to explore the spiritual dimension of our lives. There will be those who come to us knowing they hurt but are unaware that the message of the gospel of Christ will give them meaning and hope. Some people may have tried many ways to resolve their inner conflict and so discovered their need for spiritual help.

The needs displayed by people searching for spiritual help must be met with loving understanding. Our goal is reconciliation, not condemnation. Bible teaching must not only give information but also focus on the application of God's Word to a person's life. By the end of our teaching session we want to answer the questions, So what? What does God's Word have to do with the issues I face in my life?

In general, young single adults face issues of education or specialized training, establishing their career, establishing adult relationships with the same and opposite sex, and coming to grips with singleness versus marriage. Older single adults have a greater focus on "emergency room" ministry. The issues will focus on divorce recovery, widow support, single parenting, and grief recovery. "The effectiveness of our ministry is tied to a clear understanding of the needs of those to whom we are called to minister."[3]

Ministry Statement

A ministry statement is a written document that describes the group's direction and values. This document will guide your leaders and participants to know the reason for the group's existence. Defining the basic purpose and the values you hold will help determine the ministries you organize.

After your single adult task force has compiled a primary list of identified needs, formulate a ministry statement that will complete the sentence, We exist to. . . . This statement will need to be broad enough to last for a few years yet specific enough to provide direction now. Keep your ministry statement simple, using one statement or three or four key words or phrases.

A ministry statement may be written by first brain-storming with your task force. From what you compile, narrow the list down to five words or phrases that describe your ministry. Then narrow the list to three words or phrases. Using the final words or phrases, write an easily understood statement. One single adult ministry has five key words in their ministry statement—relationships, spiritual nourishment, evangelism, and involvement.

Objectives and Goals

Once you have settled on your ministry statement by answering the question, Why does this ministry exist? you should determine the areas of ministry you will provide as you fulfill the ministry statement. You may choose broad areas such as Bible study, support, education, and relationships.

Goals are specific and measurable steps to accomplish the objective you set. Your goals will have a date, number, or time attached to them. Goals need to be specific, obtainable, and measurable but flexible enough so you can make adjustments as your needs change. Examples of combining the objectives and goals would be:

1. Bible Study. Goal: Begin a 20s and 30s Sunday school class by September 1.
2. Support. Goal: Begin a codependent group by March 1.
3. Education. Goal: Begin a six-week single parent workshop by October 1 with thirty people attending, ten people from outside our church.
4. Relationships: Goal: By January 1, begin a hospitality team to greet people who attend the Sunday morning adult class. See that everyone has name tags, and follow up on visitors.

Your ministry statement, objectives, and goals don't have to be perfect the first time around; refine them as you go.

A Well-Rounded Ministry

In the process of revitalizing your single adult ministry, you may find that you are overemphasizing your contact with new people or focusing all your time together in teaching content, or completely focusing on developing an awesome commitment core of spiritual berets.

All too often in ministry we focus our attention on what we tend to know best—such as having a mini-worship service every time we get together. Consequently, we don't intentionally plan for the inclusion of uncommitted Christians or non-Christians. We also don't challenge our people to grow through a deeper commitment to Jesus Christ and to each other; therefore, we lose the great joy of seeing people reproduce themselves in ministry.

The chart that follows on page 272 contains a three-step plan of *contact, content,* and *commitment.* The plan can be a valuable aid in personal and leadership team planning.

Contact

Unless you are seeking to relate to new people who need to know the good news of the gospel, you will not have a vital, growing ministry. You need to plan nonthreatening events to reach out to the non-Christian person, times when they can come to something enjoyable, such as sporting events, cookouts, and need-related workshops. This kind of contact will help develop a mailing list and lead to follow-up for further involvement. In addition to the event being enjoyable and informative to Christians, it gives them opportunity to invite a friend to something that is positive with a purpose.

Content

The second level of the balanced ministry is the level where we encourage our people to begin a consistent commitment to the Lord Jesus Christ, to the single adult ministry itself, and to the church body at large. This commitment begins with the regular weekly meetings. The desire is for the person to start with the very basic concepts of the Word of God and move toward a more consistent commitment of time, talents, and treasure.

A concern is that the content level can become the comfort zone for a ministry. It easily moves into a ministry to "our people." It can be "safe" to minister at this level because there are few risks. You do not have to contend with very many new relationships or non-Christian people, as you would in outreach, and you don't need to stretch yourself in dealing with all those people out there who have problems.

Upon arriving in Dallas, I soon attended my first single adult ministry steering committee meeting. This volunteer team of people had developed some good Bible study ministries, held monthly dinners, kept contact with visitors, had a strong Sunday school, conducted some small group Bible studies, had a missions emphasis, and planned some good socials.

However, I was not fully prepared for the response blurted out by one of the ladies when I asked the question, "What are you presently doing to minister to divorced and single parents?" The reply came back, "Oh, they aren't welcome here!" You can imagine my shock. I'm pleased to say that within a few months we discovered there were people who wanted to become a part of developing a ministry of support for single parents and for those who were divorced.

A Well-Rounded Single Adult Ministry

	Purpose Biblical Basis for Ministry	Plan Involvement Required	Program Accomplishing the Purpose
Contact	*Lead and Equip Others* Ephesians 4:11–15 Development of mature Christians 1 Peter 4:10 God has given each of us special abilities; use them to help each other.	*Come and Lead* Be an equipper of others to develop multiplying disciples—those who will disciple others. Expose people to opportunities to serve others by leading Bible studies, mission trips, discipling others. Use your spiritual gifts to serve others.	*Meeting Needs for Growth* Leadership training, small discipleship groups, class teaching, leading outreach activities, and mission trips
Content	*Develop Spiritually* Hebrews 10:24–25 Stimulate one another toward love and good deeds; meet together, encourage one another Matthew 28:19–20 Go and make disciples.	*Come and Grow* Learn and apply basic biblical principles for spiritual growth. Build one another up through commitment to Christ and to each other. Learn to become accountable to others by being a regular attender of the ministry.	*Meeting Spiritual Needs* Church services, home Bible studies, retreats, Sunday A.M. and special seminars
Commitment	*Outreach* Acts 1:8 You will be my witnesses. Luke 19:10 Christ came to seek those who were lost.	*Come and Investigate* Come to activities and be exposed to the gospel. Become a part of activities that appeal to Christians and non-Christians. Be given the opportunity to respond to the claims of Christ	*Meeting Felt Needs* Recreation, sports, special outings, workshops (self esteem, divorce recovery, single parents, children of divorce, codependency), and evangelistic Bible studies

Commitment

The move upward to the commitment level thins out the number of those who are willing and able to give themselves to leadership and discipleship. As we challenge our people to consider opportunities to minister and be leaders, they will understand better the spiritual gifts they have to contribute to the body of believers. They will be able to discover the requirements and responsibilities of leadership, teaching, missions, caring for others, and administration.

When given the opportunity and challenged to serve, single adults will rise to the occasion with depth of dedication. Serving and impacting another person's life can be the most challenging and rewarding experience on the path of growing to spiritual maturity.

Effective prayer, planning, preparation, and communication joined with the guidelines given on the chart and a lot of hard work begin the development of a well-rounded ministry for single adults.

The progression of ministry involvement is not an evaluation of spirituality. The progression is a degree of commitment one has made of the time and energy he or she is able to give to the ministry. The plan chart helps to evaluate present ministry; it also challenges your group members to evaluate their own commitment to ministry.

Relaunching a Single Adult Ministry

We are attracted to signs that read, "Under New Management." Those who liked what was going on don't believe it can get better, and those who were dissatisfied don't believe it will be any worse. You are in a win, win position.

There are several keys to relaunching a vital ministry to single adults.

Communicate through Leadership

At this time your task force will conclude their responsibility. After they have evaluated the ministry and designed a balanced one, they will have fulfilled their reason for existence. The continued development of the ministry will be done by the present established leadership team, an entirely new team, or the present leadership team with new people added.

Depending on the size of your group, you will need several people to give oversight of each ministry. Be careful not to build ministry around one person, but let several people share responsibility. Also be careful you don't fall into the trap of running a single adult ministry like a youth group. These are adults, and they need to own this ministry.

The leadership team will need to carry the message of this ministry to others. Each of them has a network of friends at church, where they work, and where they live.

Communicate a Major Emphasis

To relaunch your ministry, focus on a key time when you can make an impact on the most people. Determine to make this a quality experience for everyone attending the event. For some churches this major emphasis will be on Sunday morning, and for others a weeknight will be best.

In one church I served, the design of the Sunday morning worship services made this the best time for inviting new people; consequently, this was our major focus time for people to sign up for seminars, support groups, trips, and recreation and then hear a message designed to meet a felt need from a biblical perspective.

At another church, we found it advantageous to use Thursday night as our inviter time. The evening was designed with a variety of ice-breakers, recreation, skits, a need-related discussion, and refreshments. The variety and the informality appealed to this group.

Determine a date for your major emphasis and design a plan to communicate it. Choose a date at least four to six weeks away. Your focus may be to start a new topics series, bring in a guest speaker, or put in a new twist such as recreation or a barbecue.

To publicize the event, design a flyer, and write a news release for the church newspaper and the local community paper.

Communicate Churchwide

Since your single adult ministry is an essential focus at your church, you and your leadership team need to let it be known that you are committed to it. As the ministry gains visibility, you will see this enthusiasm become more contagious. People want to be part of something positive.

The purpose of the big announcement is not to draw attention to you or create some unusual hype for the group but to communicate that this is an important area of focus in your church. It is essential that the senior pastor declare his support for this ministry. Make effective use of the regular publications of the church such as the church bulletin, church newspaper, and bulletin boards.

You may also gather prospects for your single adult ministry by including a single adult contact card in the church bulletin. The card will ask for people to name single adults and their phone numbers and addresses for your contact list. Many of your prospects will come from their family and friends. Contact prospects as soon as possible to let them know of your major emphasis.

Keep It Going

Whether you are the single-adult minister, associate pastor, senior pastor, or a volunteer layperson assigned to this ministry, the following steps can help you have a more effective single adult ministry.

Tend Your Own Spiritual Passion

Whether we are in ministry vocationally or as a volunteer, most of us readily acknowledge the necessity of maintaining a strong, consistent, and stable spiritual life. However, with the pressure of schedules, problems, programs, and activities, we struggle with our relationship with God. Thus, we neglect what is most important, our own spiritual maturity. Jesus told his disciples, "I am the true vine, and my Father is the gardener. He cuts off every branch in me that bears no fruit, while every branch that does bear fruit he prunes so that it will be even more fruitful. Remain in me, and I will remain in you. No branch can bear fruit by itself; it must remain in the vine. Neither can you bear fruit unless you remain in me" (John 15:1–2, 4).

Establish Your Own Personal/Family Time

You will not be effective in ministry if you are not spiritually, emotionally, and physically refreshed. You need to schedule your time so your family is the first priority after God. This applies to leaders who are married and those who are not married. Unmarried leaders need a "family" where they can be committed and accountable. Your family should complement your ministry rather than be a hindrance to it. Do not neglect your family when ministering to others.

Create a Relational Ministry

Model to your leadership team a ministry that desires to meet the needs of individuals. That caring will communicate that relationship with God and others is the basis of the ministry. In scheduled meetings plan for relationship building.

A busy executive ran through the double doors into the train station, leaving behind him the pressures of his job. His only thought was his beautiful, warm family. He dreamed of playing with his children and could almost taste his wife's good cooking. He had to hurry to catch the train out of the city to the suburbs, so he ran down the station's long, crowded corridors. As he turned the corner onto the final stretch to his homebound train, he did not see a little boy who was squatting down, playing with some marbles. The running executive ran into the boy and the marbles flew everywhere. But the man kept running, thinking, "If I stop, I'll miss my train, my time with my family, my dinner!" A few steps later, however, he stopped. He walked back to the boy and helped him gather the marbles. Amazed, the little boy looked into the man's face and asked, "Mister, are you Jesus?"[4]

May we minister in such a way that those we serve will see Jesus.

Select Leaders

Certainly we don't know what the Lord will do with gems in the rough if they are willing to be servants to others (Mark 10:42–45). It is exciting to see how the Holy Spirit works as people commit their lives to him in ministry.

A leader must be teachable, willing to follow another person's leadership, and desirous of learning to be effective. A good leader should be flexible and should also be able to set priorities so as to have enough time to serve on the leadership team.

Build the Ministry Team

The care and equipping of the leadership is an ongoing process. Our leadership team development must be based on a biblical foundation (Eph. 4:11–18).

> The importance of teamwork is found in a parable for staff members. Once upon a time a church called three members to serve on the leadership staff. The first said, "Here I am; now your troubles are over. I will do everything that needs to be done." But his job was given to another.
>
> The second said, "Here I am. You do the work while I give orders." But his job went to another.
>
> The third said, "Let us pray and plan, and work together, that we may serve Him who has chosen us and appointed us that we should go and bear fruit and that our fruit should abide." And the seeds which they sowed fell in good soil and brought forth abundantly.[5]

If the ministry is going to work, there must be a systematic plan for developing leaders. It was Jesus' "job" to develop his disciples. "Believers are to be cared for and serviced. If leadership is not being developed to provide service, growth stops."[6]

The leadership team will need to meet regularly to maintain a quality relationship with each other and to care for the various ministries. At each leadership team meeting, in addition to a time of ministry to one another and reports from ministry areas, we need to include the following steps to keep the ministry fresh:

1. *Evaluate and brainstorm.* Ask questions, tough questions. Then consider how you may improve what you are already doing. Also consider what other possible ministries you can include to meet the needs of single adults.

2. *Decide.* Consider what could be implemented from the brainstorming session. Maybe you will only decide on one thing to implement. Don't try to do everything at once, but make a decision. Trust God for the results. Be sure the ministry is compatible with your ministry statement's objectives and goals.

3. *Plan.* Put someone in charge. Consider who will be the point person for the ministry, what recruiting will be necessary, what training will be needed, and the financial responsibility for the program.

4. *Begin.* Determine a launching date. Communicate when this renewed ministry will begin, then make certain that it is a quality ministry.

5. *Evaluate again—and again.* A ministry that is worth doing now may not even be needed in six months. At your regular leadership team meetings have a mini-evaluation of your ministry through reports. At least twice a year have a leadership retreat to consider the whole ministry.

Conclusion

It is important to design a ministry model around a "family" environment that is nurturing people to spiritual, mental, and emotional health. Ministry is much more than programs.

Single adult ministry must be meeting needs within a balanced program of evangelism and discipleship. A program will die quickly if it exists only for itself.

Serving others is imperative. In service we take the focus off ourselves and place it on the Lord and the needs of others. Many people who are "too busy" or who are in crisis feel they don't have anything to give. But even in times when we don't believe we have anything to give, we grow by giving of ourselves. People need a sense of mission in which they feel they can make a contribution.

Building ministry by equipping leaders will add stability to individual lives as well as to the group. Through equipping, leaders find affirmation and healing.

As we focus our attention outward, our ministry will be defined by the needs of the community. This will sharpen our focus on continued and future ministry.

38

Developing an Outreach Ministry

Gary Gonzales

Reaching modern Americans and especially singles demands that we adopt a "go and tell" rather than a "come and see" strategy.

During this final decade of the twentieth century, it's obvious that the traditional church in America is lying flat on the mat—and the ten count is well underway. Statistics on church vitality show that more than 85 percent of churches are plateaued or declining. But why?

Cultural and Social Shifts

The last fifty years have been an era of unprecedented social upheaval and change. Most experts agree that these shifts are radical and all-pervasive. One social observer notes that as we move into the next millennium, change will be so rapid that future historians will look back with nostalgia on the last decade and refer to it as "the stable '80s."

As is too often the case, most churches are twenty years behind the times, oblivious to the implications current trends have for their ministries and are continuing to do business as usual. But these shifts are of monumental significance. Let's take a moment to review some of the major ones.

From Rural to Urban

In 1900, 90 percent of Americans lived or worked on the farm. Today fewer than 5 percent make their living on the farm. A survey revealed that 61 percent of Americans live in the thirty-nine largest U.S. cities. We have become an urban world.

It has further been suggested that within a couple of decades most of us will live in one of three "megalopoli": "San-San" (San Diego to San Francisco), "Bos-Wash" (Boston to Washington), and "Chi-Pitts" (Chicago to Pittsburgh)!

This urbanization has altered the personality and psyche of the people we're trying to reach. *The Four Spiritual Laws,* for example, although still effective with middle-class Anglo-Americans who share a common set of values, is often ineffective in evangelizing modern urban people who share a whole different set of values, beliefs, definitions, understandings, and needs.

From Homogeneous to Multicultural

A friend of mine who is an internationally known urban expert once spoke in my inner-city church. He made a striking observation: "The West Coast is no longer the backbone of America; now it's the front door of Asia." Then he added, "The United States is currently the third largest Spanish-speaking nation in the world, following Mexico and Spain." The Los Angeles public schools claim to have eighty-six language groups represented in their classrooms.

Whether you view these changes as an affront or an opportunity, the fact remains that they strongly impact the way we need to do evangelism today. Failure to recognize this rich diversity can lead to personal frustration.

While I was pastoring a church in the Los Angeles area, a well-versed man in my church asked me if I could help him understand why his evangelistic attempts were unfruitful. He had been trying to reach a number of his neighbors through lifestyle evangelistic methods for some months. He had done all the right things, but his efforts had proven unproductive.

I said, "Describe for me the kinds of people you're trying to reach." Without seeing the implications he said, "Let's see, the couple across the street just moved here from China. And then there's the

Mexican family next door. And just down the block is a black single mother my wife has been witnessing to."

I stopped him and said, "Wait a minute. Listen to what you're telling me. What you're describing is a foreign mission field!" The era of the homogeneous church is over and a new day has dawned.

From Judeo-Christian to Rampantly Secular

In about three-quarters of a century, we have gone from a Christian consensus to a caricature of pluralism. Virtually every kind of freedom of expression is available in America today, except one that embraces a belief in God.

The irony is that pollsters George Gallup Jr. and George Barna keep cranking out research that indicates the vast majority of people claim to have a personal belief in God. Of these, 25 percent admit to having had some kind of Christian conversion experience. In response to such testimony, William Iverson writes with thinly veiled doubt, "A pound of meat would surely be affected by a quarter pound of salt. If this is real Christianity, the 'salt of the earth,' where is the effect of which Jesus spoke?"

From Marriage-Oriented to Single-Oriented

Another factor often overlooked or downplayed in Bible-believing churches is the national trend toward broken marriages or postponing the marriage decision, combined with an increased willingness to choose a single lifestyle. A special report in the *Single Adult Ministries Journal* (January 1992) stated that while Protestant churches are very sensitive to the needs of families and the elderly, they are all but oblivious to the concerns and needs of single adults generally and single parents specifically.

This attitude is radically out of step with the times. While we should never value one segment of society over another, we need to know the demographics of our constituency. How else can we hope to reach them or meet their unique needs?

When I was living in Southern California, four large Presbyterian churches surveyed their congregations during a Sunday morning worship service to see how many of them were single adults. Each church was shocked to discover that over 50 percent of their regular attendees were single.

Overcoming a Hardening of the Categories

An ancient bit of doggerel can serve us well as we attempt to reach single adults for Christ in this time of change.

Methods are many;
principles are few.
Methods always change;
principles never do.

As Americans we have a built-in penchant for packaging. After all, we're a world-class consumer society. Give us a product—any product—and we know how to wrap it, advertise it, price it, position it, and market it. Even Christian ministry. Too often the focus of our attention is on method rather than principle. And while principles are timeless, methods are time-specific. Rapidly changing societies demand rapidly changing methodologies.

The key, as regards the gospel, is to translate its message into understandable terms for a new generation of hearers without transforming it. This is a delicate art, so let me try to offer some handles.

Start with felt needs rather than real needs. Right off the bat, I've attacked—and I hope, mortally wounded—a sacred cow. Felt needs are front burner, real needs generally back burner.

Most of our attempts to reach unchurched people—single and married—are too direct for our suspicious-of-institutional-religion day. For example, we invite people to come to our Bible study, on our turf, and when it's convenient for us. That usually translates into something like, "We'd like you to come to our church (or home) to study the Book of Leviticus at 7:30 on Tuesday night."

That kind of approach is doomed to failure from the start. It asks too much of seekers, although it may be just fine for believers. It expects seekers to enter unfamiliar surroundings (the current number-one fear of Americans), to study a book of the Bible they couldn't spell even if their life depended on it, at a time of day that might be inconvenient or inappropriate (how many women want to stroll urban—or suburban—streets at night in these days of random violence?).

A friend of mine faced these important issues by developing an outreach to his target audience of professionals in high finance that took place on Thursday at lunchtime (one-hour time limit) in a popular watering hole located in a large hotel that caters to business people. Following a brief lunch and informal time of conversation around the tables, he led an in-depth Bible study on Leviticus (though they never knew it) in the seminar-style to which they are accustomed. Rather than entitle his talk to these real estate and financial moguls "A Layman Looks at Leviticus," he called it "How to Stay Afloat in a World That's Circling the Drain."

Formerly a successful business entrepreneur, he spoke their language from the outset by talking about the fast-track, get-rich-quick scams that stimulated the economy of the 1980s but proved to be bankrupt in the 1990s. After several minutes of this, he introduced the biblical teaching on the Year of Jubilee into the discussion. Using sound financial principles that would cause even Alan Greenspan to smile approvingly, he showed how God had a better way to avoid reversals of financial fortune by implementing a plan of economic fairness for all.

My wife and I sat and marveled at the skill with which he held his audience in the palm of his hand without missing a biblical beat. He began with their felt needs in mind and then gently moved toward addressing their real needs—God's provision for the safety and security of mankind. The felt needs of single adults are multitudinous. There are many places to begin.

Contextualize the message. It's more than cliché to say that we are called to be interpreters of both "the Word" and "the world." To contextualize the message means, essentially, to put it in user-friendly terms for a particular class of people.

Think about it for a minute. The basic makeup of humankind hasn't changed much since Jesus' day. Was the centurion with a deathly sick slave really that much different from the father who finds out that his twenty-seven-year-old son is dying of AIDS? Or was the unwed woman at the well in John 4 faced with any more pain or pariah-status than the contemporary single-again mom who's been touched by divorce for the second or third time?

The would-be evangelist in every era must ask similar hard questions, starting with, What is the cultural key I can use in unlocking this person's heart in order to help him hear the gospel of Christ in terms he understands?

My wife, who served as a missionary in western Europe for almost a decade, found that although people held widely different political, economic, and philosophical views, they had the same desires for love, hope, health, and happiness. She and her fellow missionaries further discovered that their once-narrow view of the people they were trying to reach as "heathens" was transformed over time to an important appreciation that "these people are more like us than they are different."

Spanish philosopher Miguel Unamuno said, "If we ever got honest enough to go out into the streets and uncover our common grief, we would discover that we are all grieving the selfsame things."

Give them time to change and grow. In recent decades evangelism was committed to seeing instantaneous life change. Converts were expected to walk the aisle or pray the prayer and change once and for all. The more contemporary—and currently effective—approach is to recognize that people who have lived thirty or forty years in unbelief may need more time to be transformed. While this doesn't make salvation any less an act of God, it does suggest the need to build relationships with people who may come to Christ over a period of months rather than minutes. Friendship Evangelism operates on the premise, If you want a healthy birth, you've got to have a healthy pregnancy.

This approach is realistic and workable. But it is also difficult, time-consuming, and often discouraging.

It is difficult because there is no longer such a thing as one-size-fits-all evangelism. In today's complex world, this approach has fallen by the wayside. Prepackaged evangelistic tools and strategies will continue to have their place and may even work well on occasion, but they are far too simplistic in a pluralistic society. The other problem with relying too heavily on them is suggested by the saying, If the only tool in your toolbox is a hammer, you tend to see every problem as a nail.

Reaching people with the gospel is time-consuming—and time is increasingly viewed by moderns as their most precious resource. Microwave ovens, VCRs, and voice mail all attest to that. The myth that singles have extra free time is just that—a myth.

Most of us are reluctant to invest our limited time and energy in developing new friendships because they demand too much output from already overloaded people. Yet, reaching today's single requires just such an investment because, more than ever, the gospel has to be seen as need-meeting in a practical, day-to-day sense.

Contemporary evangelism can be a discouraging enterprise because many people we're trying to reach have deep-seated problems besides unbelief. Broken and blended families, addictions, and codependent relationships are more than mere buzz words. They are realities. The odds are high that single adults coming out of a painful past will need to be dealt with and ministered to on more than a superficial or even single-issue level.

Bill Hybels, pastor of Willow Creek Community Church near Chicago, stated in an interview for *Preaching* magazine that their church is discovering that before they can disciple new converts in earnest they must first re-parent them. That's an incredible undertaking and one for which few churches are equipped.

Don't Give Up the Ship!

The reason evangelism seems so hard today, especially among singles, is that we're living in a new world. Before we can even hope to compete on a level playing field with cultic groups, Islam, neo-paganism, and New Age religions, we've got to find the stadium where the game is being played.

However, the good news for us would-be evangelists is twofold. First, biblical Christianity has always flourished in hostile environments. It's no accident that the blood of the martyrs was the seed of the church. Today's world is tailor-made for the gospel message. Paul, the greatest evangelist of all time, wasn't kidding when he wrote, "I am not ashamed of the gospel, because it is the power of God for the salvation of everyone who believes: first for the Jew, then for the Gentile" (Rom. 1:16).

Second, we have been given the unlimited power of the Holy Spirit. Jesus promised we wouldn't have to go it alone (Matt. 28:20). He would leave planet earth, but only so the Comforter might be sent. The Greek word for comforter is *paraclete*, which literally means "advocate," or "to come alongside of." So, we're not abandoned by God in the task.

Words—and Music Too

Our culture claims to have a supernatural outlook, yet most people live with an antisupernatural bias. When Christians try to share a message of faith that is supernatural at its very core, it is often rejected in the marketplace of ideas because it doesn't conform to the self-absorbed spirituality in vogue today.

Christians too often try to evangelize lost people without taking time to listen to what they are really saying and thinking. Still more dangerous, we assume we have to be able to answer every question asked of us—and on a moment's notice. Let me remind you, A fool can ask more questions than a wise person can answer.

A better approach in today's combative climate is to turn the tables by asking questions. Ask single adults you're trying to reach not only *what* they believe but *why* they believe it. Perhaps then they will see the contradictions in their thought process. Jesus confounded the religious authorities of his day with questions. Socrates and other master teachers did the same thing. Maybe it's time for Christians to start playing offense rather than defense.

Many of today's singles see mainstream Christianity as stifling and restrictive. They may have grown up in environments that emphasized dos and don'ts. As a result, they're often angry at and antagonistic toward "oldtime religion." To try to confront or "preach" to a person with that mind-set is to invite argument and animosity. Raising pertinent questions is a far less confrontational approach and one that encourages honest dialogue.

In the final analysis, evangelism to single adults must remain a fluid process. While it ought to be done intentionally, as the old saying goes, There's more than one way to skin a cat.

I've mentioned the role of words in evangelism, yet words often get in the way. Some years ago when I was in seminary, an astute professor reminded us that we ought to play the music of the gospel before we play the words. Most of us are more tuned in to another's attitudes and actions than we are to his or her answers. I've never forgotten the wisdom of that remark.

Recently I was talking to a single man who was caught up in the drug culture and related vices of the '70s and has since returned to the Lord. Having felt the call of God on his life for some time, a few weeks ago he began attending a nearby Christian college while holding down a full-time job. He reminded me of the following story.

Some centuries ago a young priest was invited by an older priest to go to a nearby town in order to evangelize it. When they got there, all the older man did was to mingle in the town square and talk to people. After several hours the young priest grew weary and impatient with his mentor. He asked, "When are we going to evangelize people?" The wise old man said, "We just did."

While the debate will continue to rage about when evangelism is actually taking place, we must never forget that spreading the faith requires relationship. This is especially true in the single adult community where empty words and promises fall on deaf ears. The Scots have a saying, The gospel is more felt than telt.

So, back to discovering the felt needs of single adults. Then address them with a love that is genuine and with contemporary understanding.

Contextualize the gospel message to make it clear. It *is* a relevant message. Then, give God time to draw single adults to himself and bring maturity to those who respond.

Single adult ministry can provide the context and acceptance for effective evangelism. We have the infallible message. We must train and encourage singles to build relationships where God's message of salvation can be heard and received. If we don't, no one else will.

39

Developing a Missions Ministry

Gilbert E. Crowell

A prevalent myth among single adults is that missions is a unique specialty that should be pursued or investigated only by those with a professional interest in the subject. I want to dispel this myth from the outset!

As a young, unmarried Christian single adult, I was pursuing career and women, not necessarily in that order. For me, a "mission" was a bombing run by a jet pilot or a task to be completed by the supply department of a naval vessel, or a Friday night search for Miss Right at the junior officer's club!

I had no idea what missions was all about from God's perspective until one unsuspecting day when I was challenged by the single-adult pastor at my church to sign up for a two-week mission trip to Guatemala. I had the time and the money and I liked the other people who had signed up, so why not? One of my favorite pastimes was travel; after all, isn't that one of the reasons why I had joined the Navy? Boy, was I naive to the purposes of God for my life!

Single adults in missions is an issue that should be considered by every pastor, associate pastor, or single-adult leader in beginning, developing, or enhancing any ministry with single adults. God desires that we line up our lives with his sovereignly revealed will. But this poses the question, What is God's purpose for missions?

Purpose

God's purpose is found in the Bible, beginning with his promise to Abraham in Genesis 12:3: "All peoples on earth will be blessed through you." God swore that, beginning with Abraham, he would move through history using those people who understood and believed his promise to pass on the good news of how one can have a personal relationship with God forever. This promise can be traced through the Bible from Abraham to Christ to every believer living on the earth today. Jesus Christ was the full and complete disclosure of God in the flesh. Some of the last words of our Lord on this earth were, "All authority in heaven and on earth has been given to me. Therefore go and make disciples of all nations, baptizing them in the name of the Father and of the Son and of the Holy Spirit, and teaching them to obey everything I have commanded you. And surely I am with you always, to the very end of the age" (Matt. 28:18–20).

Peter declared to the Jews that this ancient promise of God was for them (Acts 3:25–26). Paul announced to the Gentiles that they were recipients of God's promise to Abraham because of their faith (Gal. 3:6–9). John's Revelation shows that God's ancient promise will be fulfilled with peoples from every tongue, tribe, and nation worshiping God around his throne (5:9–10; 7:9–10).

Surely, the greatest purpose that any single adult could have is to be involved in God's purpose for missions—the extending of spiritual blessing to yet unreached peoples of the world! The previous passages show that God's purpose includes all of us, not just a select few, and that his purpose is destined to succeed.

Facts and Objectives

A short-term missions project for a group of single adults can be as brief as one day or as long as three years, depending upon its purpose and the location. The four most common purposes are education, evangelism, service, or a combination of the three.

Depending on your location, you may want to begin with a one-day or weekend trip. For example, if you are near Los Angeles, you may want to consider a one-day educational field trip to the head-quarters of Wycliffe Bible Translators in Huntington Beach. Or, if you are near Washington, D.C., you might want to arrange with Pioneers in Sterling, Virginia, to volunteer a group of ten single adults to handle all aspects of their next major mailing. Regardless of your location, you are probably not far from the U.S. office of an overseas mission that needs your help. *The Mission Handbook to USA/Canada Protestant Ministries Overseas*, copublished by MARC and Zondervan, will give you the name, address, and telephone number of a mission agency near you.

If all of this emphasis on missions is new to you or your singles group, you might want to do some research, get some input from others who have done various projects, and learn from them. If your group is considering an overseas trip, it is definitely to your advantage to go with an agency that has several years of experience in hosting groups. For example, Greater Europe Mission has a summer Eurocorps project that is excellent for first-time exposure to overseas missions. Operation Mobilization has years of experience in leading groups to missions involvement in places like Mexico or Europe.

Another good suggestion is to talk with Bridgebuilders, an agency designed for the express purpose of helping single adult groups plan, organize, execute, and evaluate short-term mission trips. The founder of Bridgebuilders, Chris Eaton, has coauthored a book with Kim Hurst entitled *Vacations with a Purpose: A Planning Handbook for Your Short-Term Missions Team* (NavPress) that is an excellent planning resource for your team. The book comes with a leader's guide as well as a manual for each team member. Do not make the mistake of thinking you have to go it alone or reinvent the wheel when it comes to planning a missions project. There are many people who are standing by ready to help you each step of the way.

Once you and your leadership team have decided on the purpose of your short-term missions project, you are ready to set some objectives concerning agency, time commitment, skills required, and finances.

For example, one year the singles group from my church chose to do a missions service project. They investigated agencies and decided to help Habitat for Humanity build a home in inner-city Atlanta for a needy single parent. Working with a project coordinator from the agency, they established a construction schedule, raised $20,000, and constructed the home from start to finish, working together on Saturdays over the course of a summer. The home was completed on schedule with over $7,000 left over! Almost 200 single adults were involved in the various phases of the project, and they still talk about the spiritual impact it had on their lives.

Another year, the singles decided to do a combined evangelistic and service-oriented missions project. Knowing their purpose, they chose to work with the Evangelical Association for the Promotion of Education, E.A.P.E., an agency founded by Tony Campolo. Six single adults went to Haiti for two weeks that summer and assisted in the construction of a small church building during the day, then using numerous opportunities to share their faith in the late afternoon and evening. Talk about vacation with a purpose! As a result, a bond of continuing love and partnership was formed between the two churches.

The purpose of the project will lead you to the appropriate agency to assist your team in formulating the rest of your objectives. At the end of the project you will want to assess whether those objectives were achieved.

Recruiting the Right People

The first person to recruit is the pastor of your church. If *you* are the pastor of a local church and have never been on a short-term missions trip overseas, you owe it to yourself and your single adults to go with them at least once. Our pastor accompanied us on a trip to Guatemala fifteen years ago. After the first night sleeping on the dirt floor of a hut in a mountain village, he returned to Guatemala City and checked into a hotel for the remainder of our time in the country. However, rather than that being a negative aspect, it was such a positive that he was with us in the country on the trip, supporting and encouraging us from the beginning and providing high visibility of leadership for the project to our home church, that it hardly mattered in the least that he was not with us every day of the trip. Even the ribbing that we gave him about checking into the hotel was well received and endeared him to our hearts.

The next objective should be to solicit the support and encouragement of the entire church through the leadership of the pastor, the elders, the deacons, and the missions committee. Failure to request the approval and involvement of the church's spiritual leaders can severely restrict the spiritual impact of the project upon the life and ministry of the congregation.

Don't neglect the children and youth as you publicize your mission trip. Go to the early childhood classes and let them know about the project. Consider providing custom-made stickers to all the children so they can know, pray, and tell their families about what the single adults are doing to tell others about Jesus. The kids will talk about the stickers with their dads and moms, brothers and sisters when they go home from church, especially if the teachers and singles have made it fun for them and stressed the importance of their involvement. In this simple way, you can easily have the entire church talking about the missions project in their homes! It will be a blessing to everyone in the church and the single adult ministry in the long run.

Involve the youth and the adult classes in creative ways also. Car washes, dramatic skits, or sports can all be used to advance the cause. One church that I know of has an annual Run for Missions, a Saturday Olympics-style competition among the different departments, capped off by a family fun run that includes everyone.

If the single-adult leaders are committed to a unified, churchwide approach rather than doing their own thing, it will be recognized by the spiritual leaders, affirmed by the church body, and blessed by God to the building up of the entire church.

Be careful to encourage the involvement of all the single adults from the outset, even though only a select number may take part in the mission ministry. All the single adults can be involved in praying, planning, organizing, and evaluation and reporting phases. Of course, it is necessary to know the strengths, talents, and spiritual gifts of each single adult who desires to be involved so that the best possible match can be made of abilities and function. A simple survey that asks single adults their skills and interests along with the level of spiritual commitment (beginner, intermediate, or advanced) is the place to start.

Cost Factors

Sometimes the leaders of churches that have not been involved in missions look at the expense factor and fear that encouraging parishioners to give to missions will somehow drain the already stretched church budget. Nothing is further from the truth. The more involved we become in what God is doing, the greater the blessing that will be extended to others, spiritually, physically, and financially. In the time I have gone from being a nearsighted Christian to more of a world Christian, my giving to the work of the local church has increased significantly, and my support of missions has grown steadily over the past several years. Once churches realize that they exist for a far greater reason than just to pay their own bills, they become empowered by the Spirit of God to fulfill the purposes of God. Jesus himself said, "Seek first his kingdom and his righteousness, and all these things will be given to you as well" (Matt. 6:33). This spiritual principle is applicable to churches as well as individuals.

One church in Barbados was meeting in a leaky tent and desperately needed a new building. Yet they sensed that God was leading them to invest their building fund in a missions project. They did so, and a few months later God provided all the money they needed for their church building! God blesses us in order that we might be a blessing to others who have not yet heard of Christ.

Money should not be the number one issue. The money will be there. Single-adult leaders need to inspire and motivate single adults to give their lives to a cause greater than themselves, the advancement of God's kingdom on earth!

The best way to inspire singles to adopt God's cause is to lead by example. The heart of a leader will always challenge and motivate others to follow.

Even though financial support is not the primary issue, it deserves adequate forethought. It is good when the church makes a commitment to provide a certain percentage of the support for the mission team and the single adults agree to provide or raise the funding for the remaining amount. Each church will determine the percentages that work best. The numerous ways funding can be developed are really limited only by the creative thinking of the leadership or the policies established by the church. If faith promise, pledging, or even selling raffle tickets is contrary to your church's fund-raising policies, you might consider ideas like a complimentary spaghetti dinner or a pancake breakfast where the team can share the vision for the project and ask attenders to prayerfully consider supporting the project.

The single adults in my church had a Bowling for Bibles night. They took pledges based on their bowling averages, went bowling one Friday night and received almost $400, which they used to purchase Bibles for Romania. It was an event that everyone could be involved in, even the non-churched seekers. Unleash those creative mental juices to discover how God will provide the funds for your group's missions project.

Team Dynamics

The success of any team, whether it be the Minnesota Twins in the World Series or the single adult missions team in your church, is dependent upon five key elements: common goal and purpose; accepted leadership; solid relationships; good communication; and division of labor, or specialization. We have previously mentioned common goal and accepted leadership; now, let's consider for a moment the other three.

Solid relationships and good communication are the result of spending committed, quality time together. Too often missions projects are undertaken with the naive idea that the project will come off on its own. Nothing could be further from the truth! Six to nine months of planning and meeting together regularly is essential to a good short-term summer project. This time enables the group to pray for one another, to grow in their understanding and caring for one another, and to cultivate their faith for the unexpected.

The group needs to be prepared for the spiritual obstacles that they will encounter as well as the spiritual threats to their own unity that are certain to come. After all, missions is a spiritual venture into enemy-occupied territory! Be prepared for the enemy to fight back; yet resist him, firm in your faith and oneness as a team, trusting the Lord Jesus Christ for spiritual victory. Learn to work together and play together as a team.

Division of labor, or specialization, is simply the use of each team member's unique gift, talents, and abilities in functional roles that enhance the team's productivity. You would not want a defensive end playing wide receiver on a football team. The same principle holds true for a missions team. Make sure each person's talents and abilities are being used; affirm and encourage their use; and create opportunities for their use if they do not presently exist.

Except for prayer, there is probably nothing that will reduce interpersonal conflict more than giving people the opportunity to use their God-given talents and abilities in ways that fill them up rather than wear them out. Survey the team at the outset to find out their unique talents, background, experience, or training, and be a good steward of the human resources the Lord provides. Each team member should have a unique role and possess a clear understanding of what is expected. It is amazing the increase in impact that can be achieved when team members work in harmony, using their gifts and abilities to their full extent.

When the day of departure arrives, it should be a time of celebration, involving everyone in the church if possible. Such a send-off can be compared to the one a high school or college athletic team receives prior to departing for an out-of-town championship game. Win or lose, it is the memory of their supporters' love and devotion that remains in the hearts and minds of the participants. The church should do no less for its missions teams!

Reporting and Evaluating

Part of the long-term planning is the reporting phase. Like the project itself, this may be as short as one evening or as long as several months but should be recognized as a vital phase of the overall project.

Short testimonies in worship services or classes, potluck dinners in homes including a lively discussion and sharing time, or a full-length sharing service are just a few options your team will want to consider.

Don't forget to greet the team upon their return, but be sensitive to the fact that they may be fatigued from the rigors of the project and the travel time back home. Give them a chance to recuperate and prepare before asking them to share extensively about their experiences.

Times of reporting should be uplifting yet realistic and honest. The team should be prepared to share not only the glory and the successes, but the hardships and difficulties encountered as well. Communicate accurately about the host country's cultures and lifestyles. Remember, a few short weeks in a host country does not make one an expert on all the spiritual and social dilemmas a country or people group may be facing. Be sure to include opportunities for continuing and ongoing investment.

Probably the most crucial yet most often neglected phase of short-term missions projects is evaluation. The leadership team needs to be disciplined in its determination to evaluate all aspects of the project in order that the insights and experience gained will not be lost. A written report to the church leaders will enhance future missions projects, regardless of the success of the immediate project.

Did the missions project accomplish its stated purpose and goal? Was the investment of time and money a good one in terms of the return? Keep in mind that the return on investment can be subjective as well as objective. The spiritual lives of most short-term missions participants are dramatically changed for the better; believe it or not, they usually benefit even more than the target group they set out to assist or serve! In light of all that was learned and experienced, what recommendations should be made to the leadership group for the next missions project? These are the types of questions that need to be asked and answered in writing before the project is considered complete.

Conclusion

If we truly believe that God is in the process of bringing to himself representatives from every tribe, tongue, people, and nation to worship him before his throne, as the Bible so vividly describes in Revelation 5:9–10 and 7:9–10, then what remains for us to do?

The greatest destiny any of us can have is to move in the direction that our infinite, sovereign God has chosen to go. In the Bible God has clearly revealed that he is moving in the direction of world missions.

Several years ago, I went on a short-term missions trip to Portugal for two weeks. During that time, I was involved with ten American single adults and ten Portuguese singles in an evangelistic campaign. During the day we would distribute flyers at the public markets and train stations, inviting people to come to evangelistic meetings that night. I vividly remember my anticipation in waiting for all the people to show up for our meetings, after passing out over 5,000 invitations! The first night one elderly woman came. With the other twenty team members present, at least she did not know she was the only one who came! Our meetings continued, and at the end of the two weeks, three new believers in the Lord Jesus Christ were baptized in the Atlantic Ocean. What a joy it was to experience with them their excitement over their new life in Christ!

There are many, many single adults who are living and dying without a cause. As single-adult leaders, we have the opportunity to challenge them to become involved with the Lord Jesus Christ in advancing God's kingdom on earth. Let's make the most of the time and opportunity we have been given. Let's get started today!

Discipling Single Adults

Norm Yukers

One Saturday in February 1991 I was leading a workshop at an NSL (Network of Single Adult Leaders) conference. My topic was "Discipling Single Adults." I had planned for twenty participants and was surprised to see more than fifty people in the room. I realized then what I had been suspecting for a while—singles and their leaders are starved for discipleship and need the tools to develop this vital area of ministry.

My discipleship actually started in 1981. I was not attending church anymore and didn't give two hoots about God—or so I thought. But that year, someone took the time to tell me about Jesus Christ and how I needed a personal relationship with him. The next week I was in a church and two weeks later was being discipled by the pastor. Of course, I didn't know I was being discipled; I just knew I was hungry and someone was taking time to feed me.

Because of that nurturing, I was able to grow quickly. Fourteen months after my realization of a need for a personal Savior, I was leading a group of single adults on that same journey. It was at this time I felt called by God to full-time ministry as a singles pastor. Several years later, I found myself in seminary and being discipled by a professor who challenged me to begin a discipleship emphasis to my ministry.

299

A friend in my singles ministry and I set out to create a discipleship emphasis where Christians would grow up straight and tall and connected together in a common root system—Jesus Christ. We called our course "The Redwood Program." Some of our ideas and principles will be shared in the following pages.

Discipling Single Adults

Dietrich Bonhoeffer describes discipleship as "adherence to Christ." He goes on to say, "Christianity without discipleship is Christianity without Christ."

In this day of emphasis on freedom and equality, and with so many people unchurched, it is not popular to teach total obedience. But the Bible does not present any other message. Discipleship is obedience, and we should not make light of it.

What is the purpose of a singles group? It should be no different than the scriptural purpose of the church. Ephesians 3:14–21 gives us a picture of this purpose with a bottom line of *bringing glory to God.*

> For this reason I kneel before the Father, from whom his whole family in heaven and on earth derives its name. I pray that out of his glorious riches he may strengthen you with power through his Spirit in your inner being, so that Christ may dwell in your hearts through faith. And I pray that you, being rooted and established in love, may have power, together with all the saints, to grasp how wide and long and high and deep is the love of Christ, and to know this love that surpasses knowledge—that you may be filled to the measure of all the fullness of God.
>
> Now to him who is able to do immeasurably more than all we ask or imagine, according to his power that is at work within us, to him be glory in the church and in Christ Jesus throughout all generations, for ever and ever! Amen.

You may be saying to yourself, *What a profound mystery. Our singles group is to bring glory to God! But how do we know if we are succeeding?* The answer is actually quite simple. Our goals must be based on the purpose. Fortunately, the Bible gives us those goals.

Ephesians 4:11–14 clearly tells leaders that our charge is to help people mature in the unity of the faith and grow in the knowledge of the Son of God. Matthew 28:18–20 challenges us to go and make disciples, teaching them to obey all that Jesus had commanded.

Nothing glorifies God more than a Christlike person who is living out the lifestyle of Galatians 5:22–24: "But the fruit of the Spirit is love, joy, peace, patience, kindness, goodness, faithfulness, gentleness and self-control. Against such things there is no law. Those who belong to Christ Jesus have crucified the sinful nature with its passions and desires."

You might be asking, "How do I begin?" Let us identify disciples and their characteristics.

Becoming Disciples

I believe in horizontal or continuum discipleship as opposed to vertical. Jesus is the discipler, and all believers are somewhere on the continuum as disciples. One may be further along the line than another, but the learning goes both ways. Therefore, these ideas are aimed at both leaders and those they lead. Leaders need to apply these principles to their own lives as well as to their discipleship of others.

In the vertical discipleship model, there is Jesus and the disciple, but the discipler is plugged in the middle, a contact point between Jesus and the disciple. I cannot find reference to that model in Scripture.

People who want to be discipled should exhibit certain qualities. These qualities or characteristics all begin with the letter *C*.

Converted. A person must be converted in order to be considered for discipleship. Until one's eyes are opened to spiritual things, obedience at all cost is not an option.

Churched. A person must be churched. I am not saying that parachurch organizations cannot do discipleship. Rather, I am pointing out that just as Christ ordained the local church to carry out his plan, so we also should look for those individuals who are active in the local church. More will be said about this later.

Compassionate. A person must be compassionate toward the lost. This could manifest itself in at least three ways: the first and most basic is personally praying for those apart from Christ; the second is bringing an unsaved or unchurched person to a place, activity, or meeting where they would hear the claims of Christ; the third is giving personal testimony and actually sharing with someone about Christ.

Craving. A person must have a craving for the Bible (1 Peter 2:1–2). The learner should desire, above all else, to know Christ in an intimate way; through a greater understanding of the Bible, he or she can begin the journey to this intimacy. Just as a hungry person is first in line at a picnic with his plate and plastic silverware, so should a discipler be ready with Bible, pen, and paper to be fed spiritually.

Consecrated. A person must want to be consecrated. He or she should be willing to lead a Romans 12:1–2 life. Following is a wheel figure illustrating the four spokes to a life centered around Christ—a life of discipleship.

The Well-Balanced Christian Life

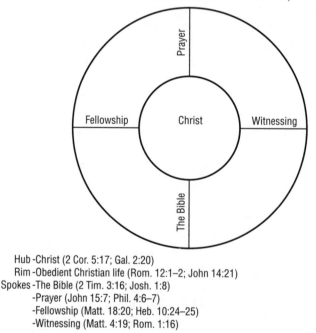

Hub -Christ (2 Cor. 5:17; Gal. 2:20)
Rim -Obedient Christian life (Rom. 12:1–2; John 14:21)
Spokes -The Bible (2 Tim. 3:16; Josh. 1:8)
    -Prayer (John 15:7; Phil. 4:6–7)
    -Fellowship (Matt. 18:20; Heb. 10:24–25)
    -Witnessing (Matt. 4:19; Rom. 1:16)

Therefore, I urge you, brothers, in view of God's mercy, to offer your bodies as living sacrifices, holy and pleasing to God—this is your spiritual act of worship. Do not conform any longer to the pattern of this world, but be transformed by the renewing of your mind. Then you will be able to test and approve what God's will is—his good, pleasing and perfect will.

A person will grow to be a Romans 12:1–2 Christian as he is exposed to the commands and teachings of Christ and has the willingness to obey them.

The Bible, God's Word

As we look at the spoke called "The Bible," we see at least five ways to get God's Word into our lives. These five ways are often illustrated as a hand.

The thumb is *hearing* (Rom. 10:17). Hearing can be listening to audiocassettes, attending preaching services, and taking notes during sermons.

The index finger represents *reading* (Rev. 1:3) the Word. There are many one-year Bibles on the market that will allow you to read the complete Bible with planned variety in a year. It is my opinion that every Christian should read through the Bible yearly.

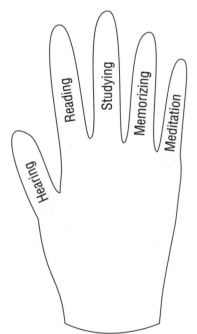

Studying the Word (Acts 17:11) is the middle finger of the hand. Many good Bible study systems are available at Christian bookstores.

Memorizing (Ps. 119:9–11) is the ring finger. Again, many good systems are available, including the Navigators' "Topical Memory System."

The pinkie finger represents *meditation.* Lately, some Christians have been frightened away from meditation, thinking it to be part of Eastern mysticism. Psalm 1:2–3 clearly tells us that meditating day and night is a good thing.

Now that we have the hand completed, let's consider our need for all these approaches to the Bible. Try to hold a book by the thumb only. Even if you could balance it, it would be very easy to snatch it from you. If you hold it with your thumb and index finger, the book is a little more stable, but still not secure. As you add each remaining finger, the stability and security increases. So it is with the Word of God. As you put yourself under the hearing of it, regularly read it, seriously study it, memorize it, and meditate on it, you will find it bringing stability and security to your life.

Prayer

The disciples asked Jesus to teach them to pray. He responded by giving them the prayer recorded for us in Matthew 6:9–13. Here Jesus was teaching not only *how* to pray, but *what* to pray. We are able to follow this pattern because we are disciples of Jesus, who mediates for us to God the Father. Because we have placed our faith in Jesus, we can pray to our Father. For an excellent treatment on prayer and discipleship, see *The Cost of Discipleship* by Dietrich Bonhoeffer.

Fellowship

The next spoke that keeps the wheel of the discipled life balanced is fellowship. As we see in Acts 2:42–47, among all the things the disciples were devoted to, fellowship was right in the middle. This is the context for disciple-making.

They devoted themselves to the apostles' teaching and to the fellowship, to the breaking of bread and to prayer. Everyone was filled with awe, and many wonders and miraculous signs were done by the apostles. All the believers were together and had everything in common. Selling their possessions and goods, they gave to anyone as he had need. Every day they continued to meet together in the temple courts. They broke bread in their homes and ate together with glad and sincere hearts, praising God and enjoying the favor of all the people. And the Lord added to their number daily those who were being saved.

In fact, the desire for community is a mark of a true disciple. Community may be two or three nurturing each other, holding one another accountable. Or, a small group of six to twelve may covenant together for spiritual growth and accountability. Regardless of the number, the communal commitment is imperative.

True disciples are a glad and joyful people and thus enjoy being with each other. A healthy and dynamic discipleship ministry for single adults will include both one-on-one and small group fellowship. This intimacy through community development is a discipleship imperative.

Witnessing

The final spoke of the discipleship wheel is witnessing. When we enter the freedom that comes with a relationship with Jesus, we carry a responsibility for sharing this with others. Some people freeze up at the thought of this area of discipleship. They think, *Oh no! Here it comes! I knew it! They want me to go in the street and pass out those gospel tracts! I'm not an evangelist!*

Instead of viewing the reproducing of our Christian lives as an action, let's view it as a lifestyle. Jesus told us that the field is ready for harvest. "Do you not say, 'Four months more and then the harvest'? I tell you, open your eyes and look at the fields! They are ripe for harvest" (John 4:35). We need to view the world and the people in it as Jesus does.

Paul told us to prepare ourselves as do soldiers preparing for battle. This preparation requires a team approach. Reproducing together through ministry teams is a powerful arena for individual growth. "Endure hardship with us like a good soldier of Christ Jesus. No one serving as a soldier gets involved in civilian affairs— he wants to please his commanding officer" (2 Tim. 2:3–4).

In *Disciples in Action* Leroy Eims wrote, "Every heart without Christ is a mission field. Every heart with Christ is a missionary." We are Jesus' plan to carry the message to those in need. A good disciple knows that and does his or her part.

For the single adult the Christian life is not easy, but if we prepare them for it in Christ, they will not be overwhelmed but can be overcomers.

Once single adults have learned and put into practice the principles shown in the wheel and hand illustrations, they are well on their way to becoming Romans 12:2 believers and true disciples of Jesus Christ.

For Further Reading

Bonhoeffer, Dietrich. *The Cost of Discipleship.* New York: The Macmillan Company, 1949, 1960.

Campus Crusade for Christ. *How to Make Your Mark* (A Manual for Evangelism and Discipleship). San Bernardino: Here's Life Publishers, Inc., 1983.

Eims, Leroy. *Disciples in Action* (Witnessing, Making Disciples, Equipping Laborers, Training Leaders). Colorado Springs: NavPress, 1981.

Pratney, Winkie. *A Handbook for Followers of Jesus.* Minneapolis: Bethany Fellowship, Inc. 1977.

Ridenour, Fritz. *Lord, What's Really Important?* (Discovering a Biblical Lifestyle). Ventura, Calif.: Regal Books, 1978.

Riggs, Charles. *Thirty Devotional Exercises* (A Discipleship Tool). Minneapolis: Billy Graham Evangelistic Association, 1980.

Part **7**

Developing Significant Ministries

Dealing with Dating Realities

Michael Platter

The dating scene has changed considerably in recent years, and the growth of the single adult population in the United States ensures that these changes are going to last a while. Dating is no longer just "kid's stuff" for teenagers experiencing puppy love, prom dances, and pimples. Now millions of widowed, divorced, and never-married adults have entered the arena, bringing with them a whole new set of concerns about dating including sexuality and, for some, Christian responsibility.

I suspect that many singles would love to close their eyes and wish the whole dating scene away, since dating causes considerable anxiety. But it really cannot be avoided. Our society has for years encouraged the dating process as the proper way for an unmarried person to find a mate. This alone makes it a weighty issue. And, as if that isn't heavy enough, our peers have also piled on additional baggage by suggesting that one's dating life is a gauge of social desirability, physical attractiveness, and sometimes even of sexual prowess or preference. Given all of these pressures on a single person, the need for good teaching on the subject is clear. Although the realities of adult dating are complicated, the valid concerns surrounding this issue are opportunities for growth and maturity, both for individuals and for single adult ministry.

What are our responsibilities as leaders when it comes to dealing with dating? Let's look at three areas that should be addressed in order to meet this issue appropriately. The first focuses on the type of teaching that can help single adults grapple with important questions. The second concerns glorifying God in dating. The third deals with how the single adult ministry group can best serve in light of the issues surrounding dating.

Scriptural Background for Dating

When it comes to proclaiming the Bible's teaching on the subject of dating, at first appearance it may seem that we have very little to work with. The Bible does not speak about dating per se because the different societies in existence at that time did not use dating as a method of selecting marriage partners. Prearranged marriages, polygamy, payment for brides, etc., were common practices in Bible times. There was no room for "Love, American-style."

However, the Bible does say a great deal about male-female relationships and about Christian relationships in general. As we look to scriptural teaching in these areas, we can apply it to dating.

Let's take a look at some of the apostle Paul's teaching regarding singleness and also his concern for proper Christian conduct with the opposite sex:

> But I say to the unmarried and to widows that it is good for them if they remain even as I [unmarried]. But if they do not have self-control, let them marry; for it is better to marry than to burn. . . . Only, as the Lord has assigned to each one, as God has called each, in this manner let him walk. . . . Let each man remain in that condition in which he was called. . . .
>
> Now concerning virgins I have no command of the Lord, but I give an opinion as one who by the mercy of the Lord is trustworthy. I think then that this is good in view of the present distress, that it is good for a man to remain as he is. Are you bound to a wife? Do not seek to be released. Are you released from a wife? Do not seek a wife. But if you should marry, you have not sinned; and if a virgin should marry, she has not sinned. . . .
>
> I want you to be free from concern. One who is unmarried is concerned about the things of the Lord, how he may please the

Lord. . . . And the woman who is unmarried, and the virgin, is concerned about the things of the Lord, that she may be holy both in body and spirit; but one who is married is concerned about the things of the world, how she may please her husband. And this I say for your own benefit; not to put a restraint upon you, but to promote what is seemly, and to secure undistracted devotion to the Lord (1 Cor. 7:8–9, 17, 20, 25–28, 32, 34–35 NASB).

These selected passages from Paul's letter to the church at Corinth suggest some important starting points for a discussion of dating. First, Paul wants to emphasize to his readers that it is all right to marry. He wants them to understand that the decision to remain single in order to give more time and energy to Christ's work (as he himself was doing) is also perfectly valid. It is even the preferred choice if it is God's particular calling for an individual. But marriage still honors Christ, Paul says, and is a calling blessed by God.

Perhaps it goes without saying, but this passage reminds me that if it is all right to marry, it must be all right to date as well. Some singles might feel that dating would threaten their relationship to God and that they may be compromising on their "undivided devotion" to Christ if they start dating. But Paul is saying here that it is fine to pursue marriage. In our culture, dating is the way to do that. Singles should be reminded that though God may have called them to singleness now, it may not be his permanent calling for them. Those who want to date should feel free to do so unless God definitely tells them no.

In other parts of this passage (vv. 10–14, 39), Paul sends a second message about a Christian's relationship with the opposite sex: *God's will is that Christians marry Christians.* Paul's approach to dating and marriage is that the Christian is to be motivated by what will honor Christ the most. Since marriage to a non-Christian is unscriptural, dating a non-Christian is certainly a risky activity. We cannot use this text to definitely say that it is sin to date a non-Christian, but certainly there must be caution against allowing a relationship with an unbeliever to progress toward deep love and commitment.

Another aspect of dating that arises from this passage is contained in the Scriptures directly preceding Paul's discourse in chapter 7. It is important to read because it sets the stage for Paul's teaching on Christian behavior between males and females.

Do you not know that your bodies are members of Christ? Shall I then take away the members of Christ and make them members of a harlot? May it never be! . . . Flee immorality. Every other sin that a man commits is outside the body, but the immoral man sins against his own body. Or do you not know that your body is a temple of the Holy Spirit who is in you, whom you have from God, and that you are not your own? For you have been bought with a price; therefore glorify God in your body (1 Cor. 6:15, 18–20 NASB).

Paul's third message is that sexual intimacy outside of marriage is a violation of God's law. This is one of the most critical concerns that single adult ministry must address. We live in a culture that has decided to cast aside God's laws regarding sexual purity, and Christian single adults are frequently tempted to buy into the values of their secular peers. But the Bible is clear on the issue: *Sex outside of marriage is a sin against God.*

Many single adults struggle with sexual issues in their dating lives. Not only are there strong natural sexual desires that are encountered in close dating relationships, but also these desires are sometimes more complicated by past sexual practices. For example, those who were formerly married were accustomed to being able to pursue their sexual desires with their spouses. But following widowhood or divorce, these newly single people must learn to restrain their sexuality during affectionate moments as experienced in dating. Yet, regardless of the sexual attraction during dating, the Christian stand is clear: God says no to sex before marriage.

Part of an approach to dealing with the issues of sex and dating should be an explanation of God's positive design for sexuality as well as his restrictions. Scripture clearly shows that God plans for sex to be enjoyable and fulfilling (Song of Solomon 7:6–8). Since God created our bodies and their particular sexual functioning, he knows the conditions in which our sexual lives will be safest and most satisfying. Therefore, the rules that he has set forth in the Bible should not be viewed as attempts to stifle our sexual pleasure but as explanations of the conditions in which sex is most fulfilling. He is the Master Designer; it is in our best interest to follow the "manufacturer's instructions." Those instructions tell us that sex outside of marriage is unsafe; it leaves people vulnerable to the increasing plagues of sexually transmitted diseases and to the psychological and sociological pains of unwanted pregnancies, abortions, sexual dysfunction due to guilt, and so forth. Add to these effects some of the other social griefs in our culture related to rampant sexuality; child molestation at astronomical rates, widespread pornography, increases in flagrant homosexuality and bisexuality, date rape and work-related sexual harassment, the AIDS epidemic, and numerous others.

Single adults need to know that God has created sexuality as a powerful force for personal pleasure and joy. But like any powerful force, the sexual urge must first be contained and then channeled in order to be useful. In this way it is like a river, a source of great power and productivity as long as it stays within its banks. But when it overflows the boundaries intended for it, floods cause widespread damage and destruction.

The bottom line for the Christian is that sexual intimacy is not to be part of the dating life of any single adult. Some of the factors in attaining sexual self-control will be dealt with in the next section.

Beyond the apostle Paul's three teachings mentioned above, other passages shed light on the Bible's expectations of Christian dating. Let's look at a few more verses from the New Testament:

> Let no one seek his own good, but that of his neighbor. . . . Whether, then, you eat or drink or whatever you do, do all to the glory of God. Give no offense either to Jews or to Greeks or to the church of God (1 Cor. 10:24, 31–32 NASB).

> For you were called to freedom, brethren; only do not turn your freedom into an opportunity for the flesh, but through love serve one another. . . . You shall love your neighbor as yourself (Gal. 5:13–14 NASB).

> And so, as those who have been chosen of God, holy and beloved, put on a heart of compassion, kindness, humility, gentleness and patience; bearing with one another, and forgiving each other, whoever has a complaint against anyone; just as the Lord forgave you, so also should you. . . . Do all in the name of the Lord Jesus, giving thanks through Him to God the Father (Col. 3:12–13, 17 NASB).

Scripture places a priority on Christians showing kindness and love to Christian brothers and sisters, seeking the good of others before one's own good, and ultimately doing everything to God's glory. It's a tall order to fill, but God's grace is available to help us to live Christlike lives—even in dating.

Christian dating should have one primary purpose—*to glorify God.* That is the first and best purpose of all Christians. Dating does not glorify God if it leads to sexual immorality or to treating others in ways that are unkind, unloving, and inconsiderate of the other's good. This is not an easy task in dating, since emotions and attractions have a way of becoming intense and easily injured when men and women become close. Still, it is a worthy motivation to date in a way that truly honors our heavenly Father.

Dating That Glorifies God

Let me suggest a few ideas you may wish to pass along to those in your ministry to help them see dating as a way to glorify God and also to keep Christian kindness at the forefront of a relationship.

Keep Your Date's Interests and Happiness at Heart

The person you have chosen to date is someone God wants to be happy, to grow, and to be a well-rounded individual. Try to do the things that your date is likely to enjoy. Go to places and do activities that are positive and uplifting and that you will both enjoy. Keep in mind that caring for another person's happiness involves more than just entertainment. It also includes contributing to his or her personal growth and to your own as well. Your date's growth can occur mentally, physically, socially, emotionally, spiritually.

Try some of the following activities to keep dating interesting, full of variety, and growth-producing: visit an art museum; take a picnic in a state park and walk on a guided trail; play tennis, badminton, or racquetball; go to sports activities; watch classic movies on video; try a variety of regional restaurants and sample international dishes; attend a concert; go to a mall and visit shops you've not tried before; take a community education class together; go to a play; try cooking a new dish, etcetera, etcetera, etcetera.

Don't Expect Dating to Bring "Mr. or Ms. Right" Your Way

Some single adults mistakenly believe that if they wait long enough and look hard enough, the perfect person will magically appear. The sad thing about this view is that many singles forget to make productive use of this waiting time. Since our goal is to live to God's glory, we should be focusing on growth, whether we are in a relationship or not. One of the best quotes I ever heard at a single adult conference was this: "Stop waiting for Ms. Right and start concentrating on being Mr. Right!" And vice versa.

Remember to "Handle with Care"

One of the frightening aspects of dating is the possibility of a painful breakup. Since only one dating relationship will lead to marriage, most single adults have experienced one or more relationship breakups. As a Christian you are to care about your partner's feelings as much as you do your own. This means that you avoid making promises concerning commitments you don't intend to fulfill. Attempt to break up kindly, with no personal attacks and without undue criticism or gossip. Be cautious about claiming affection that you don't truly feel. Leading someone on brings more pain in the long run than the painful truth at an earlier stage of the relationship.

Be Responsible with Sexual Issues

Probably the most complicated aspect of dating falls under this category. The issue of sexual purity has already been discussed, but let me add some specific guidelines that have been helpful in establishing sexual control in dating:

1. *Establish your sexual standards before you face the temptations of dating.* Short of sexual intercourse, the Bible is not specific about where to draw the line in showing physical affection between males and females. But the general teaching of Scripture is clear—you are not to become sexually intimate before marriage. In fact, you are even told to restrain lustful thoughts in your heart and mind (Matt. 5:27–30). Since you are not to be sexually impure nor engage in lust, you have a responsibility to avoid subjecting your date to undue sexual temptation. You know where your per-

sonal "line" is when it comes to lustful thoughts and strong sexual desires. If you sense that your partner is coming close to his or her boundaries sexually, you have a responsibility to cool things down. These issues are not easy, but it is your goal to glorify God and to help your Christian brothers and sisters to do the same. Know your limits, your strengths and your weaknesses. Talk about your sexuality with another person in an accountability situation, if this would help your self-control. Pray about your desire to honor God by not misusing or abusing his gift of sexuality.

Whatever you do, don't make the mistake of determining your sexual standards while in the passion of an intense romantic evening. And don't play the How-close-to-the-edge-can-I-get-without-going-over game. You are more likely to fail if you don't *prepare* to succeed in your sexual life.

2. *Plan your dates to focus on other things than unrestricted intimacy.* I remember the classic joke about a young man who asked a girl out by saying, "Hey, tonight let's go to a movie or something." Her reply was, "We'll go to a movie or nothing!" There is a nugget of wisdom in her answer. When there is no plan for the date, it is very easy for a couple to just spend time "making out" and struggling with sexual control. Some couples go through this weekend after weekend. They could avoid some of the intense temptation if they would carefully plan their dates for enjoyable social activities and leave less time for physical temptation.

Certainly couples should still plan time for romance and affection, but they should make sure that their dates include plenty of time for other activities that bring them together intellectually, emotionally, etc. rather than just physically. Because the experience of physical affection is so satisfying, it is often easy to let it take the place of conversation, discussion of values or relationship issues, etc. But this can be dangerous in the future—the enduring foundation of a good relationship is in the friendship, not in the sexual intensity.

3. *Keep in mind who your date is.* As a single person who has had to deal with these dating issues myself, I have found great strength in always recalling whom it is I'm dating. I remind myself that I'm going out with a daughter of God. As a teenager, I remember how frightening it was to meet the fathers of the girls I wanted to date.

I remember the fear I felt of what these men might do if I ever mistreated or hurt their daughters. I think it's wise for Christians to remember that whomever they are dating, that person is a son or daughter of God, and God is committed to the sexual purity and wholeness of his children. I would not want to incur his disappointment by mistreating a child of his for whom he has paid such a great price.

A Single Adult Ministry Response

Since the issues involved in dating have implications for single adult ministries as well as for individuals, I want to briefly address a few points that may need to be considered in leading a group.

Deal Squarely with Christian Dating Issues

Most single adults have a high interest in this issue. Take some time in your plan of activities to talk about dating ethics, dating problems, sexuality, etc. You may wish to have a speaker do a dating seminar, or you might read some good material on the issues and prepare your own seminar. Try tossing out some of the tough issues and questions to discussion circles or talk-it-over groups. Don't worry about not having all the answers; the issues are too broad and complicated for any leader to have complete answers; just deal with the questions.

Concentrate on Affirming Your Singles

Unfortunately, in the American culture, dating has been pictured as a game of the Haves versus the Have-Nots. Often women who are asked out on dates are seen as physically attractive and socially adept; women who seldom or never date are assumed to be undesirable physically or socially. The dating process and the values attached to it can often be cruel to those who are not dating much. Since our culture permits men greater social freedom in initiating dates, many women feel at the mercy of an unfair process and may also feel self-conscious or bitter. A man who does not date may be the object of silent concern as to his sexual orientation or be regarded as one who has never broken free of his attachments to his mother.

On the other hand, those who do date frequently may be seen as proud, easy, lacking in spiritual depth, or as having loose morals. Because our society has attached such desirability issues to the dating process, the fallout of hurt feelings or judgmental attitudes can be damaging.

Be sure to affirm the worth and desirability of each single adult through positive messages of self-worth. Let them know that you and the group accept them, believe in them, love and value them because they are created in God's image and are worthwhile, no matter how the dating scene goes.

Watch for Wolves in the Fold

In 1 Peter 5:2 we read, "Shepherd the flock of God among you, not under compulsion, but voluntarily, according to the will of God." Later in that chapter Peter reminds us that Satan prowls about like a roaring lion, seeking to devour the ones you have been called upon to protect (v. 8). One of the rough tasks of church leadership is caring for the weak and powerless among the flock of God, for Satan truly will try to hurt and injure them.

I find that in single adult groups there are a great number of people who have been hurt by painful relationships and broken commitments. I'm convinced that God dearly loves all his sheep and is especially concerned that these hurt lambs of his be in a safe place where they can find healing. You want that place to be your single adult ministry. As shepherd to these hurting sheep, guard against things that could expose them to hurt again; and particularly guard against those "wolves" who are looking for easy prey. Most likely, they will enter your group dressed as sheep, and it may take you a while to recognize them. And you must be cautious against judging—even wolves may need a safe place to heal. Your goal is not to judge but to protect the weak and hurting.

Decide some policies in advance to help you guard your flock. For example, you may decide that your ministry will not have activities where pairing off is required (such as a formal sweetheart banquet). You will definitely need to consider a policy regarding keeping phone numbers and addresses confidential. For example, our group recently switched to listing only first names on name tags in order to better protect women from unwanted phone calls from strangers.

Decide What Your Group Emphasis Will Be

What do you think God is calling your single adult group to be? Do you believe that you are to be a social network for Christian singles? Do you sense that God is particularly leading your group to focus on nonchurched single moms? Have you felt that your group is supposed to be primarily a Bible study and to keep a strong spiritual emphasis?

I'm convinced that God has a unique ministry for you and your group. I also believe that no one group is capable of ministering to the vast needs of singles in a large area—that it takes several groups fulfilling different roles to present a well-rounded ministry to a community. Find your specific calling and do your best to meet the needs that seem to be God's direction for you. You may feel that God does not wish for your group to emphasize finding a mate but instead wishes it to focus on plugging single adults into church ministry. And yet there are some single adult ministries that believe that God's leading is for them to help single adults pair off and find a possible romance. Both fulfill needs that Christian single adults have. Find your niche and fill it, and it will help to define ministry growth and spiritual growth.

Encourage Your Singles to Build Friendships

Dating relationships come and go—often they seem to mostly go. And although dating holds some great possibilities for both individual and group growth, it is wise to encourage single adults to concentrate on forming good friendships. Friendship is much more stable in a person's life than romantic attraction. It is important that single adults are grounded in the love and commitment of friends, for friends tend to stand by through the easy and the difficult times, but dates often do not have such long-term commitment. Besides, the friendship bond is the basis of all good relationships; so if single adults constantly work on their friendship ability, those skills will eventually be helpful in relationship-building with a potential date—or mate.

Developing Ministry to Single Parents

Bobbie Reed

When I was a little girl playing house, there was always a daddy. I never dreamed I would be a single parent," Donna shared.

Many single parents can identify with Donna. Parenting is at least a two-person job, and single parents face daily challenges that make them feel overloaded emotionally, physically, and psychologically. Most single parents approach their responsibilities with a serious determination not to fail. Our society accepts failed marriages, businesses, finances, ethics, careers, and almost any other kind of failure, but there is less tolerance of poor parenting. The pressure is tremendous.

Single parents must be mature enough and strong enough to take care of the needs of the children in spite of sometimes feeling needy themselves. When too harsh discipline is handed out in frustration and there is not that other parent around to say, "Well, now, Honey, maybe just this once . . ." single parents have to learn to temper their own decisions and disciplines. When children aren't coping well with the change in the family structure, single parents often acutely feel the need for the support of a spouse and fellow parent.

In order to continue to function as a family, single parents must learn to change their To-Do lists. Some tasks will just have to be eliminated, others completed less frequently, while still others

320

can be shared with the kids. Attempts to do it all and be Super-man or Wonder Woman will only wear out the parents.

Facing the challenges of parenting and failing at times to suc-ceed in all the ways they want to can result in a serious loss of self-esteem for single parents. They often feel as if one small set-back labels them a total failure. During such times, the children tend to sense the lack of confidence and leap at the chance to take control of the family.

On the other hand, there are moments of joy, times of family closeness, and exciting occasions in the single parenting experience:

- a special closeness with the children
- being able to raise them *your* way
- seeing them make progress in their own growth toward maturity
- sharing your faith and worshipping together

Ways to Minister

Wherever the single parents in your church are in their jour-neys, you can help.

Redefine the Term "Family"

In some churches the term "family" is still limited to those groupings that have two parents in the home. However, researchers say that one out of every two children born in the 1980s will spend some time living in a one-parent family. A family can be one par-ent and his or her children. If we accept this reality, our programs may also undergo some changes. Mother-daughter or father-son activities might become parent-child functions, or provisions might be made for sonless or daughterless people to be surrogate mothers and dads for the occasions.

Provide Respite

Many single parents have no family in the area, do not have ex-spouses who take the children away for visits periodically, and cannot afford childcare for anything more than the time they are at work. They have virtually no free time away from the children.

Reading a book, taking a nap, running errands alone, cleaning house without being interrupted to play judge between two siblings, or listening to quiet music are often only fantasies for single parents. One of the greatest rejuvenators you can give the single parents in your ministries is an afternoon or evening alone.

In one church four men provide free respite for the single parents by taking the children on a four-hour outing once a month. One mother who takes advantage of this offer admits to spending most of her free afternoons just sitting alone in her house listening to the quiet or taking a nap. Often married couples are willing to take single-parent children for Friday nights or a Saturday if they understand just how much their gift will be appreciated.

Check Your Program

Single adult ministry leaders will want to ensure that there is childcare provided for single adult functions. Often those who need the workshop or fellowship the most can afford it the least. Given the choice between paying $5–$10 for childcare to attend a Bible study and using that money to pay for food, the single parent will usually choose the groceries.

The single adult calendar needs to be balanced to include free activities as well as some for which there is a charge. Each month include at least one event where children are welcome.

Develop Support Groups

One of the more successful and helpful ministries for single parents is a weekly or biweekly discussion group where they can talk about what's happening in their lives. Although the discussions are on assigned topics, members are encouraged to be open about their difficulties and their successes. From this sharing, a sense of community develops and the body of Christ is edified. Shared problems remind group members that they are not the only ones with problems. Sharing what God is doing in their lives provides courage and strengthens the faith of other parents.

Teach Parenting

Unfortunately, many of us learn to be parents through on-the-job training or years too late. It is very helpful to provide workshops or a short-term weekly study series on disciplining children, avoiding power struggles, or ways to effectively communicate with children. You can usually find good speakers and teachers at a local community college. Several video series are available. Plus, it is amazing how parents can mentor other parents.

Organize Resources

Many single adult ministries have found creative ways to provide practical assistance to the one-parent families, such as an organized clothing exchange or advertising "needs" and "haves" to indicate who has extra furniture (clothes, books, etc.) and who needs some. One ministry put together a newsletter where single parents advertised services they could provide for a small fee, and then the ministry distributed it to the entire church. Work exchange days are always a big hit as singles swap their skills (sewing, cooking, painting, car repairing) with one another. One inventive singles pastor solicited services from within the church and the community for the single parents in his ministry. He was able to provide free dental exams, tune-ups, haircuts, legal work, and a number of other very valuable services for single parents. One of my favorites is the "recycled Christmas," where single parents bring toys their children have either gotten tired of or outgrown and exchange them for "new" toys to give their children for Christmas.

Assist with Opposite Sex Role Models

Single parents have a need for opposite sex role models for their children, particularly if there is little or no contact with the other parent. Men report that there is little difficulty finding women role models and mentors for their children, but mothers often have difficulty locating male role models.

Single adult ministries can help by recruiting male Sunday school teachers, childcare workers, and children's ministries workers or helpers. Or, families in the church can be encouraged to "adopt" a one-parent family for periodic outings and gatherings so there are role models available. A Big Brother type of program can be instituted with either married or single men participating. Often helping out this way can ease the pain a noncustodial father has over not being able to spend as much time with his own children as he might like to.

Give Hugs

The friendly touch of another adult says a lot to each of us. There's nothing like a bear hug from a friend. It says "I care," "I understand," and "I'm there for you." Build a time of hugging into your weekly program.

There are many ways to give "hugs," and we need to remember that some people are not comfortable either giving or receiving actual physical hugs. Find other ways to reach out and touch the lives of the single parents in your ministry. Greet them with warmth and acceptance. A friendly smile, a listening ear, a sympathetic nod, a shoulder to cry on, a funny card, or a thoughtful note in the mail can be the highlight of a single parent's week.

The effective leader will become a friend and make time available for the single parents who need extra assistance but will also begin to develop that kind of help from within the group and let members minister to one another.

Minister to the Children

The old myth that all children of single-parent families will be discipline problems must be abandoned. Some will and others will not. However, most children of divorced parents could benefit from a ministry that would help them understand and cope with the changes in their families. Curriculum is now available to set up such a program. Children learn to identify and deal with guilt, anger, fantasies of reconciliation, and fears.

Understand and Accept

Single parents respond in different ways to the reality of parenting alone. They experience a variety of conflicting emotions depending on the situation and their energy levels at the time.

Some are so overwhelmed that they believe, *I can't do anything!* They feel defeated, depressed, useless, inept, and appear nearly immobilized until they can learn to just take things one step at a time.

Others rise to the challenge with an attitude of *I'll do it or die!* And they nearly work themselves to death trying to do everything—alone. They refuse to curtail any activity or chore and work at fever pitch, getting little sleep or relaxation. These parents need to be taught to focus on essentials and to include time to relax and enjoy life.

A third response is *I'm surviving!* These single parents are hanging on by their fingernails, up one day and down the next. Once they find their balance and build their confidence, their lives begin to smooth out.

The ideal approach is *I'm doing my best!* There are no perfect parents. We all do our best with the time and energy we have. We all make mistakes. We can actually enjoy raising children sometimes when we let go of unrealistic expectations and simply do our best.

If leaders understand that these different responses are normal, and can in a nonjudgmental way assist single parents toward the fourth approach to the parenting experience, they will be of tremendous support and help to the single parents they seek to serve.

Getting Started

A successful program for single parents is one that has been tailored for the people in your ministry. This means that you cannot just copy what another church is doing and be successful. You should find out what needs exist in your own group and then set out to meet them.

Invite single parents to a planning session and have them share their needs, their dreams for a ministry, their visions for serving, and their ideas. If there is no defined need, don't start a ministry just for the sake of starting one. If there is no one willing to commit to leading the ministry, wait until God raises someone up to be the leader.

When a need has been defined and people are willing to make commitments to minister, you are ready to begin an exciting new expression of Christian love in your group.

Developing Ministry to Children of Divorce

Kay Collier-Slone

In the early 1960s, a Sunday school class of three- and four-year-olds were enjoying the day's lesson entitled, "God the Father loves you just as your earthly father loves you." The teaching series provided a drawing to color with a ghostly image of God hovering over an intact earthly family—the requisite two or maybe three children, mother, father, cat, and dog. Then the sharing time began, with children telling their experiences of fatherly love.

Tow-headed Mark spoke suddenly, his small face clouded. "My daddy doesn't love me. He went away."

In those days, divorce was still rare enough for the teachers not to have been concerned about the title and thrust of the lesson or the picture. The lesson would hold true for most of the class. Divorce was still enough of an oddity to be an embarrassment, and Mark was one of those children caught in the limbo of a family on its way to divorce.

At the end of the twentieth century, Mark's story is not unusual. And in Sunday school classes, youth groups, choirs, and in individual encounters, the children of divorce, from the smallest to the oldest, need to be given the attention, support, and assistance of the family that will not be broken . . . the church.

Periodically, someone in a church will say, "But aren't there private agencies and counselors to do that kind of work?" Certainly there are. But if the church is a Christian family doing the work of the Lord, then one of its roles is to "be there" for families who do not meet the traditional model of family, as well as for those who do. The church must "be there" in attitude as well as in activities.

Never again will this be an occasional issue or outside the norm. With the single adult population hovering around the 50 percent mark, church populations should reflect that figure in numbers of singles, single parents and, therefore, children of divorce. Numbers, however, do not mute the feelings that go with divorce, for both adults and children. And in this issue, there is no comfort in numbers, nor do the numbers normalize the experience of divorce itself. Each adult and each child still must go through the experience for himself or herself.

It is also important to remember that the church offers its responses based upon faith, upon the gospel. In secular settings, any spiritual base or content will be accidental rather than intentional.

Who Are They and What Do They Need?

Children of divorce may range from infants through adults. This chapter will be limited to the preschool through college years. It is important to note, however, that issues of divorce that occurred in an adult's childhood and were never attended to are often at the root of adult issues concerning relationships, self-esteem, and other aspects of life.

Judith Wallerstein, Ph.D., heads the Center for Families in Transition in Corte Madera, California, which counsels more divorcing families than any other agency in America. She has produced the first major longitudinal study of divorce conducted to date, a study based upon fifteen years of work with sixty middle-class families. The resulting picture of the long-term emotional, economic, and psychological effects of divorce on adults and children tells us clearly that divorce is not a short-term crisis but a profoundly life-changing event for all concerned.

Research continues to shed light on the experience of divorce in the lives of children and young people. Studies indicate that:

- Much of the damage of divorce happens during the predivorce conflict and not strictly as a result of the divorce. Therefore, some of the most severe problems may be present before the fact of divorce is known to the church, or even to the child.
- There are ranges of responses in all age groups. Some children show distress immediately—during divorce proceedings or in the subsequent changes that upset their lives and routines (moves, change of schools, one parent leaving, separation from siblings, dating or remarriage of a parent). Others may appear to weather the situation with minimal distress, but in young or later adulthood, they manifest symptoms traceable to this turbulent time.
- The child or young person does not have to be clinically "disturbed" or "unstable" to feel pain about this issue. Rarely does a child of divorce go through the experience without needing (but not necessarily asking for) some help.

Children of divorce are children who are experiencing two major losses: loss of an intact family, and loss of the daily presence of one parent. Along with the developmental tasks of their individual age and stage, children of divorce now have a complete other set of developmental tasks having to do with grief, transition, and recovery.

How Might Children of Divorce Differ?

Children of divorce might differ from those from traditional family units in many ways. Children of divorce may be on a visitation schedule with the noncustodial parent, which does not allow regular class attendance. Awards and emphasis on perfect attendance or examples that equate interest and commitment with attendance may force the child or young person into nonattendance or reluctance from embarrassment or feeling "out of things." The stress of single parenting may mean that younger children are irregular in attendance or are unable to participate in certain events. The older child may be without funds or be assuming home responsibilities not usual for his or her age.

The issue of religion may become an issue of contention between the parents and may be further complicated by remarriages, moves from the neighborhood, community, etc.

They may have repressed many feelings of pain and anger but live on an emotional edge, may be considered moody, or have shut down emotionally.

Children of divorce may have different names than the custodial parent, or surnames that differ from their siblings'.

Are There Differences by Ages and Stages?

While there are commonalities in responses to divorce, there are also predictable responses at specific ages. It is important to remember that every child or young person will respond uniquely, depending on personality and particular circumstances. The following guidelines, however, are helpful to teachers and leaders in developing a sensitivity to possibilities of behavior.

- **Preschoolers**
  Issues: Fear of abandonment; confusion.
  Behaviors: Reluctance to let custodial parent out of their sight; regression to earlier behavior, such as lack of bladder control, thumb-sucking, clinging to security items; sad, withdrawn; hitting, throwing fits to release anger.

- **Early school years (roughly 5–8)**
  Issues: Preoccupation with feelings of loss and rejection; fear of replacement in the affection of the absent parent; conflicting loyalties; guilt.
  Behaviors: Sudden tears; crankiness; lack of concentration; change in school performance.

- **Middle school years (roughly 9–12)**
  Issues: Awareness and anxiety that their practical and emotional base has been disrupted; concern for personal future; feeling insecure, out of control, powerless; angry at whichever parent they fault; grieving, lonely, confused, and possibly overstimulated by parents' dating or sexual lives.

Behaviors: Inappropriate caretaking for the family; physical symptoms such as headaches, stomachaches, and other stress-related ailments; changes or disruptions in peer relationships; delinquent behavior; manipulative behavior; change in school performance.

- **Adolescence/teen/college**
    Issues: Vulnerability to losing base of strong family structure, which they need to set their own emotional, sexual, and other impulses; fear of repeating their parents' mistakes; not sure where home is (particularly if away at school); concern for their personal future; angry, grieving; aware that society thinks they are too old to need help or be disturbed and attempting to live out that expectation; confused and often angry or jealous at parents' dating or sexual lives.

    Behaviors: May spend more time away from home; may move into premature sexual activity in search of warmth, closeness, identity; may assume more home responsibilities; may exhibit inappropriate caretaking behavior; changes in peer relationships, school performance; physical ailments. (It is important to note that though this age group acquires greater strength and independence through the crisis of divorce, many sacrifice important aspects of the teen/college experience, and become "old before their time.")

What Is Needed?

In a recent single adult class on loneliness, a woman new to both secular and church communities as a single parent said that she felt "out of it" at the church. "There is nothing here for a family like mine"—divorced with young school-aged children. A widow and long-time church member spoke of how the church had been like a surrogate family after her husband's death.

Which of these two stories accurately describes this parish church? Both are realities, spoken out of two radically different experiences.

The widow and her family moved into the church community as an intact family and were known well there for many years. After the death of the husband and father, many people reached out to them in love and concern in very practical as well as spiritual ways. There was, indeed, the experience of "just like a family."

For the new family, there was no history with the church as a traditional unit, of knowing and being known. The church offered no activities, support groups, or classes attentive to the needs of single parents. There seemed no way to develop a network, no way to sense "family." The environment felt more like form than substance in this phase of the family's life.

There is a difference to how the church looks, feels, and is represented to oldtimers and newcomers, to those who are in families or couples, and to those who are alone. There can also be a difference to how a long-familiar church looks, feels, and presents itself when a family configuration changes. However, there are things churches can do for families of divorce.

Have Awareness, Preparation, Acceptance, Love

Children and young people of divorce need an *aware, prepared, accepting, and loving environment.* These words are listed in an intentional order. A church must be *aware* of statistics, of research, of the new facts of life in this society before it can be *prepared.* If it is not *prepared,* then, at some level, it is not *accepting* reality and, therefore, the people of the reality. Without feeling *acceptance,* no one can feel *loved.* In the past, issues of divorce have been dealt with piecemeal, as deviations from the norm, individual crises that could be handled as the exceptional situation in the parish.

Does your church program advertise activities that indicate an awareness of families of divorce and children of divorce?

Does your church bulletin, directory, and other printed material list a resource for single adult ministry as well as for Christian education and youth activities?

Do the activities listed as regular offerings of the church indicate that families and couples are part, but not the total, population?

Are there support groups and education activities listed?

The church's program and promotion make a statement. Parents and children will not feel they can turn to their church in time of stress if it does not indicate both *awareness* and *preparation*. Families in stress do not always have the emotional energy or the time to search out resources. The activities listed, and the way they are targeted, is an indicator of where the church's time, money, energy, and ministry are directed. Already established members of the church who find themselves suddenly single will view their church from quite a different perspective than when they were paired. One young woman who grew up in a church, married, and was raising her children there, moved her membership to a church "where there were real efforts to help children of divorce, and people going through divorce" after her divorce. For both the prospective member and the long-time member, single parenting will be impacted by what programs are available and how they are promoted and presented.

Educate Clergy, Staff, Congregation

Have your teachers, youth leaders, and single-adult leaders been trained in awareness and sensitivity to families who do not fit old norms?

Are these leaders trained in an overall approach to ministry in which Christian education, youth, and single-adult leaders minister from a unified understanding of personal and Christian formation rather than a remedial approach?

Those who have never experienced divorce themselves or with anyone close to them may have "head knowledge" of what the experience is all about yet miss some of the ways in which the very environment of the church, its language, and its activities can be hurtful to children and adults of divorce.

One clergyman told of having his consciousness raised by a child who quite innocently told him, "The family Advent service made us cry." The puzzled pastor discovered that it was the absence of a "Reader number three" in this dad and son family unit that had proven very painful as they attempted to use the church-provided Advent guides for families.

"It made me start looking at our resources," the pastor said, "to try to deal with preparing our teachers to be sensitive." Teachers and leaders who have been trained in this manner will be more thoughtful in considering resources and using books, pictures, movies, and videos that show single parent homes as normative as well as problematic; they will recognize and choose examples that depict a wide range of family configurations. It is also important when asking parents to help with an activity or outing or when having "family pictures" taken for the directory to know that from one to four "parents" may show up, and the experience may cause pain for a child. As one teen whose parents had been long divorced said, "I just wish my family could be 'normal'—happy—*together.*" Another junior higher said, "I wish my mom could drive the carpool or chaperone sometime, but she has to work." One child may be sensitive to having both natural and stepparents present for church functions; another may be in pain because one of the natural parents is missing. Children are also sensitive about the use of correct names. The church needs to know a mother's last name, if she is remarried, and be able to call the stepfather by his name. In referring to parents in blended families, it is important to acknowledge the correct relationships. When in doubt, ask.

All clergy, teachers, and church leaders need to have facts about the new normative states of singleness, single parenting, and children of divorce. In this day and age, it is critical that all church leaders assume that some of the students in each group or class are not living with both natural parents. They need to take basic steps in identifying those students and adjusting the classroom or group to this new norm.

Clergy, teachers, and leaders need training in concepts of crisis, loss, and grief to fully understand the length of time and other aspects of the suffering process. They need to be introduced to standards of inclusivity in materials. They need available trained resources to answer questions as problems arise. Families should fill out registration forms and yearly enrollment updates that will report on family status, correct names. This information would go to the teacher when he or she receives a list of participants. When there are materials to send home, or gifts or pictures made for parents, there should be sufficient supplies to allow students extras.

Help the Children

In planning long-term goals, a church needs to consider its facilities, resources, and leadership, as well as community resources. Long-term goals might include:

- classes for children and young adults on topics such as self-esteem, loneliness, and solitude.
- a day-care program available through the week, at minimal cost.
- mentorship programs, which offer same-sex, opposite-sex role models and helpers to single-parent families.
- children of Divorce groups, with trained leaders helping youngsters through the experience. (Designs and training available by age-group.)
- carpooling, surrogate parenting, etc., which will allow children to participate fully in regular programs of the church regardless of home circumstances.
- curriculum that includes issues of self-esteem, loneliness, solitude, grief, preparation for individual as well as married adulthood, personal wholeness, internal satisfaction.

The long-term results should be young people who grow into adults more prepared for healthier living, individually and in family.

Help the Parents

Helping children often begins with helping parents. Divorced and grieving parents are often out of control, dazed, barely surviving. This state lasts much longer than is generally recognized. The effect is often as if there is no adult person in the home at all. By the time observable symptoms emerge in the child or young person, or a parent seeks help, considerable damage may have been done to the child. The church can help by offering:

- mediation training to help parents learn ways of communicating with each other that will not be so damaging to the children.
- classes in single parenting that offer practical help as well as support.
- community resources trained in special areas of need. Neighboring churches can pool such resources.
- special reference section in the church library with books on divorce, divorce recovery, custody, continuing parent rela-

tions, children's issues, etc. Keep several copies of each book on hand so that individuals who cannot afford to purchase them will have them available.

Children of divorce should have a very special place in the church family. The corporate body can offer a sense of continuity, of structure, of unbroken tradition, of stability and hope at a time when the children's lives seem devoid of these qualities. Such ministry will not only help and sustain the children of divorce through the crises in their families, but also will provide a model of family for the rest of their lives.

For Further Reading

Berger, Stuart, M.D. *Divorce without Victims: Helping Children through Divorce with a Minimum of Pain and Trauma.* New York: Signet Books, 1983.

Berman, Claire. *A Hole in My Heart.* New York: Simon and Schuster, 1991.

Bienefeld, Florence, Ph.D. *Helping Your Child Succeed after Divorce.* Claremont, California: Hunter House, 1987.

Diamond, Susan Arnsberg. *Helping Children of Divorce: A Handbook for Parents and Teachers.* New York: Schocken Books, 1985.

Kline, Kris, and Stephen Pew, Ph.D. *For the Sake of the Children: How to Share Your Children with Your Ex-Spouse in Spite of Your Anger.* Rocklin, California: Prima Publishing, 1992.

Ricci, Isolina, Ph.D. *Mom's House, Dad's House; Making Shared Custody Work: How Parents Can Make Two Homes for Their Children after Divorce.* New York: Collier Books, 1980.

Virtue, Doreen. *My Kids Don't Live with Me Anymore: Coping with the Custody Crisis.* Minneapolis: CompCare Publishers, 1988.

Wallerstein, Judith S., and Sandra Blakeslee. *Second Chances: Men, Women, and Children a Decade after Divorce.* New York: Ticknor and Fields, 1989.

Divorce Recovery—Small Group Ministry

John Splinter

There are many reasons why our church developed a fourteen-week, small group divorce recovery program. Indeed, all of the "healing" programs that we run (for victims of sexual and physical abuse, for children of divorce, etc.) now use the small group format. This chapter will provide a framework of the history, benefits, and problems of this approach.

A Brief History

We call our divorce recovery program Second Chapter. After surveying virtually all of the available divorce recovery programs, we decided there was none that met our standards. We wanted to have the very best, the top of the line approach to this ministry. We found that to get what we wanted, we had to create it.

Why fourteen weeks? We chose a fourteen-week program rather a shorter approach (four or six weeks) or weekend approach because of the group that helped create the program. All of them were divorced, and all were professionals of one type or another. Three had advanced clinical degrees. These individuals unanimously said that their personal quest for healing following their divorces took them a long time—many months and in some cases even many years. Given the level of trauma that divorce usually causes, it is not realistic to expect people to absorb within a short period of time a lot of knowledge about "how to recover from divorce."

When the spirit is deeply wounded, it is usually a quantum leap from knowledge to the application of that knowledge. The tasks of divorce recovery are serious and complex; they are like deep, multiple trauma wounds, and as such they take time to heal. They are not like a broken bone that, if set correctly into a hard cast shortly after the break, will heal itself within six weeks. Rather, they are more like severe, uneven, and infected gashes and punctures that need ongoing attention and regular cleaning over a long time.

While shorter divorce recovery programs can be helpful, it was our opinion that they are not capable of getting as deeply into the wound or providing as complete a healing as are longer programs.

Why small groups? The clinically trained members of the Second Chapter committee pointed out that the more time spent in small group interaction, the better the participants' healing would be. These small groups had to be closed to outside participants, completely confidential, and run by lay (but trained) individuals who had themselves been divorced.

One evening at our weekly Second Chapter committee meeting, a member presented a doctoral dissertation that confirmed everything we'd been discussing—from the fourteen-week length to the closed, small-group approach. It iced the cake for us, and the Second Chapter Divorce Recovery Project was officially born.

How Groups Are Run

Our groups are run following these guidelines.

Two leaders per group. Each group is built around two leaders, one male, one female. All leaders have been through divorce, most have been through Second Chapter, and all are required to be at least two years away from their own divorce.

Meetings in leaders' homes. Groups meet in the homes of leaders two and one half hours weekly.

Mixed groups, closed groups. Groups are mixed, with males and females in all groups. We do it that way because we believe it's important for both sexes to see each other struggle through divorce. It gives them a better understanding of what their ex-spouse is going through, and it destroys the tendency to generalize ("All men are jerks; all women are dependent, etc."). Once formed, groups are closed. No visitors.

Firm ground rules. There are a few ground rules that are firmly maintained, such as no dating among group members, absolute confidentiality, respect of group leaders.

Methods.

1. Each person is given a *Second Chapter* book and is expected to read one chapter a week. That chapter becomes the focus of the week's study, conversation, and out-of-group activity. (Rather than starting the weekly meeting by listening to someone lecture for an hour, we require that participants read the weekly chapter. Almost all participants do so, religiously.)
2. Each group meeting is begun with a short time of prayer, usually led by one of the leaders.
3. Although the group is free to discuss anything, most of the focus of the meeting revolves around the discussion questions provided at the end of each chapter. In this way the material is handled sequentially.
4. Group members are encouraged to accomplish the "action items" in each chapter during the rest of the week and to discuss at the next meeting how these helped in divorce recovery.
5. Meetings end with a short prayer time.

Cost. We charge $100 for each person. That fee accomplishes three important things:

1. It increases the level of commitment to the group. They've paid for something and now they want to get their money's worth, so they attend every meeting.
2. It increases the expectation level of the participant. Having paid $100, they now expect the program to be more professional and powerful; and as their expectation level increases, so also does their active participation and their healing.
3. It pays for a full-time program director. Individuals who cannot afford the full fee are helped on an individual basis; nobody is ever refused. When people have gone through Second Chap-

ter one time, they can go through it free as many times thereafter as they want or need. We've had several people take the course twice, and one person went through it three times.

Advantages to This Approach

Here are a few of the distinct advantages of using the long-term, small group approach to divorce recovery.

Cognitive input alone is insufficient. Following divorce, many try to ease their pain by reading books about the subject. Although such reading is informative, it seldom helps ease the suffering. Healing generally does not come through cognitive input.

Shorter divorce recovery programs are limited in their effectiveness; by their nature, they either provide a heavier dosage of cognitive material or limit the scope of material to be covered. This is true because they have less time in which to provide their information. There is, in fact, a very popular weekend divorce recovery program. People who have taken the class have told us that after the first two or three hours they were on such emotional and cognitive overload for the rest of the weekend that they couldn't absorb most of what was presented. Divorce recovery doesn't happen quickly, nor is cognitive information its key element.

The process approach is preferable. Obviously there must be a blend of content and process in any learning or healing endeavor. However, shorter programs must, by their very nature, focus more upon content, giving people quick solutions regarding "how to recover." Longer approaches allow for more process orientation, focusing upon issues—where the pain is, why it's there, when it hurts most, how to grow past it The group can support one's efforts to heal and grow. The longer approach also better allows for more individuality—"Bill, you're struggling with anger and bitterness. Jane, you seem to be struggling with sadness and fear. Terry, right now you're pretty deep into depression, aren't you?"—rather than rapidly offering canned solutions to fit everyone's circumstances.

Relationships wound; Relationships heal. It is the ability to share one's pain with another person while slowly and gently learning of solutions that can help mitigate or ease the pain that most effectively helps the healing. The healing process is highly relational and interactive in nature. In the field of family systems theory there is a phrase, "By the family wounded, by the family healed." Small group divorce recovery uses the group to act, in some ways, as a "family" to which each person belongs. The wounds of divorce are relational and spiritual in nature. The small group provides relationships within a gentle spiritual environment for the purpose of healing.

Relationships don't happen quickly. It takes time to build or rebuild relationships. Divorce represents a shattering of what was probably one's most closely held intimate relationship. Since the wounds of divorce are relational and spiritual in nature, it stands to reason that one does not quickly rebuild such relational and spiritual items as trust, hope, and love; nor does one quickly rebuild the openness and willingness to heal so necessary to sustain future relationships. It takes time, within the caring and supportive environment provided by a surrogate "family," to accomplish deeper levels of healing and rebuilding.

Bonding and self-examination heal. Healing after divorce usually involves lots of self-examination, and that process is accomplished best within a community of bonding and support. Such is the small group. Being together as a group on a regular basis, sharing the wounds of divorce, learning to be open and vulnerable with one's own responsibility for the divorce, watching each other struggle toward renewed wholeness, watching each other fall from time to time yet giving and receiving the support and caring that comes from the depth of each group member's heart—these are all powerfully healing factors.

Small groups represent body ministry. When presented within a format of gentle spiritual acceptance and love, the small group actually represents the body of Christ as it expresses grace, forgiveness, reconciliation, compassion, and more. Most people going through divorce experience some sense of alienation from the church, at least temporarily. The small group can be an effective means of experiencing the love and healing of Jesus Christ while the individual is emotionally or spiritually separated from the larger church.

Small groups have real flesh and bones. One method of doing divorce recovery involves an individual standing in front of a group of divorcing people and teaching methods of healing followed by an hour of discussion in groups.

It is our belief that it's far more effective to enter into the trenches with those who are wounded and touch their wounds with the love of Christ. Small group divorce recovery is flesh and bones, hands on, "We're right here with you" ministry. We do not want distance between the medic and the wounded.

The process is often very painful for the leaders themselves as they watch their "babies" struggle through recovery, but it's far more effective ministry than the lecture approach.

Small groups provide nurture and time. Almost any clinically trained person will agree that two important components of healing are nurture and time. Although the small group can't provide all of the nurturing needed for healing, it does give a large portion of it. And then it just takes time—time together with people one trusts with the deepest hurts.

To develop the depth of trust and support needed to begin healing usually takes several weeks. We have found that many people just *begin* to open up to their group after the sixth or seventh weekly meeting, and yet that's when many programs end.

Confidentiality is almost assured. Another benefit of the small group approach is that confidentiality is more easily assured. Everyone's in the same boat, so to spill someone else's beans is usually not even a consideration. This is in contrast with some divorce recovery programs in which the recovering person is with a different group of people every week.

The leaders become paths toward healing. Many people lose hope when going through divorce. Within the small group approach, they have ample opportunity to look at, question, and evaluate the lives of the leaders who take them through the program. All of these leaders were themselves divorced, and the knowledge and observation that the leaders have gone through the pain and are now whole, happy, and productive offers growth and hope.

Ministry continues after the group is finished. One of the most powerful reasons we use the small group, long-term approach is that the relationships formed continue on. The group frequently becomes a major part of the individual's support network for the next many years. In other words, people don't just go to a divorce recovery program and then walk away. They usually stay connected.

When that connection is to people who are also active within the church, the long-term nature of this approach frequently ends up drawing participants back to the church—or in many cases, to the church and Christ for the first time. Our divorce recovery program is one of the strongest tools for evangelism in our church.

The leaders develop. The long-term nature of this program means that leaders have to make a substantial commitment. This is a decidedly positive aspect of our ministry. We have found that as leaders make deep and long-lasting commitments, they grow, mature, and usually become even more deeply committed both to the ministry and to Christ.

When we don't ask anything of our people, they don't give much. When we ask a lot, they have to make a decision. If they decide to give a lot, everyone benefits—the participants, the leaders, the specific ministry, and the church body. The larger church benefits in that when the leaders feel they've done divorce recovery for enough years, they are already in a service mode and usually seek to direct their energies into some other church ministry.

The leaders benefit the most. At the end of every Second Chapter program, we ask each participant to evaluate the program, the leaders, the written material. For the most part we receive a grade of 90 to 95 percent; the program is tremendously well received.

However, as much as the participants benefit, the leaders usually gain more. In leading others through the swamp of divorce recovery, they reinforce their own paths of healing. In praying for group participants' healing, they are led to the Lord for their own wholeness. Our leaders over the past six years have come away from leading these small groups saying that they grew far beyond their expectations as a result of leading others.

Many said that initially they were very hesitant to lead for fear of returning to the emotional pain of their own divorce. This has not happened. Through leading others, they have found healing for unresolved issues in their own lives.

Pitfalls to This Approach

Any divorce recovery program will have its own strengths and weaknesses. Here are the issues that have surfaced within the past six years of our using this approach.

Leadership development takes work. It takes more time and energy to get a program like this up and running than for the alternatives. It takes time to recruit and train leaders. Some people are not willing to commit to a fourteen-week ministry, so it is important to handpick the leaders rather than asking for "anybody out there who wants to lead a divorce recovery group."

We shoot for the brightest, best leaders we can find. We seek people who are committed to the Lord, who have healed, and who have a lot on the ball. Overall, this approach builds a powerful and effective ministry. Several psychologists, psychiatrists, and attorneys in town regularly refer people to our divorce recovery program.

Deeper ministry requires better training and support. The fourteen-week, small group approach runs much deeper than a course of fewer weeks. People share in more depth, and painful wounds are exposed. Consequently, it takes thoughtful training and support to use this approach.

We provide small-group-dynamic training for all of our leaders. We also provide training to all our leaders to help them recognize individuals who might be suicidal and to know what steps to take.

We then provide a trained clinical person as a backup, on call twenty-four hours a day for emergencies. In six years we've had two potential suicides averted through the intervention of our lay leaders. Our leaders have frequently called on the clinical support person for suggestions on how to handle specific participants.

There is a slower growth rate of ministry. This approach won't "explode" a ministry into instant stardom. It takes time to build this kind of ministry. On the other hand, one church decided to use this approach and in the first divorce recovery session started their program with over 100 participants. Usually, however, the growth of this approach is slower. The long-term payoffs are much greater, but the initial growth rate is usually a little less aggressive.

Summary

If we had it all to do over again, if we were just starting a singles ministry and were trying to figure out how to do the very best divorce recovery ministry possible, we would do exactly what we have done. We'd go for long-term, small group, closed group, step-by-step, mixed group (male/female), lay led divorce recovery.

Organizing a Divorce Recovery Workshop

Andy Morgan

Once the decision has been made to develop a divorce recovery program for your church or community, the next question is the kind of program you are going to use. Options include weekend programs and programs ranging from six weeks to sixteen weeks, meeting once a week. In deciding which format you would like to develop, you need to define your goals by what you would like to see accomplished. What are the needs? What do you feel uniquely qualified to do?

It is my belief that the best divorce recovery program is one owned, organized, facilitated, and taught by local people. By not making it another thing done for you but something you do for yourselves, you benefit from knowing that you have helped build the kingdom in your community. At first the quality may not be as good as having outsiders come in and do a program for you, but ultimately, the health and well-being of your group will be stronger.

It doesn't matter how large or small your group is—you can have a divorce recovery ministry in your church. If you only have three people, you can have a program. If you know three people who have experienced divorce or the end of a long-lasting relationship, then consider purchasing a divorce recovery video series and start there. Invite some people to your home or to your church to watch the videos and then go over the workbooks or discussion questions that accompany the divorce recovery videos. It is important to remember that you don't have to have large numbers to have effective ministry.

The type of divorce recovery ministry discussed in this chapter meets once a week for eight weeks. The evening begins with one hour of teaching. Next the group breaks into smaller groups for discussion. Because of the nature of divorce recovery, discussion groups work best when they have an average of ten participants with a male and female facilitator. An evening might be as follows:

5:30 P.M. Registration and coffee

6:00 P.M. General session

8:00 P.M. Break

8:15 P.M. Small group discussion or talk-it-over

9:15 P.M. Dismiss

This schedule helps to end all the discussion groups on time. Starting and ending on time tells the participants that their time is important. This schedule provides a time when facilitators can discuss any immediate problems within the confines of small group confidentiality. The schedule also allows facilitators a time to recover if their groups were especially emotional.

The book I use as a text is *Growing through Divorce* by Jim Smoke. I believe it to be helpful for the journey through divorce recovery. It is good to have participants reading something during the week to keep their minds focused on recovery. To supplement the book, I provide handouts for each session. There are many different workbooks and materials available that make excellent supplemental material.

As you plan and develop your own divorce recovery workshop, you may want to consider the following sequence.

Eight to Ten Months Prior

Eight to ten months before your workshop you'll want to do the following.

Pull together a ministry team to brainstorm. This can be five to ten people who have gone through divorce and have a burden for ministering to others who have. Make sure that your leadership team is made up of a variety of people, i.e., custodial and non-custodial parents, individuals who were married less than ten years and those married over twenty years, male and female, etc. By pulling together a team of leaders, you have already expanded the number of people who will have some kind of ownership in the divorce recovery ministry.

Decide what kind of divorce recovery program you want. This could be a weekend, six-, eight-, or twelve-week program. Is it going to be taught by someone or are you going to use one of the video series that are available?

Start gathering material. You can get material from others who are doing divorce recovery. Develop a network of support from other organizations.

Six to Eight Months Prior

Six to eight months before your workshop you'll need to do the following.

Determine your main speaker, if you are going to have one instead of a video series. If you are going to use a video series, start reviewing different videos to see which one you would like to use.

Establish your dates. I have used an eight-session program; a weekly basis is preferable. The last session may be in a banquet or dinner format, even a potluck dinner, with music, special guests, and the speaker presenting the last lesson. I recommend the eight-week program, realizing that many people feel that they need more time than some alternatives. Indeed, recovery takes longer than eight weeks, and for that reason I always try to find other support systems, i.e., counseling centers, support groups, single parent groups, etc. within the community or church to help facilitate the recovery process.

The eight-week program should be in conjunction with other programs or support ministries within the church, i.e., singles ministry, Sunday school classes, week night fellowships, Bible studies, etc., so that when the program is over the people have many other options for continued healing and growth. When there aren't other opportunities for continued small group interaction, then a longer divorce recovery program might be beneficial.

Establish your location (church building, etc.). When selecting a room try to make it as warm and friendly as possible, providing a safe place for sharing.

1. Reserve a main lecture room for the opening sessions. This needs to be a room that will hold your expected participants comfortably. Don't have a room that is too small or too big. You don't want people to be cramped or feel lost in the room.
2. Reserve "breakout" rooms for the small groups. These rooms should hold ten to fifteen chairs in a circle arrangement.
3. If you plan to have child care available, you will need rooms for this. (Child care is recommended.)
4. Determine your sound system requirements (will you tape each session, do you need microphones, etc.). The participants need to hear the main speaker clearly. Your sound system can either enhance your program or make it very difficult for people to follow the speaker.

Determine the cost. When doing divorce recovery, I state that the charge is on a "donation" basis and that scholarships are available to those who cannot afford to pay. The donation should cover honorariums (for the speaker), books and materials you will hand out, refreshments (if provided), scholarships, child care, advertising, etc.

Determine your promotion. What audience are you trying to attract? If you are trying to reach out to the non-Christian community, putting flyers in your local Christian bookstore is not going to be successful. A better place to advertise might be in the "personals" of your local paper. Know your audience and target your advertising. Some ideas are:

1. Promotion through your own and other churches using inserts for the church bulletin (can be a very inexpensive way to get advertising into the Christian community).
2. Newspaper promotions (not just on the church page).
3. Radio promotions (public service announcements).

4. Cable TV promotions (public service promotions are often free).
5. Flyers at bookstores, counselors' and lawyers' offices, human resource departments at corporations, mental health clinics, and AA. Get together with your brainstorming team and see what other ideas you can develop.
6. Word of mouth promotions—start promoting early! Many of the participants will come from word of mouth advertising.

Make sure to develop a good ministry team that networks with others. Make the quality of the promotional material equal to what the average person sees every day. Quality advertising sends the message that what you are doing is important.

Three to Four Months Prior

Three to four months before your workshop you should do the following.

Design a brochure and registration form. Print copies for eight to ten times the number of anticipated participants. This larger quantity enables you to distribute your brochures at other places. Also, printing costs for 750 or 1,500 are practically the same. Make sure the brochure contains phone numbers people can call for information. Answer the basic questions of *who, what, where, when,* and *how much.*

Write to other churches to see what kinds of brochures they use and then design your own. (A list of churches using this model is at the end of this chapter.)

Select your facilitators. Establish the number of facilitators you will need. Try to have two per group.

1. Use facilitators who are legally divorced. Facilitators are a key to the program. Choosing divorced facilitators will allow participants to feel more comfortable, especially those who are most recently involved in the divorce process. This also avoids the subtle message that only married people are qualified to teach, lead, and facilitate.
2. Use facilitators who have gone through a divorce recovery program or who are in the process of healing. If they have

not gone through a divorce recovery program, I would recommend having them read *Growing Through Divorce* before facilitator training begins.

3. Only use facilitators who are committed Christians. Many of the principles brought out in the programs have their basis in the Scriptures; you will want people who are in harmony with the material instead of those who constantly disagree and state their own opinions.

4. Have the facilitators complete an application form. This will not only help you but will also convey the message to volunteers that this is serious business for servant leaders.

5. Inform your facilitators of their need to commit to the set number of training sessions before the program begins. It is important for the facilitators to be a part of the training session so that a team is developed that takes their role seriously. Usually people will only rise to the level of commitment expected of them. The more you expect from leaders, the more responsible they will be. Do the ministry and your volunteers a favor and let them know what you expect and the importance of their role. Have a variety of good training materials available. When training, emphasize the importance of listening, asking appropriate questions, and providing a safe place for people to share their experiences.

6. Make sure each facilitator is willing to commit time to be present for each workshop session.

Determine who will train your facilitators, and prepare the training materials. Prepare handouts for your training material and try to make your training user friendly. Be careful not to overwhelm your facilitators with excess materials and responsibilities. I emphasize that the primary job of facilitators is to be good listeners.

Eight to Ten Weeks Prior

Eight to ten weeks before your workshop you'll want to do the following.

Start distributing your promotional brochures. Put them at the above suggestions and anywhere else that your brainstorming team decided to advertise.

Take registrations from participants.

Have training sessions for your facilitators. I have traditionally used two training sessions. The first session can be two to four weeks before the beginning date. Have the second session the week before the beginning of the workshop.

Recruit other volunteer help. People are needed to:

1. assist with registration and greeting each night (hosts/hostesses). Your hosts and hostesses can have such an important impact on the overall ministry. They should treat all the people with dignity and sensitivity and remember what the participants may be going through. Divorce recovery should be a safe place.
2. assist with refreshments, if provided.
3. serve at a book or tape table, if provided.
4. run the childcare program.
5. run the sound system. This is a very important part of the program.
6. help with room setup if you don't have a custodial staff to do that.

One to Two Weeks Prior

One to two weeks before your workshop you'll want to do the following.

Start assigning participants to groups. Strive for 10–12 people per group, but you may leave the groups smaller at this time to allow for walk-ins the first or second night. Try to group people together based on their backgrounds:

1. Number of years married; suggested groupings: 0–8 years, 9–18 years, 19–26 years, 27+ years
2. Participants who have no children
3. Participants who have divorced more than once
4. Participants whose divorces have been final over five years

These groups may have to be adjusted based on the size of your workshop. It is not imperative to divide your group into these categories, but as your group grows, these categories can help make it easier for discussion in the groups.

Assign facilitators to groups. Where possible, match facilitators' backgrounds to the type of group, although this is not absolutely necessary.

Reverify all rooms to be used. Make sure custodians are aware of your arrangement needs! Custodians may be your best friends!

Organize a prayer meeting. Commit the ministry to the Lord.

Opening Night

On opening night you will want to do the following.

Arrive early and check all rooms. Check for tables, chairs, lighting, signs, and other setup items.

Test sound system setup.

Have workshop materials ready for people who are preregistered.

1. Each person should be given a packet with name, group assignment, and group meeting location written on the front. This helps make the participant feel welcome.
2. The packet should include handouts, outlines, ground rules, name tag, etc. (Note: Most people prefer to write their name on the name tag.)
3. If you are planning to give each person a book, make it available at this time.

Have registration materials available for "walk-ins." You might anticipate doubling the number of preregistrations with walk-ins the first night (so if you have fifty preregistered, you could conceivably have up to fifty more people the second week).

Place the new registrants into small groups. Do this while the first main session is in progress. Be sure that you have allowed available space in the groups to accommodate these people.

Dismiss to groups. When the speaker has completed the first main session, dismiss those people who have their group assignments. Then read off the names of new registrants and their group assignments.

Do not place new people into small groups after the second week! Bonding has occurred in the groups by this time, and new members will detract from the trust relationship. New groups may be formed. It is also important to determine at what point newcomers are encouraged only to audit the general session and then consider signing up for the next workshop series.

Some churches using this model of divorce recovery workshops are:

- Calvary Church, Grand Rapids, Michigan
- Single Point Ministries, Ward Presbyterian Church, Livonia, Michigan
- Arlington Heights Evangelical Free Church, Arlington Heights, Illinois
- Willoughby Hills Friends Church, Willoughby Hills, Ohio

Divorce recovery audio tapes, video series, participant workbooks, leaders' manuals, and the divorce recovery program on computer disk are available through Polestar Ministries.

Appendix

Networking through NSL

NSL is the Network of Single Adult Leaders. In fact, all of the chapters in this volume are written by NSL members. NSL is designed to encourage and be a resource for equipping lay and professional leaders for ministry. The network connects the lives and ministries of single adult leaders across our nation. This networking alone provides a great resource to single adult leaders. However, the wealth and volume of ministry materials and ideas provide invaluable ministry tools and opportunities. NSL is available to all churches and singles ministries. The following is its story as reported by former Executive Director Timm Jackson.

It was sure to be a great day in Vail, Colorado. Of course, every day is beautiful there, whether it is snowing, raining, or perfectly sunshiny. The terrain just seems to openly invite the lucky human to drink in the freshness and be inspired! But who could guess what would actually be born that spring day in 1980? Just what was going through the minds of those men and women who met there? They were singles leaders—some of them single themselves. Was there one present in that small group who happened to be discouraged? or overworked? or lonely? or neglected? or perhaps all of the above?! Whatever affected those special people then, we are the beneficiaries now!

Networking . . . individuals who interconnect . . . an interesting concept when used by people who share a like mind, heart, and commitment for Christ's work. The simple act of encouraging, equipping, and inspiring each other tends to make each of our tasks more fulfilling. When singles leaders, whether professional or lay, are brought together to learn and grow, the challenge of our ministry only deepens. Several denominations across the country understand the importance of such encouragement and training among singles leaders, but unfortunately the learning is often limited to denominational ties. There are many singles pastors still left in the cold, having no one with whom they can share the unique needs of single adult leadership.

The National Association of Single Adult Leaders (now known as the Network of Single Adult Leaders) was formed from those days in Vail and has grown to encompass a wide spectrum of single-adult leaders. Designed to encourage and be a resource for equipping both lay and professional leaders for ministry, NSL has begun to fulfill those goals in an interdenominational arena.

A focus on a variety of educational avenues has produced broader ministry skills in the lives of those involved with NSL. Conferences held around the United States in eight different geographic locations offer educational opportunities within driving distance. Here leaders learn the basics of divorce recovery, grief recovery ministries, counseling singles, and single ministry programs, and they discover how to incorporate this type of programming into the local church. Studying the needs of the single adult and learning how the church and Christian community can relate and respond to those needs is another learning experience provided by NSL.

The encouragement of leaders is a constant need. Inspiring them to be creative and innovative in their programming is also something that "networking" can do. Inspiration to live in the areas of cutting-edge ministry—constantly searching for new needs and new need-meeting tools—is offered to those who need to excel in their world for the cause of Christ. Another focus of the networking experience is to help participants set and attain personal, as well as ministry, goals. Allowing the members of NSL to informally hold each other accountable for excellence and growth in ministry tasks creates a unique, profitable forum for sharing gifts and experiences in practical fellowship opportunities.

NSL, Mobilized to Serve, and some denominational ministries provide many opportunities each year for single adult leaders to connect. Annual conferences are held by each of these groups.

Many regional and local leadership training workshops are also available. Some groups sponsor retreats and others offer membership opportunities to tie the leaders more closely together so they may communicate on a regular basis. A variety of ministry aids being produced and marketed through these networks supply a continuing educational experience. Books, tapes, and videos have all become useful tools in enabling single adult leaders to have a more lasting ministry.

With God's help, let us work with and encourage each other. Instead of facing discouragement, overwork, lonely moments, or feelings of being neglected, let's learn to conserve our energies by using that strength for the necessary tasks to which we have been called by God.

The organization listed below was created for a very special reason—you. We are happy to help make the network and other resources available, and we would like to do still more. NSL is only a phone call or letter away if you need a quick prayer of encouragement or a tough question answered. If more input is desired, we want to be available to you, whether it be consulting ideas for ministry, weekend leadership seminars, or ministry retreats. NSL is determined to build friendships that will enhance your ministry and help you, the single-adult leader, pastor, and friend, to personally grow in Christ and reach singles for Christ.

Network of Single Adult Leaders
P. O. Box 1600
Grand Rapids, MI 49501
Doug Fagerstrom, Executive Director
(616) 956–9377

Notes

Chapter 7: *The Single Adult Lifestyle*

1. Adapted from Michael E. Cavanaugh, "Personalities at Work," *Personnel Journal* 64 (April 1985): 255–64.

2. Alfred Montapert, *The Supreme Philosophy of Life* (Los Angeles: Books of Value, 1970), 89.

Chapter 28: *Traits of Single-Adult Leaders*

1. F. E. Bullett, "Why Certification?" *Certification Registration Information* (Research Report of the American Production and Inventory Control Society, Washington, D.C., 1981), 5.

2. W. E. Sheer, "Is Personnel Management a Profession?" *Personnel Journal* 43 (1984): 225–61.

3. James Brown "The Need for Confidentiality," *Luther Rice Journal* (spring 1984): 14, 19.

4. Ibid.

Chapter 30: *Developing a Ministry Vision*

1. George Barna, *The Frog in the Kettle* (Ventura, Calif.: Regal Books, 1990), 67.

2. Ibid.

3. Doug Murren, *The Baby Boomerang* (Ventura, Calif.: Regal Books, 1990), 76.

4. Barna, 77.

5. Jim Smoke, *Turning Points* (Eugene, Ore.: Harvest House, 1985), 115.

6. Linda Raney Wright, *A Cord of Three Strands* (Old Tappan, N.J.: Fleming H. Revell, 1987), 11.

7. Murren, 76.

8. Ibid., 77.

9. Jack O. and Judith K. Balswick, *The Family—A Christian Perspective on the Contemporary Home* (Grand Rapids: Baker Book House, 1989), 271–72.

10. H. Wayne House, ed., *Divorce and Remarriage—Four Christian Views* (Downers Grove, Ill.: InterVarsity Press, 1990), 10–11.

11. Douglas L. Fagerstrom, ed., *Singles Ministry Handbook* (Wheaton: Victor Books, 1988), 28–29.

12. Gerald L. Dahl, *How Can We Keep Christian Marriages from Falling Apart?* (Nashville: Thomas Nelson, 1988), 168–69.

13. Barna, 77–78.

14. Jim Smoke, *Growing in Remarriage* (Old Tappan, N.J.: Fleming H. Revell, 1990), 43.

15. Wes Roberts and H. Norman Wright, *Before You Say I Do* (Eugene, Ore.: Harvest House, 1978), 6.

16. H. Norman Wright, *Communication* (Ventura, Calif.: Regal Books, 1984), 138.

17. David J. and Bonnie B. Juroe, *Successful Stepparenting* (Old Tappan, N.J.: Fleming H. Revell, 1983), 12.

18. Ibid., 177.

19. Guy Greenfield, *We Need Each Other* (Grand Rapids: Baker Book House, 1984), 24.

20. Ibid.

21. Fagerstrom, 158.

22. Harold Ivan Smith, *I Wish Someone Understood My Divorce* (Minneapolis: Augsburg Publishing House, 1986), 146–47.

23. Harold Ivan Smith, *Positively Single* (Wheaton, Ill.: Victor Books, 1989), 22.

24. Jerry Cook, *Love, Acceptance, and Forgiveness* (Ventura, California: Regal Books, 1978), 11–12.

25. Murren, 91.

26. Ibid.

Chapter 32: *Developing Volunteers*

1. John MacArthur, *Ephesians* (Chicago: Moody Press, 1986), 155.

2. Don Cousins, Leith Anderson, and Arthur DeKruyter, *Mastering Church Management* (Portland: Multnomah Press, 1990), 75.

3. John Maxwell, *Injoy Life* tapes. INJOY, 1530 Jamacha Road, Suite D, El Cajon, CA 92019. Phone: 1-800-333-6506.

Chapter 33: *Developing Ministry through Spiritual Gifts*

1. Charles Swindoll, introduction to *Spiritual Gifts* (Fullerton, Calif.: Insight for Living, 1986).

2. John Koening, *Charismata: God's Gifts for God's People* (Philadelphia: Westminster Press, 1978), 59.

3. Colin Brown, ed., *Dictionary of New Testament Theology*, vol. 3 (Grand Rapids: Zondervan, 1975), 546.

4. Siegfried Schatzmann, *A Pauline Theology of Charismata* (Peabody, Mass.: Hendrickson Publishers, 1987), 67.

5. Howard Snyder, *Liberating the Church* (Downers Grove, Ill.: InterVarsity Press, 1983), 89.

6. Stuart Briscoe, *Romans* (Waco: Word, 1982), 219.

7. Elizabeth O'Connor, *Eighth Day of Creation: Discovering Your Spiritual Gifts and Using Them* (Waco: Word, 1971), 42–43.

8. Ibid.

9. George Patterson, *Obedience-Oriented Education* (Cucamonga, Calif.: Church Planting International, n.d.), 1.

10. Ibid., 15.

11. Roland Allen, *The Spontaneous Expansion of the Church* (Grand Rapids: Eerdmans, 1962), 13.

12. A good starter volume is C. Peter Wagner's *Your Spiritual Gifts Can Help Your Church Grow* (Ventura, Calif.: Regal Books, 1977).

13. Rick Blose, Heights Cumberland Presbyterian Spiritual Gifts Lay Coordinator's data results, summer 1989.

14. This material (with leader's guide) is available through the Charles Fuller Institute in Pasadena, California under the title *Discovering Your Spiritual Gifts in Small Groups* by Paul Ford. A second excellent set of materials, geared especially for larger churches, is called *Networking*, by Bruce Bugbee of Willow Creek Community Church in Chicago. It is also available through the Fuller Institute. The toll-free number for the Fuller Institute of Evangelism and Church Growth is (800) C. Fuller.

15. John MacArthur, *The MacArthur New Testament Commentary: 1 Corinthians* (Chicago: Moody Press, 1984), 295.

Chapter 35: *Developing a Leadership Team*

1. Jack D. Orsburn, Linda Moren, Ed Musselwhite, John H. Zenger, Craig Perrin, *Self-Directed Work Teams: The New America Challenge* (Homewood, Ill.: Business One Irwin, 1990), 13–14.

2. Rod Wilson, "Team Players," *Interest*, (March 1990), 16–17.

3. Elton Trueblood, *The Incendiary Fellowship* (New York: Harper and Row, 1967), 43.

4. Philip Van Auken, *The Well-Managed Ministry: Discovering and Developing the Strengths of Your Team* (Wheaton Ill.: Victor Books, 1989), 168.

5. Ibid., 163.

6. Ibid., 159–60.

Chapter 36: *Let's Begin at Church*

1. Madonna Kolbenschlag, *Lost in the Land of Oz: The Search for Identity and Community in American Life* (San Francisco: Harper and Row, 1988), 2–3.

2. "The Parish as Community," report 10 in *Notre Dame Study of Parish Life* (Notre Dame: Institute for Pastoral and Social Ministry and the Center for the Study of Contemporary Society of the University of Notre Dame, March 1987), 12–13. Quoted in Maria Harris, *Fashion Me a People: Curriculum in the Church* (Louisville: Westminster/John Knox Press, 1989), 82.

3. Avery Dulles, *Models of the Church* (New York: Doubleday, 1987), 218.

4. Harris, *Fashion Me a People*, 82. (It should be noted that Harris is using only a nuclear family definition in this quote and only partially addresses alternative forms of family later. She never indicates that never-married, childless single adults can be family as well.)

5. Raymond K. Brown, *Reach Out to Singles: A Challenge to Ministry* (Philadelphia: Westminster Press, 1979) 16.

6. Mark W. Lee, *It's OK to Be Single* (London: Collins, n.d.), 50–55.

Chapter 37: *Revitalizing Your Single Adult Ministry*

1. Terry Hershey, *Young Adult Ministry* (Loveland, Colo: Group Pub., 1986), 29.

2. Andrew Greeley, *Sexual Intimacy* (London: Thomas Moore, 1973), 161.

3. Hershey, 29.

4. Hale Goddard and Jorge Acevedo, *The Heart of Youth Ministry* (Lexington: Bristol Books, 1989), 152.

5. Dobbins Gaines, *A Ministering Church* (Nashville: Broadman Press, 1960), 91.

6. Ron Jensen, *Dynamics of Church Growth* (Grand Rapids: Baker Book House, 1981), 112.

Contributors

Doug Calhoun
  Park Street Church,
  Boston, Massachusetts

Jon Clemmer
  Church of the Savior,
  Wayne, Pennsylvania

Kay Collier-Slone
  The Episcopal Diocese
  of Lexington, Kentucky

Gilbert E.Crowell
  Eastside Baptist Church,
  Marietta, Georgia

Pamela Dodge
  Ward Evangelical
  Presbyterian Church,
  Livonia, Michigan

Robert Duffet
  Northern Seminary,
  Chicago, Illinois

Jim and Barbara Dycus
  Calvary Assembly of God,
  Winter Park, Florida

Chris Eaton
  Executive Director,
  Single Purpose Ministries,
  St. Petersburg, Florida

Doug Fagerstrom
  Network of Single
  Adult Leaders,
  Grand Rapids, Michigan

Bill Flanagan
  St. Andrew's
  Presbyterian Church,
  Newport Beach, California

Paul R. Ford
  Heights Cumberland
  Presbyterian Church,
  Albuquerque, New Mexico

Dennis Franck
  Central Assembly
  Christian Church,
  Boise, Idaho

Gary Gonzales
  Elim Baptist Church,
  Minneapolis, Minnesota

Mary Graves
  Solana Beach
  Presbyterian Church,
  Solana Beach, California

Rich Hurst
  University
  Presbyterian Church,
  Seattle, Washington

Timm Jackson
  Minister to Single Adults,
  Tempe, Arizona

Jeffrey R. King
  Bethany Community Church,
  Tempe, Arizona

Contributors

Carolyn Koons
Executive Director for Institute
for Outreach Ministries,
Azusa, California

Rich Kraljev
New Hope
Positive Singles,
Portland, Oregon

G. Jerry Martin
First Baptist Church, Oxnard,
California

Rob McCleland
Long Hill Chapel, Chatham,
New Jersey

Jeff McNicol
First Baptist Church,
Rochester, Minnesota

Andy Morgan
Christ Church of Oakbrook,
Chicago, Illinois

Bud Pearson
Orange Coast
Community Church, Orange,
California

Paul M. Petersen
Highland Park Presbyterian
Church, Dallas, Texas

Michael Platter
Springdale Church
of the Nazarene,
Fairfield, Ohio

Bobbie Reed
Single Adult
Ministry Consultant,
San Diego, California

David Savage
Trinity Church,
Lubbock, Texas

Harold Ivan Smith
Executive Director
of Tear-Catchers,
Kansas City, Missouri

Jim Smoke
Growing Free,
Southern California

John Splinter
Central Presbyterian Church,
St. Louis, Missouri

Jim E. Towns
Professor of Communications,
Stephen F. Austin University,
Nacogdoches, Texas

David Weidlich
Fair Oaks Presbyterian
Church, Fair Oaks, California

Norm Yukers
Rehoboth Baptist Church,
Atlanta, Georgia